The Nonprofit Economy

The Nonprofit Economy

Burton A. Weisbrod

Harvard University Press
Cambridge, Massachusetts
London, England

Library of Congress Cataloging in Publication Data

Weisbrod, Burton Allen, 1931–
  The nonprofit economy.

  Includes index.
  1. Corporations, Nonprofit—United States.   I. Title.
HD2769.2.U6W45   1988   338.7′4   87-23718
ISBN 0-674-62625-7 (alk. paper) (cloth)
ISBN 0-674-62626-5 (pbk.)

Designed by Gwen Frankfeldt

To my father and my late mother,
Leon and Idelle Weisbrod,
who helped me to appreciate the
importance of ideas and scholarship

and to my wife, Shirley,
for her understanding and moral
support during the preparation
of this book, and for her
help in improving its readability

Preface

Modern economies are complex systems that operate through a variety of institutional forms. There is no perfect institution that works well for all societies in all circumstances. Each society must find the particular combination of institutional forms that suits its needs at a given time. Every society confronts the problem of deciding how to encourage and restrict providers so that they furnish the goods and services that society needs. Gathering and assessing information are problems that plague all modern societies and make such evaluations difficult.

My view is that nonprofit organizations are largely a way of solving informational problems. Managers of nonprofit organizations lack the incentive of profit that might otherwise tempt them to misrepresent their products or services. Some people think, for example, that nonprofit blood banks, hospitals, or nursing homes are safer than those run for profit. A different point of view is that the profit motive encourages efficiency and user satisfaction. Still a third point of view is that the government, rather than either nonprofit or for-profit institutions, is the best resource society has for meeting its economic goals.

For various reasons (such as cultural and religious diversity and the traditional American emphasis on private initiative), nonprofit organizations play an integral role in the United States economy. We encourage nonprofits by exempting them from certain kinds of taxes and subsidizing them in various ways. In exchange, we require that nonprofit institutions refrain from distributing any profits to managers or directors. Since World War II the nonprofit sector of our economy has doubled (from 2 percent to 4 percent of national income), but that growth has not been accompanied by the economic analysis required for appropriate policy formulation. There are now nearly one million tax-exempt nonprofit organizations in the United States. The time has come for a thorough analysis of their functioning within the economy and their effects on other economic sectors.

We need to find out how the nonprofit economy works and to evaluate its success in meeting the goals our society has set for it. Is its privileged economic position justified by the effect it has on our overall economy? Or, on the other hand, does the nonprofit sector have unexpected negative effects on other parts of the economy?

We can ask the same kinds of questions and use the same kinds of economic models to analyze the nonprofit sector as those that are used to study the rest of the economy. It is commonplace that the private sector and the government intersect within our economy and that the actions of one influence the other. Nonprofits—a hybrid form of institution combining aspects of the for-profit and governmental forms—also have an effect on, and are affected by, the rest of the economy.

The Nonprofit Economy is my attempt to apply economic analysis to this neglected sector of the economy. I begin by placing the nonprofits in the context of a mixed economy of governmental, for-profit, and nonprofit institutions; I also discuss the variety of forms that nonprofits themselves may take. In Chapter 2 I introduce the concept of "institutional choice"—that society chooses among these institutional forms to meet the demands of the society. In Chapter 3 I extend the institutional choice perspective by considering the problems of rewarding performance in the various economic sectors.

The rest of *The Nonprofit Economy* analyzes the workings of the nonprofit sector per se. In Chapter 4 I introduce a "collectiveness index" to highlight the important relationship between the ways an organization is financed and the kinds of services it provides. I also describe the nonprofit sector—its overall size, composition, and changes over time. In Chapters 5, 6, and 7 I discuss the financing of nonprofit organizations in detail. I examine the effect of charitable donations both on nonprofits themselves and on governmental and for-profit institutions, as well as the factors affecting the level of donations. Then I take up a growing source of revenue for nonprofits, which is also a source of growing resentment toward them—sales of goods and services. The third major source of financing nonprofits—volunteer labor—is the subject of Chapter 7; volunteer labor may account for as much as 20–25 percent of the labor performed in the service sector.

In Chapter 8 I ask whether nonprofits behave differently from for-profit institutions. As a society, we support nonprofits in the belief that they provide outputs that cannot be provided profitably by private enterprise. But do nonprofits act differently in providing outputs that are hard for consumers to monitor or in the manner in which those outputs are distributed?

Finally, in Chapter 9 I present some public-policy recommendations. It is clear that more research must be done on the subject of the nonprofit economy and its effect on the economy as a whole. In the meantime, it is important that we think hard about our attitude toward the nonprofit sector. I hope that my suggestions will stimulate further research and an ongoing debate over the role of nonprofit organizations in the American economy.

To this end, I have addressed this book to a wide audience, for even readers with little background in economics will be able to follow the arguments I make in the text. I also think *The Nonprofit Economy* will be of interest to more specialized readers—economists and other social scientists. Notes and statistical appendixes are provided for those who wish to refer to them.

I received financial support for this research from the Twentieth Century Fund, which I acknowledge with thanks. A number of people helped me in major ways, and I wish to thank them also. I benefited from research assistance from Thomas Helminiak and Jerald Schiff, and from editorial assistance from Jocelyn Riley and Elizabeth Uhr. Christoph Badelt read the entire manuscript and provided detailed comments and valuable insights on both substance and style.

Contents

The Nonprofit Economy

Nonprofits in a Mixed Economy

The economy of the United States is mixed. It includes private enterprise, sizable governmental activity, and a commonly overlooked middle ground, the nonprofit sector.

Nonprofit organizations are all around us. We donate money to them. We volunteer our labor to them. We give government grants, tax advantages, and postal subsidies to them. Many of us send our young children to nonprofit day-care centers, our older children to nonprofit colleges, our sick to nonprofit hospitals. We go to nonprofit museums and zoos. *National Geographic* Magazine, "Up With People," and the Sierra Club are all nonprofit entities. So are the Better Business Bureaus nonprofit, as are the Boy Scouts, the YWCA, labor unions, trade associations, and, quite likely, the local country club. The nonprofit sector of the economy is large and heterogeneous, and it is growing.

The term *nonprofit* has several meanings. The one I emphasize is the restriction on what an organization may do with any surplus ("profit") it generates. The essence of this form of institution is that a nonprofit organization may not lawfully pay its profit to owners or, indeed, to anyone associated with the organization. Along with this restriction, however, come a variety of tax and subsidy benefits that influence a nonprofit's actions.[1]

There are also hybrid combinations of nonprofits with private firms on the one hand and with governmental organizations on the other. These are neither entirely private nor entirely public, but have some attributes of each. The post–World War II period has been one of active experimentation with nonprofit and related hybrid forms of organizations. The federal government has sought "newer mechanisms whereby programs of national concern can be conducted essentially outside of the federal establishment itself." Such use of private nonprofit organizations by the federal government began with the Rand Corporation.[2] Another example is the Urban Institute, in Washington, D.C., a private nonprofit research organization established by the federal government in the 1960s under the Johnson administration. At least in the early years, the Urban Institute, while technically independent, was funded primarily by the Department of Housing and Urban Development and worked largely on projects the department approved.

A more recent institutional form is a hybrid combination of a nonprofit and a for-profit. One of the largest for-profit hospital chains in the nation, Hospital Corporation of America, has formed a nonprofit foundation, the HCA Foundation, which gives grants to other nonprofit organizations.[3] In another recent institutional innovation, a nonprofit, the Enterprise Foundation, established the for-profit Enterprise Development Company, which has been described as "a tough-minded, business-like real estate development company that specializes in downtown [retail and festival] projects. It is run to make a profit, it pays its taxes. But it[s] . . . profits are plowed into programs and projects to aid in eliminating the problems of housing the poor within a generation."[4]

Yet another form of hybrid is the "joint venture" of nonprofits with for-profit firms. In 1985 a hospital was organized by the for-profit firm, National Medical Enterprises, and the nonprofit Methodist Health Systems. In fact, a survey of 700 nonprofit hospitals by the accounting firm Ernst and Whinney showed that in 1985 one-third of the nonprofits were already involved in joint ventures with for-profits and most of the others were considering it.[5]

No simple public policy will suffice for such a mixed collection. It is not clear, either, what society expects from the nonprofit sector. Many opinions and assertions are put forth about the effectiveness and desirability of nonprofits, but evidence is scarce. Especially limited is information about whether nonprofits are better or worse at achieving certain goals than for-profit firms or governmental enterprises would be.

It is difficult to formulate good public policy without knowing what nonprofits actually do, how well they do it, and how they respond to various incentives and constraints. Several variables are involved. To the Internal Revenue Service, nonprofits are a major headache, producing only trivial tax revenues but sizable administrative—and even constitutional—problems, such as whether a university that discriminates against blacks should retain its nonprofit status. To the courts, nonprofits are an endless source of litigation over such matters as how they may solicit donations and what part of their revenues, if any, should be subject to taxation; in 1985 alone, nonprofit activities were the subject of six cases before the United States Supreme Court and sixteen before the United States Court of Appeals.[6] To private enterprises, nonprofits are sources of subsidized, "unfair" competition. To the population in general, nonprofits are sometimes a nuisance, continually pleading for donations; at the same time they are outlets for the expression of social concerns. The nonprofits regard themselves, however, as socially valuable organizations, vital contributors to a pluralistic society. Are they worth the trouble?

Misperceptions about nonprofits abound. One is that they exist outside the economic mainstream. Their millions of volunteer workers are not counted in Department of Labor statistics. Their billions of dollars of contribution to the nation's economic output have not, until recently, been reported separately by the Department of Commerce. Information about what nonprofits do is uncoordinated and difficult to find. Little is reported on any regular basis as to the size or activities of the nonprofit portion of the economy. Even the term *nonprofit* itself is used inconsistently. A 1982 Census Bureau survey of the service sector illustrates the unfortunate state of statistical information and the low level of importance that is attached to the nonprofit sector. After the survey was designed, a decision was made (because of cost constraints) to omit major groups of nonprofits—such as schools and hospitals—with the result that there is little comparability between this survey and the 1977 survey.

It is also widely believed that all nonprofits are essentially the same, that all are guided by public-spirited altruists who seek only to serve the public interest or, conversely, by shrewd entrepreneurs who have found in nonprofits a mechanism for lining their own pockets. Nonprofits, however, are a varied lot.

Another common misperception is that nonprofits exist almost entirely on the donations of the citizenry. This is simply wrong. The variability of the sources of support among nonprofit organizations is enormous, as is the importance of nondonated revenues. A related misperception is the tendency to think of nonprofits as somehow not subject to the economic constraints that apply to the rest of the economy. The authors of a recent article in the *Harvard Business Review,* for example, asserted that a nonprofit hospital is "an institution free of market discipline."[7] The absence of stockholders does matter, but nonprofits—hospitals or others—are by no means free of market pressures. Some people believe that nonprofits do not respond to changes in prices or in demand, that consumers of services from nonprofit organizations do not respond to the prices of their services, and even that prospective donors are not influenced in deciding the size of contributions by the prospect of tax deductibility. These ideas, too, are wrong. Not only does charitable giving of money respond to the same kinds of factors that influence markets for "ordinary" commodities—prices, incomes, seller reputation, and so forth—but so does giving of time (volunteer labor). Although monetary revenues are certainly of enormous importance to the vitality of nonprofits, so, too, is the vast amount of nonmonetary contributions of volunteer labor services. As policymakers consider alternative mechanisms for enhancing (or, perhaps, limiting) the resources flowing into the nonprofit sector, they need to recognize that a wide array of governmental decisions influence that flow, even when the decisions seemingly pertain only to other parts of the economy.

The origins of organizations that are neither government nor private profit oriented are obscure. Whatever the motivations may have been for their development, they have been around for centuries. At first their existence had nothing to do with tax considerations, for the history of private nonprofit organizations long antedates the existence of taxes on personal income and on corporate profits. In the United States, the deduction for charitable giving was added to the federal income tax law in 1917, four years after the adoption of the Sixteenth Amendment, which permitted taxation of personal income. In 1918 an estate tax deduction was added for charitable bequests, but it was 1935 before corporations were first allowed to make tax-deductible contributions.[8] These tax deductions presumably had only a small effect on giving prior to World War II, for income tax rates were tiny until then. Now, with far higher rates of personal and corporate taxation, tax rates are a major influence on charitable giving.

In certain respects the nonprofit form of enterprise antedates governmental service agencies. Four centuries ago, in sixteenth-century England, governmental provision of civilian goods or services was modest. Yet voluntary private "philanthropies" (today we would call them nonprofits) were providing funds for a wide range of goods and activities that are now regarded as the natural responsibility of government: schools, hospitals, toll-free roads, fire-fighting apparatus, public parks, bridges, dikes and causeways, drainage canals, waterworks, wharves and docks, harbor cleaning, libraries, care of prisoners in jails, and charity to the poor.[9] Nonprofit organizations supported even such causes as "houses for young women convinced of their folly."[10] More recently, in nineteenth-century America, we find such nonprofits as the Anti–Horse Thief Society, formed in 1884 apparently to "supplement" inadequate governmental efforts.[11]

Choice of Institutional Forms

Every society makes choices about what forms of institutions it will rely on to achieve its socioeconomic goals.[12] The search for more efficient forms of institutions, including the invention of new hybrids, is not limited to the United States. The year 1985 saw the socialist economy of Hungary introduce "new management forms" that combine state ownership with elements of private cooperatives. The reforms call for less state control and more self-governance by the workers in state enterprises, the goal being stronger managerial incentives. The new institutional forms remain subject to central governmental price setting, but they have "autonomous, comprehensive budget and banking relations."[13]

Although the purely private enterprise and the government institution have many virtues, they also have serious limitations. For example, private enterprise, driven by profit seeking, cannot be relied on to undertake activities, such as pollution control and consumer health and safety protection, that would be unprofitable even if consumers valued them highly. And government enterprises face political pressures that make them excessively responsive to well-organized demands from industry and other pressure groups but far less responsive to the interests of poorly organized groups such as consumers.

In the United States, the limitations of both government and private enterprise are drawing attention to nonprofits. Although they, too, have drawbacks, nonprofits have unique features that might enable them to serve important social aims that neither the private sector nor the government can fulfill very well. The unique nature of the nonprofit economy and its relations (both competitive and complementary) with the private sector and the government are the subject of this book. I focus on four major themes: informational inequalities, diverse demands, the relationship between revenue sources and outputs, and the interdependency of the for-profit, nonprofit, and governmental sectors of the economy.

The efficiency of any institutional form depends to a large extent on *informational inequalities* in the market where it functions. Informational asymmetry can involve either underinformed consumers or informed consumers who choose to understate their true demands for collective-type services. When consumers are well informed relative to suppliers, the private sector is usually the institution of choice. But when consumers are underinformed relative to suppliers, the private sector often performs badly. In such areas as long-term medical care, day care, charity, and foreign aid, consumers are often in a poor position to determine the quality of output and thus may be ill served by opportunistic sellers.

Informational asymmetry in the reverse direction is the source of the "free-rider" problem. Consumers, in the aggregate, may highly value particular collective services, such as national defense, clean air and water, and aid to the poor and needy. But individual consumers may find that self-interest dictates acting as if they cared little, in the hope that others will pay for the services. Consumers do not have the incentive to reveal their true willingness to pay, by making voluntary payments, if they feel that they can benefit from others' contributions.

Both kinds of informational inequalities permit opportunistic behavior, which causes market "failure"—private markets that do not work efficiently. The nonprofit and governmental forms may be able to mitigate such behavior by virtue of their constraints on the distribution of profits. Indeed, the nonprofit sector includes organizations that provide services subject to both types of informational problems. Some provide services traditionally identified with the private sector that can be sold to individuals but with a consumer-protection or informational element added; nursing home services are an example. Other nonprofits provide collective-type services that are traditionally identified with the public sector—for example, basic scientific research. There are also nonprofits, such as country clubs and trade associations, in which informational inequalities play no part.

The second theme of this book, that consumers have *diverse demands,* also has important consequences for nonprofits. In a democratic society in which governments tend to be responsive to majority wants, there is a need for institutions that can respond to the demands of persons who feel intensely about particular collective-type activities, such as the preservation of Carnegie Hall or other landmarks, research on muscular dystrophy, or helping native Americans.

The third theme is that there is a close relation between an organization's *sources of revenue and the nature of its outputs*. This is true for all organizations, whether governmental, for-profit, or nonprofit. An organization that relies heavily on income from sales, for example, cannot engage in activities promoting environmental preservation that, however valuable socially, cannot be sold profitably. An organization that relies on donations to aid the poor must tailor the form of that aid to the wants of prospective donors, who are, in effect, the economic demanders of the organization's services.

Finally, the fourth theme is that *the nonprofit sector of the economy is interdependent with the governmental and for-profit sectors*. Both the outputs it provides and the revenue sources it uses bring it into competitive as well as complementary relations with the other forms of institutions. When government reduces personal income tax rates, for example—perhaps to stimulate economic growth or, as was the case in 1986, to simplify the tax system—contributions to nonprofits decline. And when nonprofits respond by extending their activities in search of additional revenues, they come into increased competition with the private sector.

Public Policy

Public policy toward nonprofits—to the extent there is one—can be described most aptly as confused. Government simultaneously encourages and discourages nonprofits—subsidizing them and restricting them, proclaiming their virtues and distrusting them. This is not surprising, since there is little consensus as to what goals society should achieve by fostering nonprofits. And without a consensus there cannot be tests of whether goals are being reached or even approached.

I believe that there should be a policy debate to help shape thinking about the role of nonprofits in our mixed—and changing—economy. The first step in such a debate is to clarify the issues. Although there are many questions, they can be classified in two categories. What kinds of activities should nonprofits engage in? How should nonprofits be financed?

To identify the appropriate range for nonprofit activities, we must recognize both the strengths and limitations of the nonprofit form of institution as well as of other forms. There is little point in encouraging nonprofits to compete with proprietary firms in activities for which the motivating force of profit spurs sellers to be efficient and innovative. There is little point, either, in encouraging nonprofits to compete with government in meeting demands for collective goods when there is broad consensus as to the types and qualities of such goods that should be provided. But the failure of private markets, perhaps because of external effects or informational asymmetries, or of governments, perhaps because of great diversity of consumer demands for collective action, may be justification for nonprofit enterprises. It is a justification, though, that may be more potential than actual. The possibility of misusing nonprofit organizations is real; costs of monitoring nonprofit activities are great enough that the potential social benefits of this institutional form can be eroded by the same types of opportunistic seller behavior that gives rise to failures of the private market—unless safeguards are in place.

Along with deciding which activities are appropriate for nonprofits, we must decide how nonprofits are to be financed. Should they be permitted to engage in profitable activities to subsidize their unprofitable, collective-type activities? If so, what limits should be imposed, in recognition of the effects of their profit seeking on the private economy? If not, are we willing to accept a reduced level of activity in the nonprofit sector? Should nonprofits be restricted to the activities for which they have been granted tax-exempt status, and restricted even further to financing only through donations? In any event, how expansively or narrowly should a particular nonprofit's tax-exempt purpose be defined, and what special restrictions, if any, should be imposed on nonprofits' fund raising? Should there, for example, be an upper limit on fund-raising expenditures, as has existed in many states? Should fund raising through direct mail advertising be subsidized in ways that other fund-raising techniques are not, as is now the case with reduced postal rates?

Deciding on the proper realm of nonprofit activities and deciding on the set of revenue mechanisms are not matters that can be resolved once and for all time. Just as the forces that lead to the failure of private markets and governments are changing, and, more precisely, just as the character and extent of informational problems in the economy change, so do the answers to the two policy questions. What should nonprofits be doing? How should they be financing those activities?

There are, of course, subsidiary questions to be resolved. Administration poses a difficult problem. What kind of governmental agency should regulate the nonprofit economy, deciding whether a specific applicant should receive the privileged status and whether violations of policy have occurred? The institutional-choice perspective proposed in this book is the best framework for analyzing the nonprofit sector of the economy. It highlights the possibility that whatever the nonprofit sector does, is or could be done by the other sectors. Whether better or worse is the question.

The Varieties of Nonprofit Organizations

Nonprofit organizations are far from homogeneous; there are as many variations among them as there are among governmental organizations and for-profit firms. Constraints differ, and so do motivations. Some leaders of nonprofits appear to be what one researcher saw as "idealists," people who wish to help others and effect social reform—which reflects the historical roots of nonprofits in charity and community; others appear to be simply income maximizers.[14] Because of the difficulty of monitoring their activities, some nonprofits will inevitably be used for socially undesirable purposes. There is no way to ensure that a nonprofit organization, once established, will be utilized for its "intended" purpose alone.[15] Consequently, although many nonprofits provide the collective-type services, including consumer information, that society expects of them, others do not.[16]

Some nonprofits can more appropriately be called "clubs."[17] Their benefits accrue essentially—and in the clearest cases, only—to their members. Although they are legal, they are treated differently from the collective-type nonprofits. They do not receive the benefits of tax-deductible donations and many other subsidies. A trade association, for example, is a nonprofit in the legal sense that any surplus would not be taxed and that it is precluded from distributing any surplus; however, while it does not seek profit for itself, it is devoted to the maximization of profits of its member firms. Similarly, labor unions are club-type "nonprofits" that exist to maximize the welfare of workers. Whether an organization calls itself a club is not important. The key to identifying this type of nonprofit is whether substantial benefits accrue to people outside the organization. The Sierra Club, for example, works for environmental preservation at the national level and can benefit many nonmembers; it is more appropriately described as a collective-type nonprofit. Yet many other nonprofit clubs, such as local philatelic and numismatic clubs, provide few benefits to nonmembers and so have little claim to public subsidization.[18]

Preferential treatment under United States tax law does not correspond precisely to this typology, but tax benefits are granted on similar criteria. Trust-type and collective-type nonprofits are the kinds that most people generally have in mind when they hear the term *nonprofit*. Charities that promote the health, education, welfare, and cultural vitality of society are the organizations that receive special income-tax treatment in the form of tax deductibility of contributions. *Trust-type nonprofits* are the nonprofits that are thought to provide trustworthy information to consumers who cannot easily judge quality of services for themselves; day-care centers and nursing homes are potential examples. *Collective-type nonprofits,* such as providers of medical research and aid to the poor, produce public-type services that bring widely shared benefits. These two types of organizations—nearly all of which are tax exempt under section 501(c)(3) of the U.S. Internal Revenue Code[19]—also benefit from a variety of other subsidies and tax benefits, such as reduced postage rates, free "public service" advertising on radio and television, and, in various states, exemption from local property and state sales taxes.

An enormous number of nonprofits do not enjoy these public subsidies. Most, including those I described as clubs, enjoy none of them except that their surplus—any excess of receipts over expenses—is not subject to corporate profits taxes. The club-type nonprofits are likely to have little or no such surplus, though, for they depend heavily for finance on membership dues, and these can be expected to be set to ensure that the clubs "break even," but no more.

A particular nonprofit may not fit neatly into any one of these categories; its activities may be of more than one type. The tax law takes into account such situations. If, for example, a nonprofit has been determined to be engaged in activities having a substantial public interest—providing trust or collective services—it will receive the subsidies noted above, but only for those activities. If it also engages in other activities—"unrelated business activities"—those are taxed as if the organization were simply an ordinary private firm.[20] Organizations, however, that engage in multiple activities—some tax exempt, others not—can shift revenues and costs among their various activities. Because of the costliness of monitoring the accounts, nonprofits can become stiff competitors of private firms; not surprisingly, a growing chorus of for-profit firms is complaining of "unfair" competition.[21]

Another type of nonprofits is the "for-profit in disguise." Acting like profit-maximizing firms, these nonprofits are of dubious legality. They exist only because incomplete enforcement of the constraint against distribution of profit permits them to abuse their nonprofit status. These nonprofits have been misclassified; they are treated by tax authorities as if they were providing trust or other collective services, but they actually pursue the private interests of managers and directors.

What happens when imperfect regulation permits the development of nonprofits that are for-profits in disguise? This question is particularly important when consumer informational handicaps are the social justification for nonprofits; sound public policy should restrain "nonprofit" providers from taking advantage of their special status to the detriment of consumers. The public often sees nonprofit status, particularly tax-deductible status, as a mark of quality—an indication that the organization is trustworthy.[22] Given the requirements of the tax code, this belief has some justification. Nevertheless, it is not always warranted.

Solid evidence of abuse of nonprofit status is difficult to find. Moreover, it is not always clear precisely what "abuse" means. The goals of non-profits are typically vague (for example, "the general welfare of the aged"), the law applying to nonprofits is hazy, and the question of what constitutes "unfair" competition by nonprofits with private firms is difficult to answer. To some firms, any competition from nonprofits is an improper abuse of a privileged position, whether it is illegal or not, but the issue has not yet been framed clearly, let alone resolved.[23]

Business leaders, however, are increasingly raising the question. At the 1986 White House Conference on Small Business, for example, "measures to prevent or discourage nonprofit groups from competing with small businesses for government contracts" was second on the priority list of ten proposals for action; at the 1980 conference this was not even on the list.[24] And charges that nonprofits are "advertising, going to shopping malls with mobile vans to offer free hearing tests, doing all the marketing things a private enterprise would normally do" are increasing.[25]

Abuse of the privileges granted to nonprofits can take many forms. Nonprofits can act as for-profits in disguise by evading the constraint on distribution of profits by dispensing profits in the form of increased wages. Disguising a distribution of profit by calling it a wage payment is illegal,[26] but given the costs of enforcement, excess payments to managers as well as to firms associated with trustees of the nonprofits can go undetected. Opportunities are abundant for directors and managers of non-profits to benefit from having their own company sell services, such as accounting, laundry, and legal representation, to the nonprofit.[27] (Such abuses also occur in the proprietary sector, of course.) The New York State Comptroller's office once charged that the state was losing millions of dollars in overpayments to both nonprofit and proprietary schools for the mentally handicapped—through payment of "inflated salaries" and through the lease of land at high prices from corporations owned by school operators.[28]

The nondistribution constraint may also be evaded when a nonprofit is controlled by a for-profit firm as a vehicle for the pursuit of profit. If the same persons own a private firm and control a nonprofit operating in a related field, the possibility of their taking advantage of the different tax treatments and subsidies for private gain is clearly present. Two recent cases illustrate not only the potential for self-serving behavior on the part of directors of nonprofits, but also the difficulty of determining the facts when there are complex relationships between nonprofit and for-profit organizations.

In 1967 a church-affiliated nonprofit organization, Second Harvest, was created in Phoenix, Arizona, to distribute surplus food to the needy. By 1983 it was a nationwide network of 61 food banks, distributing more than 100 million pounds of food.[29] Its founder, John van Hengel, was honored at the White House on March 1, 1982. To some people, though, Second Harvest had become a tool of private firms. New board members, for example, were appointed by for-profit food processors such as Beatrice Foods and Kraft and by the Grocery Manufacturers of America. When the founder of Second Harvest was ousted, critics charged that commercial firms were trying to control the nonprofit, both to prevent donated products from being resold commercially and to take advantage of corporate tax benefits.[30]

The food processors did have a stake in the amount of food that Second Harvest took and how it distributed the food. Because the donor firms could obtain substantial tax benefits from their donations, they had an interest in ensuring that their contributions would be accepted.[31] This is not a trivial issue, given the substantial amounts of goods donated. Kellogg, for example, gave 107,000 cases of a cereal that was not selling well, and Tropicana gave 2.4 million quarts of grapefruit juice that was discolored but "perfectly drinkable."[32]

The complex relationships between nonprofits and proprietary firms also appear in a quite different area—services to boat owners. The Boat Owners Association of the United States, known as BOAT/US, is "a nautical AAA, a nonprofit organization that watches out for their interests on issues such as waterway user fees and boat safety and offers its members discounts on boating gear." The organization's founders, Richard Schwartz and Richard P. Ellison, also started a for-profit organization, Boat America Corp., and allegedly used the nonprofit organization to steer business to their firm. The proprietary firm had been running membership operations for the nonprofit, at a charge of $1 million per year; but this was unprofitable, and so the work was transferred back to the nonprofit. Members of the nonprofit boat association had not been told that their leaders were also the executive officers of the profit-making company.[33]

These illustrations are not intended to pass judgment on the facts in these two cases, but they do highlight the potential for utilizing nonprofits as for-profits in disguise. Whenever there are interlocking directorates of proprietary and nonprofit organizations, there is a potential for abuse. The nonprofit economy is by no means isolated from the for-profit sector.

Whenever any nonprofit is found to have abused its trusted position, the reputation of trustworthy nonprofits also suffers; the value of nonprofit status as a signal that the organization deserves contributions of money or time is debased. Nonprofits that do not act opportunistically, as well as those that do, will find it increasingly difficult to obtain resources and will tend to be driven out of the market.[34] In the end the nonprofit market for trust-type services can disappear. This process of debasement of the "currency" of nonprofit trustworthiness can be exceedingly slow, of course, since the information required to detect abuses is itself costly.

The debasement process, which results from incomplete information, is similar to the general problem of "lemons" in the competitive market. If differences in the quality of a commodity are costly to discern—say, the extent to which various charities actually serve the public purposes they proclaim—donors may conclude that the quality of all sellers' services are indistinguishable. As a result, the high-quality, public-serving nonprofits can find their reputations, and thus their ability to obtain support, injured by the actions of the self-serving for-profits in disguise. They can disappear from the market, as better performance goes unrewarded.[35] There may be a sort of Gresham's law of nonprofits; bad nonprofits can drive out the good.

We may summarize in this way the three key characteristics of nonprofits that distinguish them from proprietary firms and that affect their actions in major ways: (1) no one owns the right to share in any profit or surplus of a nonprofit; (2) nonprofits are exempt from taxes on corporate income; (3) some nonprofits receive a variety of other subsidies—donations to them are tax deductible and they are exempt from many other forms of taxation in addition to the tax on corporate profits.

All three characteristics are important because they affect organizational incentives. Characteristic (1) exerts a potentially serious effect on the incentive to be efficient. Proprietary firms are motivated to pursue profits that can be distributed to owners and managers; nonprofits face rather different incentives simply because of the restriction on their freedom to pay out profits. As we will see, however, far more than efficiency is affected by characteristic (1).

Tax subsidies—characteristics (2) and (3)—give nonprofits an advantage in competing with proprietary firms. Tax deductibility of donations, which applies to about one-third of all nonprofits, is especially noteworthy because it has the potential to shift substantially the allocation of resources among industries and among nonprofits and proprietary firms within an industry.

The special advantages granted to nonprofits carry the potential for achieving private gain without social benefit. If characteristic (1), the "nondistribution constraint," can be evaded, characteristics (2) and, especially, (3) can turn the subsidies into private gain; nonprofits may not engage in the kinds of public-serving activities for which their subsidization is intended. And even if they do, they may not deploy their resources efficiently, since both the nondistribution constraint and the subsidies may blunt incentives to be efficient.

Nonprofits are by no means the only form of institution capable of misuse, of socially inefficient behavior. Every type of institution fails to be efficient under some circumstances. The fundamental problem of achieving social efficiency is the difficulty of measuring excellent performance and then rewarding it. Profit, the major motivation in the private enterprise economy, is the mechanism through which efficiency is rewarded. Yet profit is sometimes reaped through socially inefficient behavior. In nonprofit and governmental organizations, because sharing in organization profit is restricted, profit is not the lure to efficient behavior that it is in the for-profit economy; neither, however, does profit motivate economic behavior that is socially inefficient but privately profitable.

The overarching framework for this study is the challenge of designing institutional forms and deciding for what purpose in the economy each should be used. Within this framework I focus on nonprofits—what they do, what the justification is for their existence, how they obtain resources, and how their behavior differs from that of private enterprise and government.

Options among Institutional Forms

Three major forms of institutions are available to every society: proprietary, governmental, and nonprofit. Within these three categories, the variety of institutional forms that may exist in a society is not fixed. New forms can be, and are, invented. Institutional forms have ranged from the feudal estate, with its complex rules governing rights and obligations of land owners and serfs, to the private market, the capitalist regime, and then the corporation, which has the virtue of being able to outlive any owner. At various times in history many new forms of "non-market"—that is, not-for-profit—institutions have developed, including the private nonprofit form of enterprise, the independent governmental agency (such as the Federal Trade Commission), the condominium association, "private governments" (such as the National Basketball Association), new governmental units (such as special-purpose districts like those created to manage water or sewage services), and metropolitan-area governments. Private groups are also sometimes granted regulatory powers generally reserved for governments—as in medicine and law.

Every form of institution has advantages and constraints. The proprietary sector operates with greater decentralization of power and authority and with greater flexibility than is the case with government, and it operates on a profit-based incentive-reward system that depends on the distribution of purchasing power. Government has, in general, more centralized power and operates on the basis of political rewards.

Nonprofits are restricted from distributing profit (as is government) and are limited in the ways they may raise funds, but they are free from the taxation to which private firms are subject. Nonprofits may not levy taxes and they are not responsible to the same set of political forces that affect a governmental body, since the directors or trustees of a nonprofit are not elected to their positions by broad constituent groups. And nonprofits are far more restricted than are proprietary firms in the kinds of activities they may engage in. On the other hand, proprietary firms are not eligible for certain types of governmental grants, such as those given by the National Science Foundation,[1] that may go to nonprofits, but they do have access to the market for equity capital (that is, they may raise capital by selling shares of stock), which nonprofits do not.

Different institutional forms have different effects on society; a healthy pluralism is a continuing goal of public policy. Whether an economic system is basically private, as in the United States, or basically public, as in the socialist countries, a variety of institutional mechanisms is, in fact, inevitably used. In socialist societies the limitations of centralized governmental stewardship have become increasingly clear; inflexibility—a consequence of the high cost of information required to make detailed decisions on resource use—has led to greater need for other institutional forms. The private sector within socialist economies is sizable and growing.[2] In Hungary, for example, problems of running the country's 18,456 mostly small restaurants[3] led the government, in 1980, to adopt a policy of leasing to private operators all restaurants that had been operating at a loss or at a small profit.[4] By 1982, the Ministry of Home Trade had rented 20 percent of all restaurants to private operators;[5] by September 1983, 32 percent had been rented, and the proportion was expected to reach 45 percent by the end of 1985.[6] Leasing restaurants to the highest bidders has converted a substantial deficit into a sizable surplus.[7]

Even in the highly centralized Soviet Union there is an active private sector. Despite universal public schooling, families purchase enormous quantities of educational services through the private market. During the five-year period 1976–1980, expenditures on private tutoring alone totaled some 8 billion rubles, about one-fifth of the total national budget for all general-education secondary schools.[8] In automobile repair, the share of the private market is even more striking. A recent press account in the USSR reported that "only four out of every ten [privately owned] cars . . . are repaired at state service stations. If we assume that one private motorist in ten may do his own car work, that leaves five out of ten repairs to be done by mechanics working 'on the side.' "[9] And in even the most capitalist of societies, not everything is left to the private sector. The military, postal service, and highways are inevitably financed and operated by government. At the local level, mass transit is typically a governmental function, in the United States as well as in Western Europe. Everywhere, courts and police are governmental activities. Each institutional form has its advantages and disadvantages for meeting the various needs of the society of which it is a part.

The Proprietary Sector

The main strength of private enterprise is its efficiency in meeting consumer demands at minimum cost. The attraction of profit is a powerful incentive for managers to seek lower production costs and products that more fully meet demands. All other forms of institution, whether governmental or private nonprofit, are likely to be less efficient in this regard, simply because their managers and officials cannot share so fully in the fruits of increased efficiency; they lack the "property right" to any profit they generate.

A recent survey reviewed nearly fifty published papers that compared the efficiency of proprietary (for-profit) firms and government and, in some cases, private nonprofit organizations. Only three of the studies found lower costs in public enterprises, five found no difference, and forty found that "private supply is unequivocally more efficient."[10]

To some observers, the meaning of this literature is entirely clear: the proprietary form of institution is more efficient than any not-for-profit form of organization, whether governmental or private. The quantitative evidence on comparative efficiency is overwhelmingly focused on profit-oriented versus governmental organizations, but the conclusion reached by one pair of authors is widely believed to apply just as well to private nonprofit organizations:

> The outlines of a consensus have emerged concerning the appropriateness of public-sector activities in representative democracies such as the United States. This consensus holds that nearly every public-sector program in these nations is inappropriate, or is carried on at an inappropriate level, or is executed in an inappropriate manner . . . Both theoretical and empirical evidence suggests that the public sector cannot be and is not as efficient as the private sector.[11]

The proprietary form also has limitations. Despite researchers' preoccupation with the relative efficiency of institutions, the definition of efficiency is seldom examined carefully. Whether one form of institution is more efficient than another—in the sense of producing the same output at lower real cost—depends on the nature of the outputs. Outputs are likely to take systematically different forms or to be distributed to systematically different consumers, depending on the type of institution that provides them. Thus, the social choice is seldom between using one or another form of institution to provide a particular, homogeneous, output to a specific group of consumers; it is, rather, the choice between providing different outputs or providing the same outputs to different people.

The private market does not respond to any wants or needs unless they are accompanied by money demand. This has two important implications. (1) Consumers who are willing and able to pay will have their demands satisfied through the private market; those who are not, will not. (2) Consumers who are poorly informed—who, for example, cannot detect differences in quality of services—will not find the private market supplying higher quality when lower quality can be sold at the same price.

Lack of information is a major source of dissatisfaction with the proprietary form of institution. Producers who know more than consumers do can "chisel" away the quality of services in ways that are costly for buyers to detect. Airlines, for example, know just how thoroughly—or inadequately—routine maintenance has been done; nursing home operators know whether sedatives are being given simply to keep patients quiet. Such information is very difficult for consumers—airline passengers or patients' families—to acquire.

At the root of many social problems is a substantial inequality in the information available to various parties. Some of those problems are corruption, "chiseling," shirking, insider trading, false advertising, "cream skimming" of program applicants, "free-rider" behavior, environmental pollution, violations of trust or of fiduciary responsibilities, "diploma mills," and the difficulty of reaching mutually verifiable nuclear arms–reduction agreements. In all these cases the pursuit of individual self-interest leads to adverse effects on others, and not to the betterment of both parties, as is the outcome of exchanges between well-informed parties.[12]

Informational problems are not the only source of "failures" in the private sector (failures in the sense that consumers do not obtain the goods and services that they would demand if they were well informed). The market mechanism also fails, in this sense, when consumers demand collective-type services or when production or consumption of a commodity has "external" effects—on persons other than the buyers and sellers; profit-motivated firms will not take into account any effects of their activities that do not influence their revenues or costs. Examples of commodities that accrue large external benefits include basic research, environmental protection, aid to the poor, and national defense. These, too, are in large measure information-based activities, but in any event they are instances in which profit-motivated private enterprise cannot be relied upon to provide efficient levels of output.

The Public Sector

Collective action through government has the potential of correcting market failures. Since it has the power to tax, government can finance, subsidize, mandate, or otherwise encourage the provision of goods and services that are inadequately provided by the private sector or that are not provided to particular groups in the population. It can also provide the services itself. Conversely, it can discourage—tax or prohibit—undesired activities of the private sector.

The point to keep in mind is that government can attempt to correct market failures in several ways. It can affect the level of provision of some good or service without actually producing it. It can regulate nongovernmental providers. It can also finance production of goods or services by private firms or nonprofit organizations. How effectively government can raise funds and then use them to subsidize or make purchases from nongovernmental producers is another matter. In any event, the advantage that government has in its ability to tax, which bypasses private firms' dependence on prices or user fees, is an advantage in fund raising, not in production. Indeed, a substantial amount of the receipts of proprietary (for-profit) and nonprofit organizations comes from governments, through sales and through grants.

The legal prohibition on government officials' sharing in any surplus generated by the agencies they manage doubtless affects behavior. On one hand, it reduces incentives to take advantage of underinformed consumers. This virtue, however, may be accompanied by a corresponding loss of incentive to be efficient. Of course, if government (and nonprofit) managers can circumvent the legal restriction against distributing profit, concealing it as salary or taking it in such nonpecuniary forms as expense accounts or elaborate offices, there may be little or no actual difference among forms of institutions in the incentive to exploit consumers.

The principal limitation of government is also its basic source of strength—its reliance on the political process. No brief characterization of this process can do it justice. What is clear is that the incentives offered by the political reward structure to government officials are different from those offered their private-sector counterparts; they have less incentive to respond to consumers' economic demands and more incentive to respond to the demands of the political process with its different distribution of power. For example, the dependence of senior officials on periodic elections is not conducive to solving long-term problems. Of course, whether private entrepreneurs and managers are rewarded for long-term planning is not obvious. In addition, civil-service guarantees for less-senior government employees can reduce their incentives to be productive and creative (although for some people the greater job security may have the opposite effect). Government regulators often confront heavy political pressures from well-organized private producers that overwhelm the interests of poorly organized and disparate consumers. Government officials, looking out for their self-interest, may see on the horizon the possibility of a well-paying job with private industry and this may temper enthusiasm for strong enforcement of restrictive regulations. Finally, the same informational problems that confront the private sector exist for government; it may or may not be able to cope with them any more effectively. The net effects of all these crosscurrents are ambiguous.

The shortcomings of the private market can occur in any of three areas—the choice of goods and services produced, production processes, and the distribution of outputs. It would seem, therefore, that government could directly regulate these areas, but informational problems sometimes make that seemingly easy solution impossible or impractical. Government could, for example, alter the incentives facing proprietary firms so that they would change their behavior. Judicious use of taxes and subsidies, to discourage undesired activities and to encourage desired ones, might achieve the desired efficient and equitable outcomes; there would be no need to control either profit or its distribution—no need, that is, to foster nonprofits. If proprietary firms were polluting, a system of taxes, subsidies, and regulations could diminish the incentive to pollute; use of equipment that pollutes could be taxed or antipollution technologies subsidized, use of hazardous equipment could be taxed or safer equipment subsidized; sale of dangerous consumer goods could be taxed or safer goods subsidized.[13] "Basic" foodstuffs and housing, if deemed vital to the poor, could be subsidized directly, through food stamps and housing vouchers—without recourse to nonprofits. Indeed, each of these mechanisms is actually used.

Government can regulate, tax, and subsidize, however, only what it can monitor. The more costly the needed information—that is, the more expensive it is to gauge whether an organization has complied with a given requirement—the more difficult it is to implement a system of rewards and punishments, subsidies and taxes, to achieve the desired results. The key policy issue, therefore, is whether the disadvantages of using an indirect form of regulation—regulating the distribution of surplus, for example—are offset by greater ease of monitoring it rather than regulating production and its distribution directly.

Whether regulation is direct or indirect, it is intended to be restrictive. Thus, there is an incentive for the regulated parties to circumvent or simply to evade regulations. Enforcement costs rise with increased restrictions and resources are expended in socially unproductive searches for ways around the restrictions.[14]

Because detection of regulatory violations involves costs, all regulators—not simply governments but also private firms and nonprofits monitoring their employees—attempt to control some kinds of behavior but not others. The question of efficiency governs what is monitored. An employer may monitor the hour at which an employee arrives and departs, for example, because it is too costly to measure employee productivity directly. When government regulates nursing homes, it monitors such easily observed behavior as whether the sprinkler system is operative and whether there is a dietitian on the payroll; it does not attempt to determine whether the home is providing "tender loving care" or whether the food is tasty and attractive. Government may regulate entry into an occupation as in medicine and law, but it may do little to monitor quality once the person has been admitted to practice, since that is more costly.[15]

Recognizing these regulatory costs, government may choose to monitor what an organization does with its "profits" or surplus—that is, regulate nonprofits—because it is less costly than measuring whether an organization is producing and distributing outputs in the socially desired ways. We regulate what we can monitor easily, and we monitor what we can gauge usefully and inexpensively.[16] If and when regulation of nonprofits per se is easier than direct regulation of outputs, production processes, or the distribution of output, the nonprofit form of institution is attractive.

The Nonprofit Sector

Claims for, and charges against, nonprofits mirror beliefs about the strengths and weaknesses of private enterprise and the governmental sector. Supporters of nonprofits claim that these organizations bring about needed changes in governmental and private institutions,[17] that they provide "outlets for . . . altruism,"[18] and that they provide "trustworthy" alternatives to profit-oriented provision of day-care, nursing-home, and hospital services.[19]

In some markets buyers do not care who the seller is. For other goods and services, though, it matters a great deal.[20] A consumer who is underinformed may choose to deal with a family member, a friend, a private firm with which there is likely to be a long-term relationship, or, perhaps, with a nonprofit organization. Each may merit trust that it will not take advantage of the buyer's ignorance.[21] Consequently, just as there is often an advantage to doing business with a specific individual seller, so there can be an advantage to dealing with a specific *kind* of seller. Relationships of trust—"loyalty"—are central to many of our social and economic relations.[22]

Although the nonprofit institution, because of the constraints on it, may be more trustworthy—less likely to act opportunistically toward consumers—this feature would not be enough to make it preferred socially to proprietary firms.[23] Nonprofit managers may also have less incentive to be efficient, since efficiency cannot lawfully be rewarded. Thus, critics of nonprofits have a reasonable basis for claims that these organizations are inefficient compared to proprietary firms,[24] "insensitive to their (economic) environment,"[25] and victims of "shirking" because managers cannot retain the surplus they generate.[26] On the other hand, if managers of nonprofits derive relatively greater personal satisfaction than their proprietary counterparts do from providing a particular service, then there would be an incentive for nonprofit managers to be efficient even though they cannot benefit financially. Still, a complete comparative evaluation of for-profit and nonprofit organizations demands that we understand incentives both to take advantage of underinformed consumers and to be efficient. Previous economic research has focused on comparative efficiency—which has favored private enterprise—but that is not enough, no matter how well it is done. For a balanced view we must examine the other side—the consequences of informational problems and the ensuing difficulty of rewarding performance in various forms of institutions.

There is still a third position regarding whether the private nonprofit institution is or is not socially desirable—that it is no different from a proprietary firm! In the nursing-home industry, one writer asserts, "The roughly 15 percent of American nursing homes classed as nonprofits are not significantly different from their profit-making (proprietary) brethren."[27] And in the hospital industry, "there is little distinction between a for-profit institution and a not-for-profit institution."[28]

Of the many claims, the one that nonprofits are no different from proprietary firms, although possible, is least plausible. The legal constraints that influence nonprofit and proprietary organizations differ markedly— the nondistribution constraint,[29] of course, but also the restriction on nonprofits from selling shares of stock as proprietaries may do, and the tax subsidies, which favor nonprofits. These are almost certain to produce unequal behavior, even when the two kinds of organizations compete against each other.

Hybrid institutions such as nonprofits exist because neither the proprietary nor the governmental form is fully satisfactory—individually or in combination. Consumers are not equally informed about any particular commodity. They differ in the efficiency with which they can obtain and interpret information and, because they have different preferences and wealth, they attach different levels of importance to being informed. The for-profit market will thus work more satisfactorily for well-informed consumers than for others. In some industries, multiple forms of institutions may be desirable—none being preferred by all consumers.

If we think of an economy as a system of for-profit, governmental, and nonprofit institutions, then the institutional-choice problem has two parts. One is a choice between for-profit organizations and the other forms; this choice hinges on the nature of the commodity involved—in particular whether it is essentially a private good or has collective-good qualities. Basic medical research and consumer information are collective goods, which the for-profit market is presumably less efficient in providing than are alternative institutions. The second choice is between governmental and private nonprofit institutions. Both face the nondistribution constraint, but they differ in other dimensions, particularly in the political constraints on governmental decisions and in nonprofits' access to capital markets. The public sector is the institution of choice when consumer demands are homogeneous. The nonprofit institution is attractive in meeting heterogeneous demands from minorities who are willing to pay for high levels of service.

The rationale for the nonprofit sector, then, has two components: nonprofits are useful in providing collective goods when consumer demand is heterogeneous. These components are complementary, not alternative, justifications for nonprofits.[30]

Meeting Diverse Demand for Collective Goods

In a democratic society, government must make its services available to everyone who meets certain conditions—the "equal access" constraint. Inevitably, some people who benefit from governmental services are unintended beneficiaries; they are included only because of the cost of excluding them. At the same time, some who do not obtain the services are excluded unintentionally, victims of the high costs of targeting the consumer population more accurately. Determining eligibility for any government program thus presents a dilemma: (1) eligibility can be more comprehensive, which would avoid excluding any intended beneficiaries but would increase the cost of the program by including some unintended beneficiaries, or (2) it can be more restrictive, which would reduce costs and decrease provision of services to unintended beneficiaries but in the process would inadvertently exclude more people for whom the program is intended.[31] In some cases a more decentralized, nongovernmental institutional mechanism, such as the nonprofit, may have better access to diverse, localized information, thereby overcoming some of the problems of over- and underutilization.

Dealing with diversity—which is fundamentally a problem of information—is a major problem for government. If all consumers had identical demands for public action—whether for trust-type, consumer-protection services, or for other collective goods—this problem would disappear. When demand is diverse, though, whatever quantities and qualities of services government provides will oversatisfy some people and undersatisfy others.[32] Can the nonprofit form of institution respond?

All governmental units are defined by geographic boundaries—of a country, state, province, district, municipality, and so on. The smaller the unit, the more its residents are likely to be similar—in income, wealth, religion, ethnic background, education, and other characteristics that lead them to have similar economic demands. The geographic mobility that permits such sorting is, however, imperfect.[33] The demands for any specific collective-type service normally vary among the persons within a geographically defined governmental unit; whatever the combination of governmental services and taxes, some people will demand more, others less.[34]

In addition to relocating, other potential adjustment mechanisms are available to unsatisfied consumers, but all involve costs. Attempts can be made to change the "rules of the game"—the tax-pricing system, the process by which the level and pattern of governmental activities are determined, and the definition of the boundaries and functions of governmental units. Yet, because of the costs required to pursue these options, there will inevitably be both oversatisfied and undersatisfied demanders—persons who, given the tax prices (tax per unit of output) they pay, prefer either diminished or expanded public services.

Undersatisfied demanders for collective-type services can turn to the private market for substitutes for the governmentally provided outputs; the private good (shipboard radar) can substitute for the public good (lighthouse); home and office air purifiers can substitute for a public clean-air campaign; private sprinkler systems can substitute for public fire departments; outdoor lighting of individual homes can substitute for public street lighting; alarms, locks, guards, and dogs can substitute for police.[35] These private goods are not perfect substitutes for the governmental form of output. The principal advantage of the private good is the individualized control that its owner can exercise—for example, being able to turn one's house lights on and off as desired, rather than having to abide by collective decisions. The principal disadvantage of the private good in this regard is its higher cost per consumer.

Undersatisfied demanders can also turn to the private nonprofit sector. Nonprofits reflect the diversity of demands upon government; Robert Clark has even referred to private nonprofit organizations as "mini governments."[36] The undersatisfied demand for collective-type goods is a governmental "failure" analogous to private market failures. That is, the combined willingness of part of the population to pay for some additional collective-type goods exceeds the incremental cost of providing them and yet government, responding to majoritarian interests, does not provide them.

If the nonprofit sector exists to respond to diversity of demands for collective goods, its size relative to government should differ across nations. The private nonprofit sector does seem to be particularly noteworthy in the United States, a country of unusual diversity. The separation of church and state, with its concomitant requirement that governmental spending on religion be zero, is unique to the United States, with its religiously diverse society. This is what the demand-diversity model would predict—if government responds to the demands of the majority and the nonprofit sector responds to the demands of the undersatisfied, then the greater the diversity of demand the larger the size of the nonprofit sector will be, other things being equal. And if the diversity is sufficiently large, the quantity of a specific good or service demanded by the majority can be zero; if a good or service is demanded by only a minority of consumers—that is, if it is a collective-type commodity only for them—governmental provision would be minimal or absent.[37]

Similarly, when it comes to support for the poor and needy, some new evidence shows a remarkably higher level of nonprofit activity in the United States as compared with Japan, a country of less cultural and economic diversity. In 1982, "Community Chest" contributions per capita were ten times as great in the United States as in Japan. Since per capita income in the United States is about 1.5 times that of Japan, some difference would be expected, but the question posed in a recent Japanese newspaper column—"Why is Japan's per-capita donation so small?"—is not likely to be answered by the subtitle of the column, "Are Japanese tightfisted?"[38] Rather, it is more probable that the greater consensus in culturally more homogeneous Japan leads to a larger role for government, to greater satisfaction of demand, and to a smaller role for the nonprofit sector.[39]

If the private nonprofit form of institution is to correct governmental failures associated with undersatisfied demand, it must overcome the free-rider problem. How should the true demands for collective goods by undersatisfied demanders be determined? How should output be financed? If government could determine the demands, it could tax the undersatisfied demanders and provide more output, thereby satisfying the diverse demands. Can private nonprofit institutions obtain information on individuals' willingness to pay any more efficiently than governments can? Even if they can, are they able to get people to pay, given that the nonprofits cannot compel payment? The two questions are somewhat related and the nonprofits have an arsenal of instruments for dealing with them.

Nonprofits have two principal instruments for encouraging consumers to reveal their demands. One is a stick: social pressure; the other is a carrot: subsidies. Individual pursuit of self-interest sometimes needs to be harnessed if collective goals are to be achieved. The agricultural "commons" may need protection from overgrazing and the fishery from overfishing, lest the total resource be destroyed by individually sound but collectively irrational actions. Littering needs to be curbed, pollution limited, and aid to the needy stimulated. Sometimes embodied in the law, but often simply part of the social fabric, such rules and norms of expected behavior are inculcated by the social system. Schools, churches, and other social institutions teach what society expects of each of us—to behave in ways that harmonize our individual self-interest with the collective social interest. Thus, many people donate to charities and do not litter simply because they have been socialized to believe that one is desirable and the other is not. These attitudes are reflections of "invisible institutions: the principles of ethics and morality"; they involve "agreements, conscious or, in many cases, unconscious, to supply mutual benefits."[40]

Sometimes these societal pressures amount to taxation, as when an employer, customer, or friend "asks" for a "donation" of money or time. However they are perceived, the effect of such requests is the channeling of private contributions for the provision of collectively valuable activities. These activities provide benefits primarily not to those who contribute or who apply the pressure, but to others—be it the poor, in the case of antipoverty organizations such as CARE; the disabled, in the case of Goodwill Industries; or the victims of particular diseases, in the case of the various medical research and caring activities of the American Cancer Society and American Heart Association.[41]

Donations to "charitable" organizations engaged in furthering goals in education, health, welfare, scientific research, and so forth are encouraged through a variety of subsidies to both nonprofit organizations and their financial supporters. The organizations' activities in the charitable (collective-good) realm are not subject to federal tax on profits; donations to them are tax deductible on federal and state income tax returns; the organizations are, in most states, not subject to real property taxation or to sales taxation on their purchases; they obtain subsidized postal rates, are sometimes exempted from minimum wage laws, and have until very recently been permitted to opt out of the Social Security system.

These subsidies help to overcome free-rider tendencies, thereby increasing organizational revenues, in two ways. First, the deductibility of donations on the donor's individual income tax return stimulates giving because it reduces the after-tax cost to the donor. Second, the various tax subsidies to the organization increase the amount of output that a donor can buy for any given donation. Both have the effect of rewarding people if they reveal—even partially—their willingness to pay for particular collective goods.[42]

In the United States, income tax deductibility is used to encourage donations. In the United Kingdom, by contrast, there is no tax deductibility for charitable donations. Donations are, however, partially matched by governmental grants to the recipient organization. In both countries the private cost to a donor of transferring a dollar (or a pound) to a charitable organization is less than a dollar (or pound). A significant difference between the two systems is that whereas the matching rate in the United Kingdom, at least between 1946 and 1981, did not depend on the level of the donor's income, the U.S. system has had the effect of making the matching rate greater for persons in higher marginal income tax brackets. The difference in effect between these two systems is that the U.S. approach gives greater incentives for higher-income persons to contribute, and so it gives them a stronger voice in determining the level and pattern of activities in the nonprofit sector.[43]

Whatever the form of governmental encouragement, it is only partial; there is a private cost to the donor. Yet, despite the cost, people donate to charities, "public" television, schools, hospitals, museums, libraries, medical research, and so on. The invisible institutions—social conventions, ethical norms, and "demands of conscience"[44]—provide implicit rewards for giving.

Nevertheless, free-rider behavior is a real source of private market failure whenever collective services are involved. Experimental evidence shows that the pursuit of narrow self-interest by potential beneficiaries leads to private underprovision, although not to a zero level.[45] Similarly, research shows that fund raising—that is, advertising—increases contributions; this would not occur if donors acted strictly as free riders.[46] The question, however, is whether high demanders reveal their preferences and high willingness to pay any more fully to a nonprofit organization than to a government or to a proprietary firm. The undersatisfied high demanders of collective goods may be people for whom the sense of social responsibility is strongest; while they may prefer that more people shared their intensity of concern about certain collective goals, they may feel that their own obligations are not diminished by the lower intensity of others' contributions.

Tax-subsidy policies encourage high demanders to reveal their demands. Whenever donations are deducted from taxes, tax revenue is reduced. In effect, taxpayers in general subsidize those particular taxpayers who will reveal their greater willingness to pay for collective goods by donating. The subsidy is understandable insofar as there are taxpayers with lower but still positive demands for collective goods; they, too, would benefit if the high demanders would increase their contributions. Tax subsidies therefore represent, in effect, contributions from low demanders to stimulate the high demanders to contribute. Moreover, in the process of encouraging donations, society is also making a statement about social norms—about which types of behavior are to be encouraged and appreciated. Thus, the subsidies have a double-barreled effect on contributions.

There is no necessary reason that subsidies should work only through nonprofit organizations. They could be given for donations to governments or to private firms.[47] Donors of funds to proprietary firms are understandably likely to be concerned. Those firms may not use the funds as donors intend, given the difficulty that donors have in monitoring what is done with their donations. Because of the informational handicap, donors may prefer to deal with an organization—such as a nonprofit— that is legally constrained not to pay its surplus to its managers and that is monitored by a governmental regulator (the IRS).

Even if donors prefer not to deal with a proprietary firm, because of the greater cost of monitoring it, nonprofits would not be needed if contributions could be made to a government agency responsible for providing the desired service. It seems plausible, however, that people who are already paying taxes to governments will prefer, when it comes to financing additional output, to fund other providers. They may feel that their voluntary contributions will lead not to increased governmental output, but to an offsetting decrease in tax-financed expenditures. Although a voluntary contributor to a government agency may be quite uncertain that the contribution will actually increase governmental output, the possibility that a contribution of money, goods, or time to a nonprofit organization will diminish governmental activity in that area, while not absent, is seemingly weaker. High demanders may therefore prefer to contribute to voluntary organizations rather than to government.

The effect of a donation, whether it is made to a proprietary, governmental, or nonprofit organization, on the level of tax-financed governmental expenditures is not yet known. At issue is the magnitude of "crowding out"; increased private donations may decrease what government would otherwise have done.

Prospective donors do not always have the option of donating to governmental organizations. Robert Monks, the wealthy head of a U.S. Department of Labor pension program unit, recently attempted to make a donation to the federal government. He found, first, that federal law barred him from refusing his $67,800 salary. Second, he could not even donate it to the department in order to hire additional staff! So Monks donated the money to nonprofit charities in Maine.[48] Although the federal government may restrict donations to support particular activities, the very essence of a nonprofit organization's appeal to donors is that donors can increase the level and even change the direction of the recipient organization's activities.

Managerial Sorting

Nonprofit organizations may act differently from private firms not only because of the constraint on distributing profit but also, perhaps, because the motivations and goals of managers and directors (hereinafter I will refer to both as managers or decisionmakers) differ. If some nonprofits attract managers whose goals are different from those of managers in the proprietary sector, the two types of organizations will behave differently. Whether this "sorting" of managers, if it occurs, is an advantage or a limitation of the nonprofit form of institution is another matter.

Do nonprofit and proprietary managers have different goals? The question is whether managers of the different forms of organization are selected or sorted in ways that cause for-profit and nonprofit, and also governmental, organizations to have systematically different goals. Is it true, for example, that managers of nonprofits are more interested in serving the public and less motivated by financial opportunities than are their proprietary counterparts? If they are, then depending on how "public service" is seen by prospective consumers or donors, donors might or might not prefer to deal with a nonprofit rather than with a proprietary firm.

If all decisionmakers had the same preferences and goals, it would make no difference, from a social perspective, which ones worked for governments, which for private nonprofit organizations, and which for proprietary firms. Preferences do vary, however, and that they do has important implications. One is that the restrictions that are imposed on any form of institution—such as the nondistribution constraint—will be more restrictive for some managers than for others. Indeed, for some decisionmakers a particular constraint will not be limiting at all; people who enjoy helping the needy, for example, will be affected little by a requirement that the organization for which they work must limit its activities to the poor.

Managers will, therefore, sort themselves, each gravitating to the types of organizations that he or she finds least restrictive—most compatible with his or her personal preferences. As a result, nonprofit and proprietary organizations, having different legal regulations, will attract managers with systematically different goals. The two types of institutions will behave differently for two reasons—the constraints on them differ, and the goals of their managers differ.

There has been little study of the process of managerial sorting in proprietary and nonprofit organizations. In two studies of students in the Graduate School of Management at Vanderbilt University, striking differences were found among students who subsequently entered the for-profit and nonprofit sectors—differences in personality, values, and behavior.[49] A battery of tests disclosed no significant differences in their problem-solving ability, intelligence, or creativity. Those choosing the nonprofits, however, had previously scored significantly higher on the California Psychological Inventory tests of "personal relations," "dominance," "capacity for status," "social presence," and "flexibility." On a test of values (Rokeach Value Survey), persons preferring to work in the nonprofit sector gave higher rankings to being cheerful, forgiving, and helpful. By contrast, those preferring the proprietary sector attached more importance to financial prosperity, ambition, neatness, obedience, and dependability; they also displayed greater "need for power" and less "need for security" (as measured by the Ghiselli Self-Description Inventory).

Evidence of sorting was also found in a study of law school graduates' choices between working for a proprietary law firm or for a nonprofit "public interest" (PIL) firm. The two types of law firms served different kinds of clients and were financed in different ways: the for-profit firms depended on user fees from clients, whereas the nonprofits relied heavily on contributions, largely from foundations. The PIL firms focused on informational and organizational problems of "underrepresented" groups in such areas as discrimination in employment or housing, preservation of wilderness areas, or the content of advertising on children's television programs.[50] PIL lawyers were earning less than they could earn in private law practice, they were aware of it, they did not expect the PIL experience to let them make up the shortfall later in their professional careers, and judging from the limited evidence on lifetime career paths of PIL lawyers—most of whom, when they did leave PIL work, went into relatively low-paying jobs in government, teaching, or legal rights— they did not make it up. Despite the financial sacrifices, 97 percent of PIL lawyers who were asked whether they are satisfied with their career choices answered yes. The overall attractiveness of PIL work to the lawyers engaged in it was apparently sufficient compensation for their lower financial rewards.[51] Background information was consistent with the view that preferences between private-sector and PIL lawyers differed. Nonprofit PIL lawyers were more likely to be politically "liberal," to have been involved in political activity in college or law school, to be Jewish, and to have grown up in a larger city—factors that suggest differences in attitudes and goals.[52]

Two or three studies cannot demonstrate conclusively that different constraints on organizational behavior necessarily leads to managerial sorting. Nor can they prove that organizational behavior is affected materially by such sorting as does occur. The evidence, however, is quite suggestive on both counts.

Similar sorting of managers may well occur between the nonprofit and the governmental sectors, depending on differences in constraints in those sectors. Although the nondistribution constraint applies to both governmental agencies and nonprofits, the other respects in which they differ make it likely that further sorting of managers does occur between them; differences in behavior would then result. Evidence on this is lacking.

Differences in Efficiency

Institutions differ in their ability to address the social goals of efficiency and equity. One aspect of "efficiency" that largely escapes attention is that proprietary and nonprofit (as well as governmental) suppliers provide systematically distinct forms of output. The social choice among forms of institutions, therefore, is a choice not among alternative instruments for providing a given mix of services, but for providing different mixes and often for distributing outputs to different consumers.

If one form of institution is more efficient than others, that would be a major argument for utilizing it. Whether one or another form of institution is most efficient depends, first, on the state of consumer information. The proprietary form is preferred on grounds of efficiency when consumers are well informed; a profit-constrained form—government or private nonprofit—is preferable when consumer information is limited. Second, efficiency depends on the diversity of consumer demands for collective action, to deal with either informational handicaps or with other collective wants. Government is likely to be preferred when there is greater homogeneity in demand; the nonprofit form has greater advantages the more heterogeneous the demands for collective action.

A society's choices among forms of institutions does not depend on their efficiency alone; considerations of equity also matter. Nonetheless, the comparative efficiency of proprietary, governmental, and nonprofit organizations is certainly an important issue, and many people hold strong positions on it. What do we really know about the comparative efficiency of the three forms of organizations?

Cost per unit of output depends on the quality of output. If public and private producers did not provide essentially identical outputs, their costs might well differ, but we could not say that one producer was more cost efficient than the other. With quality potentially differing in many dimensions, it may or may not even be possible to say which producer is providing higher quality, let alone how much higher. Thus, if differences in production costs are associated with differences in qualities of output, it is meaningless to say which producer is more efficient.

Analysts have attempted to control statistically for such differences in order to answer the question: holding constant the quality of output for public and private producers, do costs differ? These statistical efforts, in general, are seriously flawed. In the hospital industry, for example, are proprietary hospitals more efficient than governmental or nonprofit hospitals? If there are systematic differences in the types of services provided, then it is not appropriate to ask which form of institution is a lower-cost producer when service levels are held constant at any particular level. Indeed, the answer can depend on the level considered.

The problem of making sense of the question, which form of institution is more "efficient"—let alone of answering it—is complicated further insofar as the size of producers varies. In fact, proprietary short-term hospitals are generally smaller than nonprofit (as well as public) hospitals; they have an average of 120 beds, compared with 211 beds in the average nonprofit hospital.[53] If the reason for the smaller size is that proprietaries offer a more limited scope of services, then the difference in size is a systematic, not a random, difference; it is a result of the output mix of the institution. As such, it should not be held constant in a quantitative analysis of the effect of institutional form on cost efficiency.

Figure 2.1 shows how the average cost of production varies with the form or quality of output, for two hypothetical groups of providers—one public or, perhaps, nonprofit, the other proprietary.[54] Costs increase with quality of output and each form of institution is more cost efficient in a different quality range. There is no way to decide which type of provider is more cost efficient. At quality level 1, private providers are

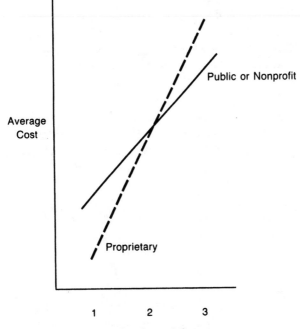

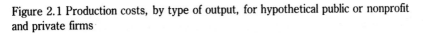

Figure 2.1 Production costs, by type of output, for hypothetical public or nonprofit and private firms

more efficient; at level 3, public providers are more efficient; and at level 2 there is no difference. If each type of institution was providing the type of output it could produce most efficiently, the proprietary sector would have a lower average cost but also a lower "quality" of output.

Is this hypothetical situation at all likely? Granted its possibility, precisely which cost relationships have actually been estimated in the empirical studies that have compared "the" efficiency of public and proprietary providers?

Generally speaking, researchers making statistical comparisons of institutional efficiency have assumed—usually only implicitly—that the public and private producers being compared produce outputs with essentially the same attributes, or at least that the cost functions (or other measures of efficiency) do not cross, as they do in Figure 2.1. Most have done little more than compare some measure of performance— "costs," prices, passenger-miles carried, and so forth—of public and private providers while alleging that the quality of output is sufficiently similar to pose no serious problem. In the case of one study of public and private garbage collection, the author simply assumed that, for example, once-a-week curbside collection is a standardized, homogeneous unit of output. There was no adjustment for the possibility that systematic differences in quality exist between public and private providers—differences in, say, reliability of service, neatness of the pickup, and type of waste collected (grass clippings and other yard waste, bulky waste such as large appliances and furniture).[55] Similarly, discussions of the comparative efficiency of the U.S. Postal Service and the private United Parcel Service typically fail to consider differences in the number of free pickup points, the variety of sizes of articles accepted, and the geographic distribution of delivery points.

In an excellent study comparing the productivity (output per unit of input) of the privately owned Canadian Pacific Railroad and the publicly owned Canadian National, the authors use statistical models to control for factors that would influence costs independently of ownership form but which are correlated with ownership form.[56] These factors included, for example, the length of haul and the type of commodities being carried. In the context of Figure 2.1, some producers were supplying output at quality level 1—rail transportation of long-haul, bulk cargo—while others were supplying higher-cost, level-3 output—short-haul, finished goods. The statistical model for estimating productivity employs averages of the effects of length of haul and type of commodity carried, which would provide estimates of comparative cost efficiency somewhere between levels 1 and 3 in Figure 2.1. The results of this study are in contrast to most estimates of comparative institutional efficiency. "Contrary to the property rights literature, . . . [there is] no evidence of inferior performance by the government-owned railroad."[57] This is precisely what Figure 2.1 shows for the "average" quality of output.

If governmental, nonprofit, and proprietary suppliers provide unequal quality, or serve consumers who are unequally easy to reach, then the failure to account for these differences leads to bias in the resulting cost comparisons. If certain dimensions of quality or of consumers are omitted, the form of institution that provides more of them will be found, erroneously, to have higher cost, even though it is actually providing a different type of output. Thus, from a statistical viewpoint the issue is one of how accurately "outputs" are measured. When outputs are viewed and measured in a way that focuses on the qualities of the private sector, the special qualities of public or nonprofit suppliers are overlooked. When proprietary, governmental, and nonprofit sellers coexist, they are likely to provide systematically different types of services or distribute them in different ways, but when costs are compared, the private firm is considered the standard of comparison. Nonprofit and governmental organizations may well provide more outputs in forms that the private market does not reward. If society wants to encourage production of these outputs, these institutional alternatives to the private market have a place.

Some outputs can be measured well; others, only poorly or not at all. The janitorial staff at a major midwestern public university includes a large number of deaf-mute and mentally handicapped people. Since such persons are seldom employed in proprietary firms, it may well be that, given minimum-wage rules, it is more costly per unit of janitorial services to employ them. Their employment by the public institution could reflect simply the inefficiency of organizations in which property rights are limited. Yet hiring the handicapped is itself an output having collective value. A private employer would be expected to hire a janitor only for the services he or she would provide, whereas the public or nonprofit employer might be purchasing janitorial services and also providing employment opportunities for the handicapped. It is true, however, that employment of the handicapped could be increased in the private sector with appropriate governmental subsidization. Thus, even if private firms do hire relatively fewer handicapped workers than do nonprofits or governmental agencies, it would not follow that the latter forms of institutions would be preferable. It would demonstrate only that under current conditions the overall pattern of activities varies across types of institutions—and, as a result, their comparative efficiency cannot be assessed without adjusting for those differences.

Determining whether the social value of the output "employing the handicapped" justifies a greater cost per unit of the output "janitorial services provided" for nonprofits and governmental organizations—assuming there is a difference in cost—is another matter. This public organization, the university, not only provides conventional educational services, but also provides output in the form of employment opportunities for the handicapped. To disregard the latter is to assume that its social value is zero. If such examples are not only common but typical—and I believe they are—there is systematic undercounting of the outputs (or quality) in public and nonprofit institutions; for that reason, studies of comparative institutional efficiency are, in general, erroneous—biased in favor of private firms.

"Unmeasured outputs" take varied forms and are found throughout the world. In Canada the government entered the railroad business, establishing the publicly owned Canadian National Railways (CN), after World War I, when it took over three privately owned rail systems that were nearly bankrupt. The CN was legally restricted from abandoning its "excess trackage." Public ownership was adopted to achieve more than one broad social goal—"to avert the repercussions which would have followed the bankruptcy of several railroads" and also to encourage development of a sparsely populated region of the country.[58] Any comparison of cost efficiency that disregards these additional outputs of the public railroad system gives a misleading picture; the public system provides some outputs that the private railroads in Canada do not. The value of such outputs, however, remains to be examined, as does the cost of providing them in other ways, but as long as their value is not zero, no determination of which system is more "efficient" can be made without assessing that value. Cost efficiency cannot be compared when the bundle of outputs is different.

The same type of bias results when the cost efficiency of private and government-owned coal mines is compared. Governments are likely to take over the more marginal mines; thus, costs per ton of coal extracted can be expected to be higher. However, governmental operation of these mines is part of a policy to reduce burdens on workers who would otherwise be displaced; the "uneconomic" employment of labor is a substitute for income maintenance and social welfare programs.[59] The private coal mine produces only coal; the government mine produces coal plus income maintenance. In Britain, where coal mines are nationalized, some 55 percent of coal is produced at a loss; some mines have costs that are more than double the pithead price.[60] The social wisdom of maintaining production in all these unprofitable mines is very much in question.[61] Still, to ask whether public or private mines produce coal more cheaply, while disregarding the other output, is poor statistical methodology.[62] It is also not a sensible basis for public policy choices among forms of institutions. At the same time, providing income maintenance through employment in coal mines need not imply public (or nonprofit) ownership; private firms would provide the employment with appropriate subsidization.

The argument that public and private nonprofits may be more trusted than proprietary firms implies that when proprietary and nonprofit (or governmental) organizations operate in the same industry, providing what are ostensibly the same services (such as nursing homes, day care, or coal), they may well be providing certain attributes in common but not others (those that the proprietary market does not reward adequately). Similarly, they may be providing the same services but to consumers who are selected by different criteria—ability to pay in the case of the proprietaries, and "need" or some other criterion in the case of nonprofits and governmental providers.

Prisons illustrate the sometimes subtle differences in output that can exist between proprietary and other forms of institutions. Prisons, customarily restricted to governmental organizations, have recently come within the domain of the private, for-profit sector. Corrections Corporation of America and Behavioral Systems Southwest are two of the largest firms in a growing private sector. There are privately run jails in Arizona, California, Colorado, Tennessee, and Texas already. Nearly twenty states are purchasing or negotiating to purchase jail services from private firms.[63]

Objections to the use of private-enterprise jails seem to reflect concerns about unmeasured forms of output. Some civil-rights lawyers "fear that once strict state supervision is removed, abuses might go unchecked." Perhaps for that reason, most states still ban private ownership of prisons.[64] The opponents are concerned, appropriately or not, about subtle, hard-to-detect activities of proprietary prisons that have the potential for increasing profits at the expense of socially undesired practices. Although Corrections Corporation of America charges the Immigration and Naturalization Service one-third less than the previous cost incurred by the government agency,[65] we cannot determine whether this saving represents greater cost efficiency or lower quality.[66] Studies of comparative "efficiency"—in easily measured terms such as cost per inmate-day—would overlook these differences.

If society simply wants "minimal" custodial care from a prison, there should be no problem contracting with a proprietary firm to provide it. If, however, society wants some more complex bundle of services encompassing subtle attributes such as "humaneness" and "encouragement," it may be difficult indeed to develop a contractual arrangement that would provide the appropriate incentives to profit-oriented firms. Governmental or nonprofit providers, having different incentives, might pursue goals that are more consistent with providing such prison services. Evidence, though, is hard to find.

Do private prisons attempt to maintain occupancy by making it more difficult for inmates to accumulate the "good behavior" points necessary for parole? More broadly, as the executive director of the Association of Criminal Justice Planners, a research organization, put it, "Does the government want to emphasize such a mercenary value as profit in its response to a social problem, as opposed to such values as fairness, equity and personal accountability?"[67] The answers are far from clear; managers and workers at government prisons also have incentives (their very employment) to sustain occupancy, and whether the important values of fairness, equity, and accountability are less fully realized in private firms remains a matter of conjecture.

The systematic failure of statistical comparisons to account properly for differences in the full mix of outputs produced by proprietary, governmental, and nonprofit organizations results from a fundamental oversight. An important question has rarely been asked: Why does a particular industry have a public or a nonprofit component at all? In effect, it has been regarded as a matter of pure chance that the mix of institutional forms among industries varies so much. Surprisingly, the more reasonable explanation has been overlooked: the public or nonprofit forms of institution exist because of a deficiency in the proprietary sector's economic behavior! The result: when proprietary firms coexist with public or nonprofit providers, there are systematic differences in the form or quality of outputs or the way they are distributed to consumers. In Chapter 8 I present some new quantitative evidence testing this proposition.

The employment of the handicapped in the public sector and government ownership of coal mines illustrate the importance that society attaches to distributional goals; we care not only about producing janitorial services and coal, but also about providing decent employment opportunities and earnings rather than welfare or unemployment compensation. The Canadian National railroad highlights the social goal of regional economic development. The debate over for-profit prisons illustrates the relevance of subtle, hard-to-monitor forms of output. Private enterprise undervalues certain outputs that may be of importance to society as a whole, and it can be difficult for government to contract with private firms to provide these outputs.

The Problem: Rewarding Contributions to the Public Good

A major strength of private enterprise is the incentive for its managers of greater rewards for greater efficiency and responsiveness. A second strength is its relative independence from government and political constraints. Its weakness—which is a corollary of its strengths—is that the pursuit of profit sometimes results in social inefficiencies and inequities. The private interest in profit and the public interest are not always synonymous.

The institution of government has different strengths and weaknesses. Its strength lies in its power of compulsion—to regulate and to tax. Its handicaps are its political entanglements and the weak incentives it provides for efficiency.

Private nonprofit organizations combine some of the strengths and weaknesses of government and profit-oriented organizations. Nonprofits, like for-profits, have no power to compel action. Nonprofits are like governmental organizations, though, in being restricted in the use of any surplus they generate. Because of this constraint, their managers have limited ability to benefit from taking advantage of informational superiorities. Thus, like government, nonprofits may be a more "trustworthy" form of institution than the private market; as such they may be capable of overcoming some of the problems that beset the for-profit sector in the provision of goods and services that are costly for consumers to evaluate. And because nonprofits are nongovernmental, they can be more flexible in meeting the heterogeneous demands of consumers for collective action. Nonprofits are a potential safety valve.

Society cannot expect the institutions that have the greatest incentive to be efficient and responsive to consumer demands, which requires managerial freedom and unrestricted opportunities for rewards, to be concerned simultaneously with social goals that are costly to reward. In the search for an optimal balancing of institutional mechanisms, no single form will do.

Many of the advantages and disadvantages of the various forms of institutions hinge on their success in coping with informational problems. These underlie the central institutional-choice problem—how to reward behavior that contributes to the public interest.

THREE

Incentives and Performance

The nonprofit form of institution is designed to prevent an entrepreneur or manager from reaping monetary rewards by taking measures that increase the organization's surplus. This is akin to tying one arm of a fighter behind his back. What sense does it make for society to handicap an organization's efforts to win greater support from consumers and, in the process, to augment profit? The nonprofit organization is only one of a number of institutional forms that society uses to limit rewards—for satisfying consumers or voters. Making sense of such limitations requires an understanding of when and why it is sound policy to drive a wedge between performance and reward.

Choosing when to use the nonprofit form of institution and when to use another is a social welfare problem. Which institutional form will be most successful in rewarding socially desirable behavior? When consumers are well informed, they will reward producers that provide what consumers demand at least cost. When meeting those demands does not affect the well-being of others—that is, when there are no real external effects—private enterprise is very likely the preferred form of institution; the inducement of profit encourages excellence of producers' performance. When consumers are poorly informed, however, it is neither efficient nor equitable to reward producers for meeting demands; the lure of profit is counterproductive when sellers are rewarded for providing what consumers purchase mistakenly.

The advantages and disadvantages of every form of institution are crucially related to informational problems. Information, in turn, is critical because without it we cannot reward people or organizations that do what society wants or punish those who do the opposite. In short, the success or failure of any type of institution lies in its ability to obtain information on product quality and consumer demand and in its incentive to convey to consumers information on the extent to which its product meets that demand—that is, to use the information in socially desirable ways. For-profit, governmental, and nonprofit institutions differ both in their ability to obtain information on social wants and demands and in their incentives to act on it. As a result, each has a distinct niche to fill in an economic system. Institutional pluralism is vital.

"Performance" can be rewarded appropriately only if it can be measured appropriately. The danger of rewarding performance when it is measured poorly was dramatized in 1971 in an influential book on the market for human blood. Explaining that a serious, often fatal, disease—hepatitis—was far more common in the United States than in the United Kingdom, the author argued that the cause was institutional, the reliance in this country on the profit-oriented market. Richard Titmuss's *Gift Relationship* did not reach the best-seller list but it did have a major effect on social scientists, and, eventually, on policymakers. It led to legislative changes that sharply curtailed for-profit blood banks.[1]

Informational problems were central to the argument for the superiority of nonprofit institutions in this case. Individual "donors" (providers) of blood know their health conditions and whether they are using unclean needles to inject drugs—factors that affect the probability that their blood carries the hepatitis virus (and, as we now know, the AIDS virus)—better than do buyers (blood banks and hospitals). In such a market the truthfulness of the blood donor is crucial. In the United States, said Titmuss, private commercial gain was the motive for giving blood, whereas in the United Kingdom all human blood was given freely and with absolutely no compensation or reward. The moral Titmuss drew is that a profit-oriented market for blood—but presumably also for a far-wider range of activities—is inferior to a nonprofit system (which he assumed implicitly was altruistic).[2]

The "facts" presented by Titmuss were far from persuasive. Whether the lower rate of hepatitis in Britain was materially related to that country's lesser reliance on paid blood donors, as Titmuss asserted, was by no means clear; indeed, even the greater dependence of the United States on paid donors was open to debate. Nevertheless, the fundamental point was important—when buyers are underinformed, sellers can gain by acting opportunistically. Nonprofit organizations could be less likely to do so, as Titmuss claimed. If, indeed, managers and directors of non-profits cannot benefit from opportunistic behavior, because of the constraints they face, they will have less incentive to deal with opportunistic sellers—persons who are suspected of withholding vital information. (See Chapter 8 for evidence on differences in behavior by for-profit and non-profit organizations.)

Even when informational inequality is substantial, proprietary firms are not necessarily inferior to nonprofit organizations. Two centuries ago Adam Smith, in *The Wealth of Nations,* captured the essence of an economy based on private enterprise: "It is not from the benevolence of the butcher, the brewer, or the baker that we expect our dinner," he said, "but from their regard to their self-interest."[3] Competition ensures that self-interest will prevent sellers from taking advantage of consumers. Trust is needed only when a person can be harmed in a transaction because the other party can take advantage of superior information. In that case, the better-informed party can be rewarded—and can reap profits—even when performance is less than satisfactory. For competition to drive out opportunism, consumers must be able to distinguish—and, hence, to reward—the honest sellers, to do so at modest cost, and to switch suppliers easily when the truth is learned or specify in a contract appropriate penalties for opportunistic behavior. Sometimes these conditions hold; sometimes they do not.[4]

Consumer protection through competition is an important feature of private enterprise. Government, too, is used to protect underinformed consumers,[5] as are nonprofit organizations. Professional associations and related codes of ethics are still another means of consumer protection, although there is some evidence that such codes sometimes restrict competition and harm consumers.[6] Nevertheless, given the imperfections of every form of institution, it is good to have variety. Competition among forms of institution is desirable, just as is competition among private firms.

The informational advantage of the seller often disappears rapidly after purchase. This has an important implication for choosing an institutional structure: the private, for-profit market can work quite satisfactorily—rewarding producers effectively—even when sellers have the advantage at first, provided that buyers eventually close the information gap.[7] Buyers can, under these conditions, reward the desired performance. Furthermore, warranties in the private market and product liability under tort law mitigate the effects of consumers' initial handicaps. As such, they, like nonprofits, are components of a wide-ranging informational strategy for consumer protection.[8]

When some types of services are purchased, however, there is no way of ever learning for certain what would have happened if the service had not been performed or if it had been purchased from another seller. If, in the case of health care, the patient improved, was it because of, or in spite of, the care received? Would an elderly, infirm resident of a nursing home have been better off at another home? The buyer of legal services will never learn whether he or she would have been better off dealing with another attorney; was a lawsuit won (or lost) because of or in spite of the attorney? When college education is purchased, would the student have received a "better" education elsewhere? When a charitable contribution is made to an organization, what would have happened to the needy if the donation had not been made?

In all these cases the seller, although far from fully informed, often knows more than the patient, client, or donor. For the consumer, rewarding performance is difficult. Not surprisingly, in these service markets there are large elements of collective intervention into, and alternatives to, the proprietary market. There is extensive reliance on governmental regulation, on self-policed—or, in the case of the legal community, court-determined—codes of professional ethics, and, particularly in health and higher education, on nonprofit organizations. Alternatives to the socially unconstrained private firm are the rule[9]—the nonprofit form of institution is only one alternative. It is difficult to gauge performance outside the proprietary marketplace, since certain activities are more likely to be undertaken in governmental and private nonprofit institutions precisely because society wants particular outputs that are difficult to monitor. And what cannot be easily monitored cannot be easily rewarded. Therefore, although some elements of behavior in the public and nonprofit sectors can be observed and the producers rewarded accordingly, other elements cannot.[10]

It is difficult to gauge the success of governmental and nonprofit organizations in providing services with hard-to-measure attributes. A great deal of literature in public administration highlights the "vagueness and intangibility" of public-sector outputs; it underscores "the unique difficulties in specifying and quantifying performance measures in the public sector."[11] Since the economic statistical literature largely overlooks this and fails to measure certain outputs, it systematically undervalues the outputs of public and nonprofit providers relative to proprietary-sector outputs.[12] The view that "if a superior performance is desired, then privatization [of publicly owned assets] is the appropriate policy"[13] is a common one. But "superior" performance is a tricky notion when consumers cannot monitor easily outputs that are nevertheless important to them.

When society uses a particular form of institution—for-profit, governmental, nonprofit—to provide output it is implicitly rewarding certain types of behavior. There are several bases for rewarding excellence in performance; that is, there are several ways of measuring performance— by organizational structure, by process, or by outcome.[14] Ideally—were it not, that is, for costs—performance would always be measured by outputs or outcomes. In health care the output is the enhancement of the patient's health. In schooling it is the student's learning or, perhaps, ability to earn in the marketplace. In the case of aid to the poor it is the raising of living standards. In the criminal justice system it is the punishment of the guilty and the protection of the innocent.

Ideal information on outputs is often unobtainable or excessively costly. Indirect, or proxy, measures can then serve as a basis for judging rewards. These may be "structural" variables (such as the number of social workers relative to the number of poor families) or the institutional form of the supplying organization (such as the nonprofit). Alternatively, they may be "process" or "procedural" variables, such as response time of an ambulance to an emergency call, use of a set of prescribed rules said to constitute "due process" in a legal setting, or use of a "peer review" process for judging the quality and publishability of professional research. When the direct contribution of an activity to final outcomes cannot be determined, such indirect, procedural measures are often employed.[15]

Indirect (structural and procedural) measures are always imperfect— and perhaps extremely so. As a result, whenever they are used as a basis for rewarding performance of individuals and organizations, the desired behavior is not really rewarded. The same is true for the use of the nonprofit form of institution; it can have merit, at best, as an indirect and imperfect mechanism for achieving particular outcomes, such as provision of certain (trust and collective) services or distribution of outputs to particular classes of consumers.

The difficulties of rewarding socially desired behavior are evident. Some attempts to solve the problem involve the use of nonprofit suppliers; some do not. All involve lack of information for rewarding "good" performance and the resulting search for indirect measures. A recent report on primary and secondary education, recognizing the danger of incomplete measures, lamented the increased use of "merely quantifiable criteria" for assessing skills.[16] An advocate of rewarding good teachers opposes "merit pay" because "teacher performance, unlike the work of, say, an insurance salesman, is not easily gauged by objective standards of productivity."[17] In a federal court case involving a segregated law school, the court found that evaluating an educational setting requires more than an assessment of the buildings, curricula, and other tangible factors: minorities were not receiving equal educational opportunities because of "those qualities which are *incapable of objective measurement* but which make for greatness in a law school."[18]

When outcomes are costly to measure, a choice must be made between rewarding what is easily measured, even though that would not reward the desired outcomes, and incurring costs in other forms—by devising better measures or, alternatively, by not rewarding performance at all. Using a poor and incomplete measure may well be worse than not rewarding performance at all. Paying all teachers equally could be preferable to paying the "good" teachers more if our ability to identify the good teachers is sufficiently limited; it is noteworthy, in this connection, that salaries of federal judges do not vary with the judge's "performance." The incentive to excel may be affected adversely, but there are countervailing advantages in reduced acrimony over how to judge excellence. Similarly, the nondistribution constraint on nonprofits exerts an adverse effect on incentives to increase profits, but the advantages, in markets where informational problems are severe, may justify those effects.

Should Performance Be Rewarded When "Performance" Is Costly to Observe?

Imagine that every commodity is a bundle of attributes. Some attributes—type 1—are easy for a buyer to observe and evaluate. Other attributes—type 2—are very costly to observe and evaluate.[19] The taste of a chocolate cookie and the location of a nursing home are of type 1. The extent to which a nursing home actually provides "an atmosphere of love, courtesy and understanding"[20] and the success of police in preventing crime are type-2 attributes. Although consumers are poorly informed about the type-2 attributes, producers are often better informed.

Buyers place different values on each attribute of an output, ranging from zero to infinity. For simplicity, we can distinguish four classes of attributes—class A has low information costs and high value; B is high cost, high value; C is low cost, low value; and D is high cost, low value. Table 3.1 portrays the four cases and illustrates each. Class D is uninteresting because, with the value of information being low but the cost of getting it high, that information will not be provided through any form of institution, but focusing on the first three classes of attributes is most useful.

Every good can be located on a spectrum according to the ratio of the value, to buyers, of its type-1 (easy-to-monitor) attributes to its type-2 (hard-to-monitor) attributes.[21] At one extreme of the spectrum, all characteristics of the good are readily monitored; that is, there are only type-1 attributes. This is the textbook case of the fully informed consumer, or, more generally, of symmetric information, buyers and sellers being equally informed. The taste of a "chocolate cookie" is a type-1 attribute; consumers can easily decide whether they like it and can switch brands at low cost (relative to income) until the preferred brand is discovered. At the other extreme, all important characteristics of the good are opaque to the consumer. Some attributes may be easily observed, but they are not important to the consumer; those that are important are not observable. This extreme is illustrated by national defense. The important attributes are not the military hardware or manpower, which are observable, but "security," which is not. Another example is complex, technology-intensive medical procedures; certain physical properties of the equipment are readily observed, but what consumers care about, its effectiveness, is not. Most goods fall between these extremes. A used car, for example, has a number of easily monitored (type-1) attributes, including age, model, presence of manual

Table 3.1 Commodities classified by the costs and benefits of information

Costs	Benefits	
	Low	High
Low (type 1)	Taste of a chocolate cookie (class C)	Volume of gasoline left in auto tank (class A)
High (type 2)	Detecting when a light bulb is about to burn out (class D)	Tender loving care in a nursing home; crime prevention by police; national defense (class B)

transmission, and so forth. Other attributes are costly to monitor (type 2); these give rise to the "lemon" problem[22] and to jokes such as "Would you buy a used car from this person?"

A profit-oriented producer choosing between providing goods with type-1 attributes, for which there are rewards, and goods with type-2 attributes, for which there are not—because consumers find it costly to evaluate them—has the incentive to concentrate on type 1. The reward system, in effect, distorts producers' decisions away from providing "tender loving care." If the reward structure were neutral for type-1 and type-2 attributes, producers would not face incentives to distort the allocation of their resources. For nonprofit organizations, the reward structure is closer to being neutral than is usually the case for private proprietary firms; the nonprofit manager cannot benefit as much as a manager of a private firm—at least if the nondistribution constraint is enforced—from additional profit that could be obtained by concentrating on outputs that have easily measured and rewarded attributes.

Realistically, of course, managers of nonprofit organizations or public agencies are not fully insulated from rewards for the more easily measured components of output. The difference as compared with for-profit organizations is one of degree. Because of the cutting, or at least weakening, of the tie between the level of the organization's profits and the manager's rewards, the nonprofit manager has less incentive to capitalize on consumers' lack of information.

The distorting effects of reward structures are common, but so is recognition of the problem. The tempest over "merit" pay for teachers is a clear example of how the high cost of measuring differences in output makes it impossible to reward merit without adverse effects. As the president of the National Education Association put it: "if student achievement is used as a measure of merit, then a teacher with a class of gifted and motivated children would be far more apt to be selected [for higher rewards] than one with less-willing students."[23] And as one syndicated writer put it: "No test yet devised can measure love, dedication, patience, warmth, and some of the other elements of successful teaching."[24] Utilizing a relatively simple, low-cost measure of a complex phenomenon to reward people is likely to influence behavior—in this case by teachers—in surprising and undesirable ways. Perhaps unwittingly, people are encouraged to concentrate their efforts on raising their measured performance; in the process, they may devote too little effort to elements of performance that, although unrewarded, are more important.

Police services—also provided largely outside the private market—similarly illustrate the importance of the distinction between type-1 and type-2 attributes. Apprehension of criminals is a type-1 activity, relatively easy to monitor; the prevention of crime is a type-2 activity. It is substantially easier to determine whether a violator has been apprehended than it is to determine whether a violation has been prevented, and so the former is more likely to be rewarded. As a result, police resources are likely to be distorted toward apprehension, with too little going toward prevention. Police officers, who are pressured to issue tickets to speeding drivers or pedestrian jaywalkers, frequently complain about quotas of tickets,[25] but preventing violations of the law—for example, by working to forestall domestic violence, teenage drug use, or property crime—does not lend itself to a quota system.

Although there may be no "quotas" for preventing crime, there surely have been many efforts to reduce the overall crime rate in a community, state, or the nation. These efforts also show the distorting effects of rewarding measurable proxies rather than the behavior one wants to encourage. The title of a recent newspaper article tells the story: "Do Lower Statistics Mean Less Crime?" Commenting on the decline in the national crime rate, the writer reports that Justice Department officials regard the figures with "cautious reserve." Caution is in order partly because not all crime is reported. "Some think the matter too personal or not important enough, some lack faith in authorities, some may fear retaliation, and some are reluctant to get caught up in the slow-moving machinery of the criminal justice bureaucracy." A second difficulty with interpreting the reduction in reported crime as a reduction in actual crime is that local authorities, from which the national data are aggregated, "have their own reasons to over- or under-report the amount of crime in their jurisdictions."[26]

This much seems clear: the more individuals or organizations are rewarded for reducing "crime," the greater will be the incentive to do things to bring down the measured number of crimes. Because the measured rate can be reduced either by decreasing the actual amount of crime or by changing what is "officially" counted, there is a danger that the easily monitored crime rate—a type-1 measure—will become the basis for rewards and resources will be shifted toward reducing that measure rather than reducing the true crime rate. Law enforcement authorities can succeed without really succeeding.[27]

A similar distortion can occur in response to governmental regulation of hospitals. Economist Martin Feldstein testified before the Senate Health Subcommittee that hospitals can comply with cost-cutting regulations even though they are not really achieving reductions in costs. "Hospitals can also circumvent the effect of regulation by . . . wasteful distortions that produce the appearance of compliance. By admitting more patients whose conditions require relatively short stays or relatively less nursing or laboratory services, a hospital could appear to reduce the rise in its cost per case. By reorganizing to spin off services like pathology or laboratory testing, a hospital might also be able to reduce its adjusted cost per case. The totally inadequate system of hospital accounting makes such circumventions extremely difficult to prevent."[28]

A third example concerns eligibility of the poor for food stamps. How should "poverty" be defined? The recent Presidential Panel on Food Assistance recommended that eligibility for food stamps should be limited to households having less than $2,250 in assets (compared with the existing level of $1,500), excluding an automobile, for which an increase of the exemption from $4,500 to $5,000 was proposed.[29] Measuring eligibility in this way requires only reasonably available information. What is available may not be what is really desired, however. Such definitions of eligibility might, for example, encourage people to turn over their assets to relatives in order to qualify for aid. The attempt to measure and "reward" particular circumstances can affect behavior in undesired ways.[30]

In all these cases there are measurable components of output, but because there are other outputs that are not easily measured, the use of the easy measures as a basis for rewarding performance poses genuine problems. If we reward what we can measure, we distort behavior; if we do not, we discourage efficiency.

These examples are all drawn from the public and nonprofit sectors, the institutional forms that are most likely to be used when outputs that are believed to be significant are costly to measure.[31] Oftentimes cause and effect are confused on this matter; the emphasis is misplaced when it is said that "we do not yet know how to measure public sector productivity." This statement implies the need for "a new obsession with measuring *results*—developing public equivalents of business' bottom line . . . The question is not how many sanitation men and how much equipment work how faithfully for how long—but whether the streets get clean. "[32] The author of this article on "making government accountable" is correct, as far as he goes. But what he did not seem to recognize is that certain activities are in the public or nonprofit sector largely *because of* the complexity of assessing them. Because these activities are not easily monitored and therefore rewarded (the strength of the private sector), society turns to other sectors to carry them out.

There are both costs and benefits of rewarding incomplete measures of performance. The benefits—favorable effects—result from the fact that producers of desired attributes are rewarded and, hence, have an incentive to provide them. The costs—unfavorable effects—result from the inability to reward important attributes of output that are difficult to measure, because the lack of reward leads to an excessive allocation of resources toward producing outputs with more easily measured attributes.

Owing to such distorted incentives, it may be efficient not to reward the easily monitored forms of behavior, to devise reward structures that are more neutral toward the more and less easily measurable kinds of behavior. There is a "price" to be paid for such structures, but it is sometimes smaller than the price paid for rewarding the measurable components of output while in the process distorting effort away from the less-measurable components.

A number of seemingly strange reward structures can be understood as mechanisms for coping with the dilemma of encouraging efficiency in production without distorting effort. Civil-service protections, employment tenure for academicians and federal judges, and limits on the number of terms that an elected official may serve are understandable in this light. They do not involve nonprofits per se, but they illustrate the logic for, and the variety of, restrictions on rewards; the nonprofit form of institution is but another kind of restriction. In all these cases, there are both observable and unobservable dimensions of output, but the latter are so important that rewards for the observable dimensions have been severely restricted.

Civil-Service Guarantees, Tenure, and Maximum Terms for Elected Officials

Complaints about the effects on efficiency of civil-service rules are legion. These rules have been justified as ways to protect workers and, indeed, the public from abuses of the political "spoils" system. They have, however, an unfortunate side effect—insulating unproductive workers from discharge. What sense can be made of a system that establishes such severe obstacles to disciplining an employee as to virtually guarantee continued employment regardless of effort or productivity?

If the "productivity" of a civil servant can be measured well in all of its relevant dimensions, rules that prevent incompetent workers from being demoted or discharged or that prevent unusually good workers from being rewarded are simply inefficient. But that is an important "if." On the other hand, if the "productivity" of a postal clerk were measured and rewarded by the number of pieces of mail handled at the post office window, the clerk would tend not to spend time with a confused or hard-of-hearing patron who had a complex problem. If being helpful to such people is a socially desired output, then, given the operational difficulty of determining when a patron deserves special attention and then of devising a system to give additional rewards to a clerk who provides the "appropriate" assistance, it may be preferable to forgo measuring productivity altogether, except in a very gross fashion, such as presence on the job. Rewarding by the number of hours worked—independent of amount of mail handled—may be quite sensible, indeed efficient. It leaves the worker facing a reward structure that is neutral toward attending to the easy versus the difficult patrons. Productivity is not always difficult to monitor, but when it is, society does, and should, search for reward mechanisms that balance the advantages and disadvantages of rewarding only what we can monitor easily.

Job tenure for academicians has a somewhat different rationale. It has been justified historically to protect academic freedom, the freedom to examine or espouse unpopular or unorthodox ideas. The fundamental position is that a scholar should not be penalized for such activities; employment security, salary, and other rewards should not be influenced by the political popularity of the professor's scholarship.

That is the theory. If it were easy to determine whether a particular professor were being punished inappropriately for his or her ideas, a contract could be written to prevent it, with compensation for anyone who fell victim to it. Desired performance would be rewarded regardless of its form.

Economist Richard Cyert argued that "the faculty member on tenure and the government worker on civil service . . . tend to concentrate on approaches that will make it easier for them to do their jobs while at the same time perpetuating themselves. Thus it is unlikely that labor-saving techniques will be introduced."[33] But tenure has another face; it encourages free inquiry, as its holders are undaunted by the elusive, hard-to-measure "validity" or "legitimacy" of ideas.

In principle, tenure presents a scholar with a reward structure that is neutral toward the popularity of his or her research. In the process it does two things: it eliminates, or at least reduces, the rewards that would come from doing "approved" research—and this is socially desired; but it also reduces the incentive to do any research at all, since employment is ensured in any event—and this is not efficient.[34]

An even better example of the use of job tenure to deal with hard-to-measure outputs is the appointment of federal judges. Judges are guaranteed (1) employment for life, the retirement decision resting entirely with the judge, and (2) a salary that is the same for all judges at a given judicial level. Federal judges thus face a remarkable situation: except for the possibility of promotion to a higher-level court or of leaving the bench, their tangible rewards bear essentially no relation to their performance! This reward structure is quite unlike that for academicians, for whom salaries for, say, full professors can vary enormously, even within a given department, let alone across departments, schools, or universities. Whether federal judges work long hours or short, whether they hand down many decisions or few, whether their decisions are regarded as models or are frequently overturned upon appeal, their employment and salaries are unaffected. What sense can be made of such a chasm between performance and rewards?

One answer is that society recognizes that there are some aspects of a judge's activities that are very difficult to monitor but are nonetheless very important. If, say, the number of decisions made, which is easily monitored, affected rewards, judges would be encouraged to allocate little effort to any single decision, no matter how difficult it may be. Quality, however, is far harder to measure. There are indicators of quality, such as the frequency of favorable citations and of decisions overturned upon appeal. Still, it remains difficult to determine whether a given judicial decision was influenced by the judge's beliefs about whether a superior will "like" it. If such rewards by superiors are possible, legal decisions may well be affected.

By contrast, with a reward structure that is largely independent of judgments about performance, federal judges have scant incentive to have their decisions influenced by prospective rewards. In the overwhelming majority of other jobs, it is costly for a subordinate publicly to attack a superior; by greatly restricting the "superior's" power to punish federal judges, however, tenure provides greater independence to the subordinates. It is hard to imagine a justice of the United States Supreme Court severely criticizing the chief justice if the chief justice were in a position to determine the "quality" of a justice's performance and then to determine whether employment would continue and, if so, at what salary. Tenure guarantees, which cut the tie between rewards and measured performance, may help to explain the willingness of an associate justice of the Supreme Court, John Paul Stevens, publicly to criticize Chief Justice Warren Burger, charging him (and other Supreme Court justices) with "ill-considered" legal opinions.[35] In a landmark prisoners'-rights case, Stevens chastised the chief justice, in remarks delivered from the bench, for disregarding constitutional guarantees and for inconsistency in proclaiming the rights of institutionalized persons in the abstract but disregarding them in a specific case. The chief justice may well have been angered, but Stevens was insulated from retributive actions.

Perhaps federal judges would work harder if extra effort were rewarded, but the distortionary effects of such rewards are potentially quite serious for society; thus a neutral reward structure—one that does not reward any dimension of performance—may be optimal.

Another seemingly strange reward structure is limitations on the number of terms an elected official may serve. It seems irrational for voters to say, "We will not reelect a particular official no matter how well he or she has performed in office." If a political leader were doing a truly superior job and were expected to continue doing so, we would be wise to retain that person's services. Yet society does impose limits on terms in high political office—for president of the United States, for many governors and mayors. Some universities even limit the terms of academic deans and department chairpersons.

In reality, however, there are good reasons for restrictions on the number of terms that may be served by a person in a position of power—regardless of the quality of performance. Those reasons have to do with the limits of voters' ability to gauge performance. Voters may believe, on the basis of everything they can learn at low cost, that a leader is performing splendidly and so deserves to be rewarded by reelection or reappointment. Yet the information available pertains to the type-1 attributes of performance. There are also type-2 attributes about which voters are likely to be systematically underinformed.

The "systematic" nature of the information gap should be underscored. It is very much in a candidate's self-interest to provide voters with full information about his or her accomplishments. If, however, a candidate is engaged in activities that are illegal, illicit, of doubtful morality, or otherwise likely to be "punished" by voters, that information is not likely to be forthcoming. The forces of political competition as well as the activities of investigative reporters serve to bring forth some type-2 information. Nonetheless, society has reason to be concerned that some crucially important elements of behavior may go undetected until serious and irreversible damage has been done.

Because serious errors can result from inadequate information, it is quite rational to pay the price of losing the services of a candidate whose easily monitored behavior seems very favorable. It is clear that the longer a person is in a position of power the greater the danger of undetected flaws.

Restrictions on length of service are most likely to be utilized in situations in which type-2 attributes are important. Such restrictions are less likely to be employed in the proprietary sector. In government as well as in the private nonprofit sector, both of which are more likely to be engaged in activities having a large type-2 component, limiting length of service is more commonplace.[36]

Rewards and the High Cost of Information

Maximum terms in political office and *minimum* guarantees of tenure may seem to be contrary sides of the same coin, but both are understandable as adjustments to type-2 informational problems. Both involve balancing the advantages of rewarding performance against the distorting costs of the inability to measure all relevant dimensions of behavior. Similarly, the nonprofit form of institution explicitly limits the rewards available to managers and directors, regardless of the surplus that organizational performance generates, in exchange for greater neutrality of managerial incentives. Because neutrality is valuable only to the extent that type-2 dimensions of output are significant, the nonprofit institution has a restricted—albeit important—social role to play.

Social choice among forms of institutions is a choice among incentive structures. The crucial question is how effectively the various structures actually reshape—redress—incentives. Organizations that face different incentives do not necessarily behave differently. They could be constrained in ways that prevent the differences in incentives from being effective. If, for example, government legislation mandated that all organizations in some industry—regardless of ownership type—would be paid for services on a cost-reimbursement basis, then even if there were no differences in behavior across types of institutions, that would not imply that there would be no differences if the cost-reimbursement rules were relaxed or eliminated. In a large part of the health-care sector of the United States such rules have been in effect over the last two decades, until late 1983; they have the effect of blunting differences in institutional behavior that would otherwise develop.[37] Restrictions on incentives can limit differences in the behavior of public and private, for-profit and nonprofit organizations; they may or may not eliminate the differences.

FOUR

Anatomy of the Voluntary Nonprofit Sector

The nonprofit sector is a microcosm of a modern economic system, a mixture of heterogeneous organizations engaged in a variety of activities. How shall we define the "nonprofit" sector? How large is it? How is it changing over time? To what extent do nonprofits compete with for-profit firms and with governmental organizations? And, finally, should society be satisfied with the current pattern of nonprofit activity?

Despite the enormous variety of nonprofit organizations, we can sort them into a few principal classes on the basis of their similarities to private firms and to government. These similarities can be captured, in some measure, by a "collectiveness index," which highlights the important relationship between the financing of any organization and the kinds of services it provides. The index also links a nonprofit organization's sources of finance to its competitiveness with the for-profit sector of the economy. The nonprofit economy has assumed a larger role over time. It is important to study its interaction with the dominant proprietary and governmental portions of the economic system.

There are three general categories of nonprofits—one private and two public types. The private type consists of "commercial" or "proprietary" nonprofits. Although they do not operate to reap profit themselves, they are instruments for generating profits for their constituents—private firms or members. Proprietary nonprofits include trade associations as well as clubs and associations that do little but seek the betterment of their own members—country clubs, dog and garden clubs, farmer cooperatives, mutual insurance companies, and chambers of commerce.

There are two forms of "public"-type nonprofits—collective and trust. A "collective" nonprofit provides services that generate sizable "external" benefits to persons who do not help to finance the organization's activities—for example, medical research, museums, wildlife sanctuaries, environmental protection, and aid to the poor. The activities of collective nonprofits are virtually indistinguishable from those of governmental agencies. Some nonprofits, for example, finance research on causes and cures for diseases, and various United Way organizations aid the poor and handicapped. The work of these nonprofits is essentially the same as that performed by the National Institutes of Health and the U.S. Department of Health and Human Services, as well as various state and local governmental agencies.

The second public-type nonprofit provides "trust goods"—combinations of a private good and consumer protection. Nursing homes, daycare centers, and blood banks are potential examples. They sell their services, just as proprietary firms do, but the services they sell are of the kind about which consumers are often poorly informed. Some consumers may prefer to deal with a nonprofit organization in the belief that it will take less advantage of consumers' informational handicaps than a for-profit seller would.

Although these three categories—proprietary, collective, and trust nonprofits—are useful, the nonprofit sector is more complex than they would suggest. There are borderline cases, such as organizations that ostensibly provide collective or trust goods but may actually take advantage of their privileged position to operate as a proprietary nonprofit would. This can happen because the high cost of regulating nonprofits permits some organizations to take advantage of their opportunities and subsidies and reap private rewards for the organizers or managers. For example, two exporters of used clothing were charged in the federal district court of Philadelphia with paying kickbacks to Salvation Army officers to ensure a steady supply of clothes for shipment abroad; the case involved an alleged misuse of a public-type nonprofit for the attainment of private profit.[1] Enforcement of the laws constraining the behavior of nonprofits poses the same problems as are found elsewhere in society.

In the United States, the tax laws determine which organizations are classified as nonprofit. The governmental "nonprofit" (or tax-exempt) classification is useful for two reasons. First, the determination of tax-exempt status through a democratic decision-making process gives a nonprofit organization some legitimacy. Second, the IRS makes available data it gathers on organizations so classified. Simply designating an organization "nonprofit" does not, of course, change its objectives or its behavior. The nondistribution constraint, however, applies to all organizations that receive tax-exempt status by the IRS.

The tax law defines nonprofits as organizations that are "organized for charitable or mutual benefit purposes." (Note the inclusion of *both* purposes.) It includes more than two dozen major classes of organizations, such as "Corporation[s] and any community chest, fund, or foundation, organized and operated exclusively for religious, charitable, scientific, testing for public safety, literary or educational purposes, or to foster national or international amateur sports competition (so long as none of its activities involve the providing of athletic facilities or equipment) or for the prevention of cruelty to children or animals, no part of the net earnings of which inures to the benefit of any private shareholder or individual, no substantial part of the activities of which is carrying on propaganda, or otherwise attempting to influence legislation, and which does not attempt to participate or intervene in any political campaign."[2] These are the organizations that are exempt from taxation under section 501(c)(3) of the Internal Revenue Code; contributions to these organizations, and with a few exceptions only to them, are tax deductible on the donor's individual or corporate tax return.

An organization can also qualify as a nonprofit, tax-exempt organization—although not as a tax-deductible organization—if it is a "Civic league, an organization not organized for profit but operated exclusively for the promotion of social welfare, or a local association of employees . . . and the net earnings of [the organization] are devoted exclusively to charitable, educational, or recreational purposes"—section 501(c)(4). Or it could qualify as a "Labor, agricultural, or horticultural organization"—section 501(c)(5); a "Business league, chamber of commerce, real estate board, board of trade, or professional football league, not organized for profit"—section 501(c)(6); a "Club organized for . . . nonprofit purposes," a "fraternal beneficiary society," and so forth.[3]

There is, in short, an enormous diversity of organizations that the Internal Revenue Service can certify as tax exempt. To some people, the nonprofit sector is interesting because of its charitable or "philanthropic" activities, such as may be engaged in by organizations that qualify for tax deductibility of donations—largely the 501(c)(3) organizations—or, perhaps, by those organizations plus those that would qualify were it not that they engage in a "substantial" amount of legislative lobbying—the 501(c)(4) organizations.[4]

To some people, the broader set of philanthropic organizations is the epitome of the nonprofit sector, whereas to others a narrower definition, including only the tax-deductible organizations, is of interest; others prefer a still broader concept that includes in the nonprofit category not only various other formal organizations but also informal self-help groups as well as organizations such as neighborhood associations that have no legal structure. Some definitions would not include "mutual" organizations and "cooperatives." The foregoing distinction between the government type and the private or commercial type of nonprofits takes into account the heterogeneity of nonprofits.

The present state of quantitative knowledge of the nonprofit sector has grown out of a hodgepodge of definitions. There is currently no consistent basis for portraying the nonprofit part of the economy, how it relates to the public and the private for-profit sectors, and how these interactions have changed over time. Despite the lack of data, however, the nonprofit sector is far from negligible overall, and it is especially important in particular industries. Moreover, nonprofit organizations interact with the rest of the economy in ways that are complex, frequently troublesome, and little understood.

The Size of the Nonprofit Sector

Organizations in the United States that are legally classified as nonprofit (that is, tax exempt) are far more common than most people would guess. They engage in hundreds of distinct activities; they are growing at the rate of thousands per year; they employ millions of workers; and they have hundreds of billions of dollars of annual revenues and assets.

In 1967, 309,000 organizations were designated tax exempt by the IRS. In fewer than twenty years that number nearly tripled, approaching 900,000 (Figure 4.1). The tax-deductible, "charitable" nonprofits have similarly leaped in number, from 138,000 in 1969 to 366,000 in 1985—an increase of over 160 percent; these are the nonprofits that have been granted special privileges, presumably because they are thought to provide substantial public benefits (collective or trust). Nonprofits are growing at a more rapid rate than are for-profit corporations, which increased by 100 percent—although from a larger base—from about 1.5 million in 1967 to 3.0 million in 1983, the most recent year for which data are available. (For details see Table A.1 in Appendix A.) The total revenues

Organizations
(millions)

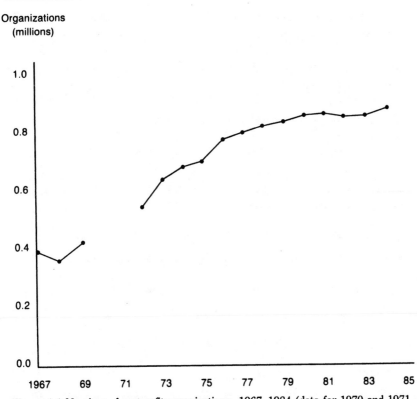

Figure 4.1 Number of nonprofit organizations, 1967–1984 (data for 1970 and 1971 not available). *Source:* Table A.1 in Appendix A

of the charitable nonprofits have also increased markedly in recent years, from $115 billion in 1975 to $314 billion in 1983.[5]

Even more striking is the recent tidal wave of applications for tax-exempt status. Through the late 1950s and early 1960s the IRS was receiving some 7,000 applications for tax-exempt status annually. In one year, however—1965—the number more than doubled, to over 14,000, probably as a consequence of the Great Society programs of the federal government; by 1984 it had more than quadrupled again, to over 64,000, although it dropped substantially in 1985, to some 59,000 (see Table A.2).

Throughout this period, the IRS continued to approve 70 to 80 percent of applications for nonprofit status. The result: the number of new nonprofits rose dramatically. The IRS approved about 5,000 new nonprofits per year through 1963; in 1964, the IRS approved nearly 40 percent more—7,000. This was only the beginning of a new era for the nonprofits. In 1965, the IRS approved nearly 12,000 applications; by 1977 the IRS was approving over 35,000 applications annually, and in 1984 and in 1985 more than 44,000 new nonprofits entered the economy (Table A.2).[6]

The number of nonprofit organizations says nothing about their size, of course. Nonprofits are typically small and, overall, they own only 1.8 percent of the nation's assets. It would be a mistake, though, to dismiss this share as inconsequential. Many nonprofits provide government-type services (collective and trust). If nonprofits are compared with government, a very different picture emerges. Assets in the nonprofit sector are substantial when compared with those of the federal government— 3.9 percent of national assets—or with the assets of all state and local governments—8.5 percent (see Tables A.3 and A.4). Thus, assets of the nonprofit sector equal nearly 50 percent of the assets of the federal government and some 15 percent of the assets owned by all levels of government in the United States. Moreover, assets of the nonprofit sector have been growing, whereas those of government have declined. (Assets are defined here as the value of land, reproducible consumer durables and semidurables, and financial assets; they do not include the value of subsoil assets, standing timber, research and development expenditures, and unfunded pension liabilities, which would increase national assets by about one-third. See Table A.3.)

The nonprofit sector's contribution to national income has also been growing, but cyclically (Figure 4.2).[7] Peaking at the depths of the Great Depression, the nonprofits' importance reached a trough during the affluent years of World War II, when unemployment essentially disappeared and government was taking financial responsibility for the health and welfare of a growing number of military personnel and their dependents. Since World War II, the relative importance of the nonprofit sector has shown an almost uninterrupted climb.[8]

Because nonprofit organizations are typically labor intensive, they are far more important as employers of labor than as contributors to national output. As of 1977, when the U.S. Department of Commerce last comprehensively surveyed employment in the service sector, nonprofit organizations employed well over 5 percent of the entire national labor force. The reported total of 4.95 million paid workers in the nonprofit sector[9] was clearly an understatement, however; the survey included

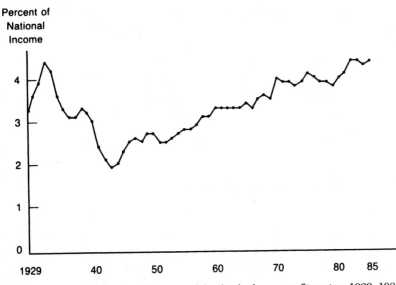

Figure 4.2 Percent of national income originating in the nonprofit sector, 1929–1985.
Source: Table A.5 in Appendix A

only 166,000 nonprofit establishments whereas the Internal Revenue Service shows double that number of tax-exempt, nonprofit organizations filing tax returns. Moreover, another half-million nonprofit organizations did not file tax returns because they had too little activity (less than $10,000 of receipts) or were churches that were not required to file. Surely this half-million generated some employment, if only part-time.[10]

I have estimated employment in the nonprofit sector using another approach and find a considerably higher level. I assume that employment in the nonprofit sector bears the same relation to total revenue of the sector as it does in other parts of the economy. Depending on whether the standard for comparison is (a) the economy as a whole, which has 5.50 full-time equivalent (FTE) workers per million dollars of revenues, (b) government enterprises, which have 6.31, or (c) the service sector, which has 7.19, the nonprofit sector accounts for employment of from 7.9 million to as many as 10.3 million workers.[11] Because much of the nonprofit sector engages in activities similar to those of government, the ratio of employment to revenue for government enterprises, 6.31, may be a more appropriate basis for estimating employment in the nonprofit sector. By this standard there are an estimated 9.0 million FTE employees in the nonprofit sector—80 percent more than the Census Bureau figure (which was clearly an underestimate) and fully 12 percent of the nation's FTE labor force of 74.4 million workers in 1976. Even by the lower standard the number of FTE employees was surely greater than 4.95 million; and it was almost certainly no higher than 10.3 million. Understanding the nonprofit sector is clearly handicapped by the lack of solid data obtained regularly and according to a definition of nonprofit organizations that is consistent with that used by other agencies that keep statistics, such as the IRS. In any case, the range of estimates shows that the nonprofit sector employs a substantial portion of the labor force.

Whatever the true number of paid workers in the nonprofit sector, the total amount of labor working in this part of the economy is considerably greater. The difference is unpaid volunteers, who supply billions of hours of time annually.[12] The most recent estimate, based on a 1985 survey, put time volunteered to formal organizations at the equivalent of 5.7–6.7 million FTE workers (depending on whether a work year of 2,000 hours or 1,700 hours is assumed);[13] this was some 6 percent of the employed labor force, 106 million, in that year.[14] Since paid employment in the service sector is about 20 percent of the total labor force, volunteer labor, which I assume is essentially all in that sector, constitutes a gigantic 30 percent addition to paid labor in the service industries. Volunteer labor is an even larger percentage in the charitable social services subsector (see Tables A.7 and A.8), where nonprofits are concentrated!

The supply of volunteer labor (as well as revenue in monetary form) is influenced a great deal by public policies, but unsatisfactory record keeping is a major handicap to our understanding the full extent of this influence. Volunteer labor is unpriced, so it is not included in Department of Labor statistics on employment and unemployment. The 1979 report of the National Commission on Employment and Unemployment Statistics recognized this omission, noting that information on volunteer labor is needed to "provide policymakers with better indicators of the potential labor supply." The commission recommended "that information on volunteers and their work be collected every 3 years in a special supplement" to the Current Population Survey, but the recommendation has not been implemented. A large minority of the commission even favored including volunteer labor in the regular monthly Current Population Survey, which is the source of official data on employment, unemployment, and the labor force.[15]

Even the definition of "volunteer" labor is vague and inconsistent. Two Gallup surveys sponsored by Independent Sector, in 1981 and 1985, asked about "volunteering" broadly, including informal help to friends, relatives, and neighbors as well as donations of labor organizations. (See Table A.8.) The principal previous survey to consider the issue, undertaken in 1973 by the University of Michigan's Survey Research Center and sponsored by the Commission on Private Philanthropy and Public Needs, included only those services provided to organizations. (See Table A.7.) None of the surveys defined volunteer work carefully; respondents were simply expected to understand what was meant.

What Does the Nonprofit Sector Do?

Nonprofit organizations, as defined by the Internal Revenue Code, engage in literally hundreds of activities: they operate schools, churches, hospitals, museums, advocacy and civil-rights campaigns, and scientific research centers—most of which qualify as tax-deductible "charities" serving a "public purpose"—as well as trade unions, mutual insurance companies, and far more, as Figure 4.3 shows. These latter organizations—along with country clubs (code 280), farm bureaus (code 231), chambers of commerce (200), and fraternities or sororities (036)—pursue the private interests of their constituents or members and have only modest or nonexistent external benefits to outsiders. These are the private or commercial nonprofits; their effects can be judged, and their behavior understood, in terms of their influence on the profit or welfare of their members rather than in terms of their own revenue surplus or "profit." That they benefit their members does not imply anything improper, inefficient, or inequitable, let alone sinister, about them; in this respect they are much like private proprietary firms.

The heterogeneity of the nonprofit economy is the outcome of interactions among several forces: (1) rules determining eligibility—explicit legislative actions that have defined which activities are eligible for nonprofit status and what special opportunities and constraints will apply to each class of organizations; (2) legal interpretations and IRS regulatory enforcement of those rules of eligibility; and (3) the many social, political, and technological aspects of the economy. These forces and their in-

Code

Religious Activities

001 Church, synagogue, etc.
002 Association or convention of churches
003 Religious order
004 Church auxiliary
005 Mission
006 Missionary activities
007 Evangelism
008 Religious publishing activities
--- Book store (use 918)
--- Genealogical activities (use 094)
029 Other religious activities

Schools, Colleges and Related Activities

030 School, college, trade school, etc.
031 Special school for the blind, handicapped, etc.
032 Nursery school
--- Day care center (use 574)
033 Faculty group
034 Alumni association or group
035 Parent or parent-teachers association
036 Fraternity or sorority
--- Key club (use 323)
037 Other student society or group
038 School or college athletic association
039 Scholarships for children of employees
040 Scholarships (other)
041 Student loans
042 Student housing activities
043 Other student aid
044 Student exchange with foreign country
045 Student operated business
--- Financial support of schools, colleges, etc. (use 602)
--- Achievement prizes or awards (use 914)
--- Student book store (use 918)
--- Student travel (use 299)
--- Scientific research (see Scientific Research Activities)
059 Other school related activities

Cultural, Historical or Other Educational Activities

060 Museum, zoo, planetarium, etc.
061 Library
062 Historical site, records or reenactment
063 Monument
064 Commemorative event (centennial, festival, pageant, etc.)
065 Fair
088 Community theatrical group
089 Singing society or group
090 Cultural performances
091 Art exhibit
092 Literary activities
093 Cultural exchanges with foreign country
094 Genealogical activities
--- Achievement prizes or awards (use 914)
--- Gifts or grants to individuals (use 561)
--- Financial support of cultural organizations (use 602)
119 Other cultural or historical activities

Other Instruction and Training Activities

120 Publishing activities
121 Radio or television broadcasting
122 Producing films
123 Discussion groups, forums, panels, lectures, etc.
124 Study and research (non-scientific)
125 Giving information or opinion (see also Advocacy)
126 Apprentice training
--- Travel tours (use 299)
149 Other instruction and training

Health Services and Related Activities

150 Hospital
151 Hospital auxiliary
152 Nursing or convalescent home
153 Care and housing for the aged (see also 382)
154 Health clinic
155 Rural medical facility
156 Blood bank
157 Cooperative hospital service organization
158 Rescue and emergency service
159 Nurses' register or bureau
160 Aid to the handicapped (see also 031)
161 Scientific research (diseases)
162 Other medical research
163 Health insurance (medical, dental, optical, etc.)
164 Prepaid group health plan
165 Community health planning
166 Mental health care
167 Group medical practice association
168 In-faculty group practice association
169 Hospital pharmacy, parking facility, food services, etc.

Code

179 Other health services

Scientific Research Activities

180 Contract or sponsored scientific research for industry
181 Scientific research for government
--- Scientific research (diseases) (use 161)
199 Other scientific research activities

Business and Professional Organizations

200 Business promotion (chamber of commerce, business league, etc.)
201 Real-estate association
202 Board of trade
203 Regulating business
204 Better Business Bureau
205 Professional association
206 Professional association auxiliary
207 Industry trade shows
208 Convention displays
--- Testing products for public safety (use 905)
209 Research, development and testing
210 Professional athletic league
--- Attracting new industry (use 403)
--- Publishing activities (use 120)
--- Insurance or other benefits for members (see Employee or Membership Benefit Organizations)
211 Underwriting municipal insurance
212 Assigned risk insurance activities
213 Tourist bureau
229 Other business or professional group

Farming and Related Activities

230 Farming
231 Farm Bureau
232 Agricultural group
233 Horticultural group
234 Farmers' cooperative marketing or purchasing
235 Financing crop operations
--- FFA, FHA, 4-H club, etc. (use 322)
--- Fair (use 065)
236 Dairy herd improvement association
237 Breeders association
249 Other farming and related activities

Mutual Organizations

250 Mutual ditch, irrigation, telephone, electric company or like organization
251 Credit Union
252 Reserve funds or insurance for domestic building and loan association, cooperative bank, or mutual savings bank
253 Mutual insurance company
254 Corporation organized under an Act of Congress (see also 904)
--- Farmers' cooperative marketing or purchasing (use 234)
--- Cooperative hospital service organization (use 157)
259 Other mutual organization

Employee or Membership Benefit Organizations

260 Fraternal beneficiary society, order, or association
261 Improvement of conditions of workers
262 Association of municipal employees
263 Association of employees
264 Employee or member welfare association
265 Sick, accident, death, or similar benefits
266 Strike benefits
267 Unemployment benefits
268 Pension or retirement benefits
269 Vacation benefits
270 Group Legal Services Plans
279 Other services or benefits to members or employees

Sports, Athletic, Recreational and Social Activities

280 Country club
281 Hobby club
282 Dinner club
283 Variety club
284 Dog club
285 Women's club
--- Garden club (use 356)
286 Hunting or fishing club
287 Swimming or tennis club
288 Other sports club
--- Boys Club, Little League, etc. (use 321)
296 Community center
297 Community recreational facilities (park, playground, etc.)
298 Training in sports
299 Travel tours
300 Amateur athletic association
--- School or college athletic association (use 038)

Code

301 Fund raising athletic or sports event
317 Other sports or athletic activities
318 Other recreational activities
319 Other social activities

Youth Activities

320 Boy Scouts, Girl Scouts, etc.
321 Boys Club, Little League, etc.
322 FFA, FHA, 4-H club, etc.
323 Key club
324 YMCA, YWCA, YMHA, etc.
325 Camp
326 Care and housing of children (orphanage, etc.)
327 Prevention of cruelty to children
328 Combat juvenile delinquency
349 Other youth organization or activities

Conservation, Environmental and Beautification Activities

350 Preservation of natural resources (conservation)
351 Combatting or preventing pollution (air, water, etc.)
352 Land acquisition for preservation
353 Soil or water conservation
354 Preservation of scenic beauty
--- Litigation (see Litigation and Legal Aid Activities)
--- Combat community deterioration (use 402)
355 Wildlife sanctuary or refuge
356 Garden club
379 Other conservation, environmental or beautification activities

Housing Activities

380 Low-income housing
381 Low and moderate income housing
382 Housing for the aged (see also 153)
--- Nursing or convalescent home (use 152)
--- Student housing (use 042)
--- Orphanage (use 326)
398 Instruction and guidance on housing
399 Other housing activities

Inner City or Community Activities

400 Area development, re-development or renewal
--- Housing (see Housing Activities)
401 Homeowners association
402 Other activity aimed at combatting community deterioration
403 Attracting new industry or retaining industry in an area
404 Community promotion
--- Community recreational facility (use 297)
--- Community center (use 296)
405 Loans or grants for minority businesses
--- Job training, counseling, or assistance (use 566)
--- Day care center (use 574)
--- Referral service (social agencies) (use 569)
--- Legal aid to indigents (use 462)
406 Crime prevention
407 Volunteer firemen's organization or auxiliary
--- Rescue squad (use 158)
408 Community service organization
429 Other inner city or community benefit activities

Civil Rights Activities

430 Defense of human and civil rights
431 Elimination of prejudice and discrimination (race, religion, sex, national origin, etc.)
432 Lessen neighborhood tensions
449 Other civil rights activities

Litigation and Legal Aid Activities

460 Public interest litigation activities
461 Other litigation or support of litigation
462 Legal aid to indigents
463 Providing bail
465 Plan under IRC section 120

Legislative and Political Activities

480 Propose, support, or oppose legislation
481 Voter information on issues or candidates
482 Voter education (mechanics of registering, voting, etc.)
483 Support, oppose, or rate political candidates
484 Provide facilities or services for political campaign activities
509 Other legislative and political activities

Advocacy

Attempt to influence public opinion concerning:
510 Firearms control

Code

511 Selective Service System
512 National defense policy
513 Weapons systems
514 Government spending
515 Taxes or tax exemption
516 Separation of church and state
517 Government aid to parochial scho
518 U.S. foreign policy
519 U.S. military involvement
520 Pacifism and peace
521 Economic-political system of U.S.
522 Anti-communism
523 Right to work
524 Zoning or rezoning
525 Location of highway or transportati system
526 Rights of criminal defendants
527 Capital punishment
528 Stricter law enforcement
529 Ecology or conservation
530 Protection of consumer interests
531 Medical care system
532 Welfare system
533 Urban renewal
534 Busing students to achieve ra balance
535 Racial integration
536 Use of intoxicating beverage
537 Use of drugs or narcotics
538 Use of tobacco
539 Prohibition of erotica
540 Sex education in public schools
541 Population control
542 Birth control methods
543 Legalized abortion
559 Other matters

Other Activities Directed to Individuals

560 Supplying money, goods or servi to the poor
561 Gifts or grants to individuals (oth than scholarships)
--- Scholarships for children of emplo ees (use 039)
--- Scholarships (other) (use 040)
--- Student loans (use 041)
562 Other loans to individuals
563 Marriage counseling
564 Family planning
565 Credit counseling and assistance
566 Job training, counseling, or assistance
567 Draft counseling
568 Vocational counseling
569 Referral service (social agencies)
572 Rehabilitating convicts or ex-convi
573 Rehabilitating alcoholics, drug abusers, compulsive gamblers, etc.
574 Day care center
575 Services for the aged (see also 1 and 382)
--- Training of or aid to the handicapp (see 031 and 160)

Activities Directed to Other Organizations

600 Community Chest, United Fund, etc.
601 Booster club
602 Gifts, grants, or loans to other organizations
603 Non-financial services or facilities to other organizations

Other Purposes and Activities

900 Cemetery or burial activities
901 Perpetual care fund (cemetery, columbarium, etc.)
902 Emergency or disaster aid fund
903 Community trust or component
904 Government instrumentality or agency (see also 254)
905 Testing products for public safety
906 Consumer interest group
907 Veterans activities
908 Patriotic activities
909 4947(a)(1) trust
910 Domestic organization with activiti outside U.S.
911 Foreign organization
912 Title holding corporation
913 Prevention of cruelty to animals
914 Achievement prizes or awards
915 Erection or maintenance of public building or works
916 Cafeteria, restaurant, snack bar, foo services, etc.
917 Thrift shop, retail outlet, etc.
918 Book, gift or supply store
919 Advertising
921 Loans or credit reporting
922 Endowment fund or financial servic
923 Indians (tribes, cultures, etc.)
924 Traffic or tariff bureau
927 Fund raising
928 4947(a)(2) trust
930 Prepaid legal services plan exemp under IRC section 501(c)(20)

Figure 4.3 Activity codes of exempt organizations listed by the Internal Revenue Service. *Source:* IRS form 990 tax return instructions

terplay are not well understood, but there is little doubt that public policy has provided many, and changing, incentives for nonprofits to form and to grow, as well as restrictions on them, and that the monitoring and enforcement of those restrictions and eligibility requirements have influenced both the size of the nonprofit sector and the composition of its activities. The effect of public policy can be seen in the changing number and types of nonprofit organizations. The total number of nonprofits listed by the IRS doubled between 1969 and 1980, increasing from 416,000 to 846,000, and by the end of 1985 it surpassed 886,000 (see Table A.9). The largest class of nonprofits—about 40 percent of the total—includes the educational, health, welfare, scientific, or cultural organizations that benefit from being tax exempt under section 501(c)(3) of the Internal Revenue Code; donations to them are tax deductible. These are most of the organizations whose requests for donations arrive in our daily mail—to help the poor at home and abroad, to support medical research, to foster a local theater, art, or music group, to aid "public" radio and television, to facilitate a college's educational activities, and so on. They include such diverse groups as the American Statistical Association, the Fellowship of Christian Athletes, the American Museum of Natural History, the National Wildlife Federation, and the Grand Rapids (Michigan) Symphony Society. This is also the class of nonprofits that has grown the most. Nearly 49 percent of the total growth between 1969 and 1985 in the number of nonprofits was in this philanthropic class, which grew by nearly 170 percent.

Growth in the number of nonprofits has by no means been limited to the tax-deductible organizations. There is another group of social welfare nonprofits that is very similar to this class except that donations to it are not tax deductible because the organizations engage in a "substantial" amount of legislative lobbying; Sierra Club, an environmental protection organization, is a prominent example, and Common Cause is another. So, too, are the Veterans of World War I, the Conference of Presidents of Major Jewish Organizations, and the National Hot Rod Association. (These organizations are tax exempt under section 501(c)(4) of the tax code.) Despite nondeductibility of contributions to these organizations, their number has grown somewhat since 1969, although most of the growth was prior to 1976 (Table A.9).

The revenues of both deductible and nondeductible social welfare nonprofits are also rising dramatically. Between 1973 and 1982, gross receipts of the tax-deductible, 501(c)(3) nonprofits quadrupled, rising from

$57 billion to $234 billion, while receipts of the 501(c)(4) organizations, although nondeductible, grew nearly as rapidly, from $15 billion to over $58 billion. The combined receipts of these, the two most numerous groups of nonprofits, totaled 5.4 percent as much as the gross national product in 1973, but rose to 9.5 percent as much by 1982 (Table A.10).[16] The growth of charitable giving to the 501(c)(4) organizations is particularly impressive because contributions to them are not tax deductible to the giver. Other classes of nonprofit organizations are also growing in size. The number of business leagues—501(c)(6) organizations—nearly doubled between 1969 and 1984, from some 28,000 to 53,000; and rapid growth occurred among the fraternal and other beneficiary societies—exempt under sections 501(c)(8), (9), and (10)—particularly between 1969 and 1976.

Growth has not occurred, though, among all groups covered by section 501 in recent years. In the last decade, between 1976 and 1985, while the total number of nonprofits grew by 16 percent (124,000 organizations), there were actual decreases in the number of nonprofit labor and agricultural organizations, or (c)(5) groups; fraternal beneficiary societies, (c)(8) groups; and mutual insurance companies, or (c)(15) groups (see Table A.9). Much more than tax deductibility must be involved in explaining the growth or decline of any subsector of the nonprofit economy—for with few exceptions, only the 501(c)(3) nonprofits can receive tax-deductible contributions.

The tax-deductible nonprofits have been singled out for special subsidization on the assumption that without public encouragement there would be "too little" of those particular services provided. These nonprofits thus fit, presumably, into the category of providers of collective services or trust services; they help to meet the demands of persons who are unsatisfied by the level or quality of governmental provision of such services. In the process of supplementing governmental output, however, these nonprofits do more than help to satisfy their financial supporters, who tend to have unusually high levels of demands: they contribute to the well-being of other people who also care, though less so, about cleaner air, less poverty, increased medical research, and greater confidence that the more vulnerable members of society are receiving protection. There is, therefore, a justification for subsidizing such organizations—provided that it is not excessively costly for regulatory authorities (currently the IRS) to monitor their actions to assure that they provide the public-type services expected of them. Thus, organizations that finance scientific research on diseases (activity 161 listed in Figure 4.3), such as the Cancer Society and Epilepsy Foundation, those that supply money, goods, or services to the poor (activity 560), and those supplying legal aid for the indigent (activity 462) benefit many people, not merely the donors and recipients.

The same may be said for public-type nonprofits that provide trust rather than collective services. These offer a "package" of a private service and of information (consumer protection). Consumers' demands for information, as for other goods and services, vary a great deal. Responses to those demands involve a panoply of informational mechanisms in the private-enterprise economy and in government; but consumers who seek protective information can also turn to the nonprofit sector. Among the nonprofit organizations that provide information and trust in combination with private-type outputs are blood banks (activity code 156), nursing homes (code 152), and day-care centers (code 574). Consumers who feel underinformed about the quality of what they are purchasing may prefer to deal with nonprofit organizations, since nonprofits have less apparent incentive than proprietary firms to take advantage of consumers' lack of information. In effect, such consumers would be choosing to purchase information by dealing with a nonprofit supplier. Society at large, not only those consumers, supports mechanisms that enhance more informed decision-making.

The largely proprietary, or commercial, nonprofits—receiving little in donations, and none of it tax deductible—that are exempt from taxation under Internal Revenue Code subsections other than 501(c)(3) or (4) are as varied as the social welfare nonprofits. There are worker and trade associations, such as the Major League Baseball Players Association, the National Livestock Producers Association, and the Shade Tobacco Growers Agricultural Association, all of which are 501(c)(5) nonprofits; the U.S. Professional Tennis Association, the National Association of Women Lawyers, the National Association of Pharmaceutical Manufacturers, and the Memphis Cotton Exchange, which are 501(c)(6) organizations; the North American Falconers Association, the Model T Ford Club of America, and numerous country clubs, which are 501(c)(7) nonprofits; the Association of Russian Imperial Naval Officers in America and various Elks lodges, which are exempt under section 501(c)(8); pension funds such as the Great Neck (New York) Teachers Association Insurance Trust Fund and the Construction Workers Welfare Fund—(c)(9) organizations; the National Association of Extension 4-H Agents—

a (c)(10); and company credit unions, such as Sanford's Employees Credit Union (Bellwood, Illinois)—a (c)(14). The consequences of granting so many kinds of organizations immunity from income taxation, even if not eligibility for tax-deductible donations, are only vaguely understood, the effects on related activities in the proprietary sector even less so.

We get a clearer picture of the activities of nonprofits from a 1977 survey by the Census Bureau of the service sector of the economy, where nonprofits are overwhelmingly concentrated. Organizations that provide health services are a major component of the nonprofit service sector. They include only 7 percent of the 166,000 tax-exempt service organizations covered in the survey, but they accounted for nearly 50 percent—2.4 million—of the 4.95 million paid workers in the industries surveyed (Table 4.1). Hospitals alone employed some 86 percent of the 2.4 million workers in health services. The number of employees of nursing homes has grown appreciably since 1977, both absolutely and relative to the number of hospital workers.[17]

Education is the second-largest employer in the nonprofit service sector. The 9,160 educational organizations in the survey, including mostly schools but also some 1,400 nonprofit libraries, comprised another 19 percent of total employment in the nonprofit service sector. There are nearly twice as many social service nonprofits as there are for health and education combined, but they are typically small. Encompassing family social services, job training and vocational rehabilitation, child care, and so on, social service nonprofits constitute one-quarter of all nonprofit establishments. Despite their prevalence, they are responsible for only 14 percent of paid employment and 10 percent of the payroll of the nonprofits surveyed.[18]

Among the private-type service nonprofits, membership organizations, including some 23,000 labor unions and 12,000 business associations (for details see Table A.11), are extremely numerous. Although they constitute half of all the nonprofit service organizations, they are relatively small employers. They employ 600,000 people—only 12 percent of the total—but their impact on the economy is surely understated by either their share of employment or their share of expenditures, which is 14 percent of the entire service sector. Private membership organizations are much like clubs, organized to benefit their members. Just how much they benefit others—or, indeed, even impose costs on them—is a matter of continuing debate.

Table 4.1 Tax-exempt service industries, 1977

Industry	Number of Establishments	Employees (thousands)
All tax-exempt service industries	165,614	4,950
Public-type		
Health services	12,307	2,431
Educational services	9,160	932
Social services	40,983	676
Legal aid organizations	1,101	12
Museums, art galleries, and botanical and zoological gardens	2,252	32
Proprietary-type		
Membership organizations, except religious	82,666	600
Amusement and recreational organizations	7,138	122
Hotels and lodging houses operated on membership basis	3,096	13
Commercial laboratories	446	36
Other: sporting and recreational camps and noncommercial educational, scientific, and research organizations	6,465	95

Source: U.S. Bureau of the Census, *1977 Census of Service Industries: Other Service Industries* (Washington, D.C.: Government Printing Office, 1979), x. For additional data, see Table A.11 in Appendix A.

Another type of membership organization is the "civic, social, and fraternal" nonprofit, of which there are more than 34,000. The Census Bureau classified these quite dissimilar organizations together, but they ought to be distinguished. Many civic and fraternal organizations provide important public-type services for their communities even while they are in other respects providing proprietary, club-type services to their own members. Difficult as it is to differentiate organizations by their contributions to nonmembers, that is what must be addressed in any public policy debate; public subsidies ought to reflect public benefits.

About 4 percent of the nonprofit service organizations exist to promote "amusement and recreation," and most of them are proprietary-type nonprofits. More than 80 percent of them—5,910—are membership sports and recreation clubs, which presumably bring benefits to members alone; the balance are orchestras and other entertainment organizations, which typically charge admission fees. The social desirability of public subsidies to entertainment organizations has not been clearly resolved in this country, although such subsidies are commonplace in Europe.[19]

In 1982 the Census Bureau repeated its survey of the service sector of the economy, but with some unfortunate omissions. Blaming "budgetary restraints," it omitted major industry groups that had been included in 1977—specifically, all hospitals, elementary and secondary schools, labor unions, and political organizations—on the grounds that data about them were often available from other (though unspecified) sources. (This short-sighted change in the survey illustrates the need for a national policy for gathering data on nonprofits regularly and consistently.) The organizations omitted from the survey in 1982 accounted for 20 percent of the organizations covered in the 1977 survey, but a gigantic two-thirds of the paid employees![20]

In each of the nonprofit service industries that were covered in both the 1977 and 1982 surveys, the number of establishments increased (Table A.12). The most rapid growth was for social services and nursing homes, both of which increased about 30 percent; their payrolls increased by 80 percent and 115 percent, respectively—considerably more than the 59 percent increase in the consumer price index (CPI). Other nonprofit industries grew at slower rates, with the number of membership organizations increasing by only 5 percent and their payrolls increasing by little more than the CPI.

The distinction between public-type and proprietary-type nonprofits is too simple. Although some nonprofits are "purely" proprietary and some, at the other extreme, are virtually purely public, there are many intermediate positions between these poles. Wise public policy should make such distinctions and treat organizations that are at various positions on the spectrum differently. Even the hundreds of detailed activity groupings shown in Figure 4.3 are not homogeneous. The legislative classification of all tax-exempt organizations as either tax deductible or not is a blunt instrument for public policy that masks the variation among organizations in their wider social contributions.

The Collectiveness Index

A nonprofit's position on the spectrum from purely private to purely public can be approximated by a "collectiveness (or publicness)" index. A collectiveness index is both a measure for describing the manifold types of nonprofits and a potential basis for designing public policies that will encourage nonprofits in accord with the societal benefits they bring.

The collectiveness index reflects the causal relationship between the way an organization obtains revenues and the nature of its outputs. A private for-profit firm sells outputs that benefit only the buyer; in return it receives revenues from sales. It is typically a provider of "purely private" goods or services and an accurate measure of "collectiveness" would be an extreme score—say, zero. Similarly, an organization that, even if it is called a "nonprofit," provides only private goods or services for its members or constituents and not for others should also be characterized by a zero. Such a nonprofit would generally obtain all its revenue either from sales of goods and services or from membership dues.

By contrast, and at the opposite extreme, any private organization that provided purely collective goods—virtually all of the benefits from which accrued to persons who did not pay for them—should receive the highest measure of collectiveness, say 100. These are, arguably, the organizations that most justify public subsidies. They would receive little or no revenues either from sales or from membership dues; if they received any revenue at all, it would be in the form of contributions, gifts, or grants (CGG). A cancer research organization, a charity aiding the poor or disabled, or a legal aid organization, for example, would have a high collectiveness index, since most of its benefits would accrue to persons who had not donated to the organization.

An accurate collectiveness index, in short, would reflect the degree to which an organization provides external social benefits. Collectiveness is measured here by the percentage of an organization's revenue that is in the form of CGG.[21] This focus on an organization's sources of revenue is a proxy for the external benefits the nonprofit generates for nonpayers; these, after all, are the benefits to which public subsidies are presumably directed. The point is that people whose purchases produce "sales" revenues for nonprofits are not financing the same types of activities as are people who make contributions, gifts, and grants.

The wide range of collectiveness indexes found in the United States economy is portrayed in Table 4.2, which shows the proportion of revenues consisting of CGG for a number of the industries or activity codes listed in Figure 4.3. From the standpoint of understanding the nonprofit sector or of developing policy toward it, there is little to be gained from aggregating into a single, "nonprofit" sector both "mutual organizations, which, in the aggregate, receive 1 percent of their revenues through CGG, and legal aid organizations, which, overall, derive 97 percent of their revenues from CGG. The first are essentially providers of private services to paying customers; the second are not. (There is, of course,

Table 4.2 Collectiveness index—contributions, gifts, and grants (CGG) as percent of revenues—of nonprofit organizations, 1974–1977, by industry

Industry[a]	Donations as Percent of Revenues
Litigation and legal aid	97
Civil rights	65
Inner city and community development	51
Conservation and environment	46
Welfare	43
Advocacy	40
Instruction and training	37
Housing	31
Culture	27
Legislative and political action	18
Education	18
Employee or membership benefit	15
Scientific research	14
Health	8
Farming	7
Business and professions	5
Sports, athletic, and social clubs	4
Mutual associations	1

Source: IRS form 990 data tapes. Data apply to all organizations with gross revenue above the filing requirement, $10,000, for at least one of the years 1974–1977.

a. Organizations are classified by the first activity code listed on the tax form by the organization, although an additional activity code, or even a third code, is sometimes listed.

variation within each industry in the collectiveness index for individual organizations.)

The collectiveness index (CI) is not a flawless indicator of an organization's external benefits and so it is not a perfect basis for public subsidization. Differences in donations to various organizations do not necessarily reflect differences in the intensity of demand for their services, whether intensity is gauged by citizens' true willingness to pay or by some other measure. Moreover, the donations to an organization do not reflect any negative external effects of the organization's activities—such as the opposition of animal-rights activists to certain scientific research or the objections of anti-abortionists to pro-abortion educational activities. (There are, of course, also anti-abortion organizations and animal-rights organizations and they, too, receive donations.)

The proposed CI carries the implication that if two organizations had the same absolute level of CGG but one had more revenue from sales, that one would have a lower CI value and so would be a smaller contributor of external benefits. While the validity of such a measure can be debated, it is plausible that greater dependence on providing output that is salable diminishes an organization's ability to concentrate on its "charitable" activities; thus, a higher level of sales activity for a nonprofit would diminish the social value of a given level of donations to it.

The issues are complicated and the policy choices are untidy. What the disparity in collectiveness indexes suggests, however, is that society's treatment of different types of institutions should reflect not whether the institution does or does not "serve the public" but whether it demonstrates a greater or lesser degree of "publicness." Sources of an organization's revenues can be used to approximate the degree of publicness through the collectiveness index. From this argument follows a policy proposition: the greater the proportion of revenues an organization receives from sales and dues—and, hence, the smaller its collectiveness index—the weaker is its claim for public subsidization, other things equal.

The variation displayed in Table 4.2 is not simply the result of tax considerations. The particular nature of an organization's activities also affects the willingness of potential donors to contribute. Some nonprofits that do not have tax-deductible status nevertheless receive sizable amounts of donations. Common Cause and Ralph Nader's Public Citizen lack tax-deductible status (because of their lobbying activities), yet 31 percent of Common Cause revenues consist of CGG and 86 percent of Public Citizen revenues are from these sources.[22] By contrast, even nonprofits with tax-deductible status differ enormously in their dependence on CGG. Such donations range from 1 percent to 96 percent in the sample of nonprofits shown in Table 4.3.

The collectiveness index highlights the differences even among nonprofit organizations that report engaging in the same activity. Table 4.4 shows a sampling of industries in which both tax-deductible and nondeductible nonprofits coexist. Two facts are striking. First, with one exception the tax-deductible organizations have average collectiveness index values of 40 or less; that is, they receive a majority of their revenues from sources other than donations. Second, the nondeductible organizations, although less dependent on donations, receive significant shares of their revenues as donations.

Curiously, any particular tax-deductible nonprofit is likely to be either extremely dependent on donations, receiving 75 percent or more of its revenues in this form, or, at the other extreme, rather independent financially from donations, receiving less than 25 percent of its revenues from donations; 80–90 percent of tax-deductible organizations are at these extremes. Table A.13 in Appendix A shows this bimodal pattern for the tax-deductible organizations in a number of industries, but the pattern also holds for 501(c)(4) nonprofits and for all other nonprofits combined.

Table 4.3 Collectiveness index for selected tax-deductible organizations, 1976

Organization	Collectiveness Index
Associated Students, University of Redlands, California	1
Visiting Nurse Association	7
Meals on Wheels of Greater Steubenville, Ohio	16
Up With People	22
Grand Rapids Symphony Society	46
Cincinnati Historical Society	66
Detroit Sparks Wheelchair Athletic Association	84
National Council on Employment Policy	96

Source: IRS form 990 data tapes, 1976.

Table 4.4 Collectiveness index for tax-deductible and nondeductible nonprofit organizations, selected industries, 1976

Industry (Activity Code)	Percent of Organizations That Are Tax Deductible	Collectiveness Index	
		Tax-deductible Organizations[a]	Other Organizations[b]
Faculty group (33)	58	20	6
Singing group (89)	53	27	7
Business promotion (200)	*	37	14
Employee association (263)	*	37	14
Hobby club (281)	2	34	15
Day-care centers (574)	98	37	1
Product testing for public safety (905)	22	40	14
Museum, zoo, etc. (060)	81	33	20
Scientific research (diseases) (161)	68	37	15
Defense of human and civil rights (430)	58	57	19
Money, goods, and services to the poor (560)	92	40	12

Source: IRS form 990 data tapes, 1976.

a. Tax-deductible organizations are defined here as those that claim tax exemption under section 501(c)(3) of the Internal Revenue Code.

b. Other organizations include those that claim tax exemption under any section of the Internal Revenue Code *other* than 501(c)(3) or 501(c)(4). In this table section 501(c)(4) organizations have been omitted from calculations of collectiveness indexes but are counted in total number of organizations for purposes of figuring tax-deductible organizations as a percent of the total, in column 1.

* Less than 0.5 percent.

Obtaining much, if not most, of their revenues from sales and dues rather than from donations has an important implication for nonprofits: they are able to sell some private-type goods and services, just as for-profit organizations do. In the process of making sales and charging dues, nonprofits are likely to come into competition with proprietary firms. This competition produces economic strains on both the nonprofit and the proprietary sectors and leads to interdependency between the two economic sectors.

The Life Cycle of Nonprofit Organizations

The creation of new nonprofits and the survival rates of established nonprofits are influenced by economic and political conditions. Indeed, a good deal of social, economic, and demographic history is reflected in the ages of nonprofits. Yet little is known about the life cycle of nonprofit organizations, about how public policy has affected that cycle, or about whether public attention should be directed to the entry, growth, decline, and exit of nonprofits, either individually or collectively. Do nonprofits tend to be long-lived or short? Do they start small and remain so, or do they grow and if so, at what rate? Do they tend to reach a peak size and then level off, or do they eventually tend to decline in size and then exit from the industry? Has expansion of the nonprofit economy occurred through the growth of existing organizations or the entry of new nonprofits?[23] Should government restrict entry or exit of nonprofits? Should there be a "sunset" provision limiting the life of a nonprofit?

It is clear, despite the paucity of information, that the nonprofit economy reacts to changing forces; it is far from a static sector. In recent years the growth of the nonprofit sector has resulted in the existence of kinds of organizations very different from the nonprofits of decades ago. In some areas of activity there has been rapid expansion of the number of nonprofits; in other areas there has been little expansion. As a result, the ages of nonprofits in various industries differ markedly (Table A.14). In 1977, for example, the average age of tax-deductible, section 501(c)(3) schools was thirteen years. The tax-deductible nonprofits engaging in "inner city or community" activities such as area renewal and attracting industry had an average age of only about five years. "Political and legislative" tax-deductible nonprofits, at the other extreme, had an average age of over forty years.[24]

Nonprofit industries have responded to differing conditions of demand and supply. Nonprofits engaged in litigation and legal aid, for example, are a product of the Great Society era of the 1960s; 99 percent of the nonprofits in this area that existed in 1977 entered since 1965, and 96 percent entered since 1971 (Table A.15). At the opposite extreme, nonprofit conservation or environmental groups are of longer standing; only 26 percent of these organizations were formed after 1970 whereas 60 percent were formed by 1965. The life cycles of advocacy nonprofits—those engaged in activities 510–559 in Figure 4.3, including organizations attempting to influence public opinion concerning such matters as firearms, sex education, urban renewal, and national defense—show still another growth pattern. Not only were almost all (94 percent) these organizations formed since 1965, but only 18 percent were begun after 1970; that is, 76 percent came into existence between 1965 and 1970. By contrast, only 2 percent of the nonprofits engaged in scientific research entered in the same five-year period.

Should we care whether the growth of the nonprofit sector comes through the expansion of a few existing nonprofits rather than through the entry of new organizations? This is a dimension of public policy toward nonprofits that has totally escaped attention. In part the answer hinges on cost structures in nonprofit organizations. How substantial are the economies of scale? There is surely no general answer that applies to all nonprofits. It makes little sense to generalize about economies of scale in nursery schools, nursing homes, legal aid offices, and museums, let alone trade associations, labor unions, and country clubs.

In contrast to regulation of public utilities, where government restricts entry of new firms, nonprofits may enter freely; all that is required under current law is that the IRS must determine that the organization would engage in the types of activities specified by law. Such questions as what effect a new entrant would have on other nonprofits and whether there would or would not be cost efficiencies from having fewer but larger nonprofits in any particular industry and market area are irrelevant under existing law.

There is no doubt that the answers to these questions are neither known nor easily knowable. Moreover, even if economies of scale did support a policy of restricted entry, the matter would not be closed; even among nonprofits, the benefits of competition, including the generation of new ideas and the economic, social, and political advantages of diversity and pluralism, might justify some cost inefficiencies. Yet existing policy reflects an implicit and questionable assumption: that in none of the hundreds of activities in which nonprofits engage are there economies of scale that even *might* justify restricting the number of nonprofits beyond whatever effects occur through natural forces of competition among nonprofits and between them and other, public and private, producers.

Economies of scale appear to be relatively limited in the service sector, in which nonprofits are a prominent force. In health and education, 30 percent or more of urban nonprofits are very small, with gross annual receipts under $10,000; only about 5 percent are large, with gross receipts in excess of $1 million. Economies of scale in the environmental industry are apparently even more modest; virtually all the nonprofits are small. (Table A.16 shows the information for a number of cities in 1976, the latest year for which data are available.)

Although most nonprofits are very small, a relative handful are typically large enough to dominate each nonprofit industry in each urban area. In the health and welfare sectors, the largest four nonprofit organizations account generally for 30–50 percent of nonprofits' total revenues in a large city.[25] Cultural organizations are even more concentrated; the largest four nonprofits typically have 40–60 percent of revenues. Among advocacy groups, the concentration ratios for the top four organizations are generally in the 60–90 percent range (Table A.17).[26]

In some fields we have evidence that economies of scale have favored the growth of existing organizations, whereas in others growth by an increase in number seems to be favored. In nursing homes, child care, and legal aid, for example, the advantages of larger scale are apparently small; the number of establishments in these industries grew substantially between 1977 and 1982 but the level of real expenditures per establishment changed little (Table A.18). By contrast, activity in nonprofits devoted to education and research and in business associations increased substantially in this period but with virtually no increase in the number of establishments; growth in average size of these organizations suggests advantages of larger scale in these industries—in production costs, marketing, or both. Whether government should restrict entry of new organizations in these fields is not clear, however. Government does regulate public utilities, such as electricity, natural gas transmission, and water supply, but economies of scale in these industries are so great relative to market demand that maximum efficiency dictates a single provider. Regulation is justified both to restrict entry and to prevent abuse of the resulting monopoly power, but the commodity being sold is relatively homogeneous—or at least easily monitored—and so the key regulatory instrument is the selling price. In the case of nonprofits, though, the complexity of output—more precisely, the difficulty of monitoring quality—is often a key element, indeed the fundamental element.

When output quality is costly to monitor, the reputation of a seller is likely to be important to consumers. Although reputation develops over time and new organizations face a difficult task, there appears to be little reason for restricting entry unless a case can be made that poorly informed consumers are misled by new entrants. Opportunistic new organizations might take advantage of nonprofit status and consumer ignorance to reap short-term gain by acting as for-profit firms in disguise. Still, the advantages of competition, even within the nonprofit economy, would appear to outweigh the costs of such abuses, although this remains a quantitative judgment that deserves further study.

Geographic Distribution of Nonprofit Organizations

Current policy has given rise to an interesting geographic distribution of nonprofit organizations. When a uniform set of tax-subsidy rules is applied to a geographically diverse set of circumstances, nonuniform results can be expected.

Both the number of nonprofit organizations per 100,000 population and the level of their expenditures per capita show sizable geographic variation. There are 32 percent more nonprofit organizations in the West, and 61 percent more in the Northeast, than in the South, after adjusting for differences in population size. Differences in expenditures by nonprofits are even more pronounced—expenditures per capita being two-and-one-half times as much in the Northeast as in the South (Table A.19).[27]

The geographic diversity of nonprofits is particularly striking for nursing homes and hospitals. In 1980 there were some 1.5 million nursing home beds in the United States, 22 percent in nonprofit homes, 70 percent in for-profits (proprietaries), and 8 percent in governmental facilities. In California and in Texas, though, only 13 percent of nursing home beds were in nonprofits, and in Mississippi nonprofits accounted for a mere 7 percent of beds; in New York, by contrast, nonprofits accounted for 35 percent of all nursing home beds, in Pennsylvania it was 39 percent, in Minnesota, 43 percent, and in North Dakota, 74 percent.[28] In other words, nonprofits have a disproportionately large share of the nursing home market in the Northeast and North Central regions, and the opposite in the South and West (Table A.20).[29]

Nonprofit hospitals, like nursing homes, are most dominant in the older parts of the country, while proprietaries have their greatest strength in the Sun Belt. (Rapid population growth stimulated demand, to which the private sector appeared to respond more quickly.) In the New England states—Connecticut, Maine, Massachusetts, New Hampshire, and Rhode Island—93 percent of all short-term community hospital beds are in private nonprofit hospitals, and fewer than 1 percent are in proprietary hospitals; however, in the West South Central region—Arkansas, Louisiana, Oklahoma, and Texas—only 48 percent of hospital beds are in nonprofits, and 22 percent are in proprietaries (Table A.21).

Competition among Nonprofit, For-profit, and Governmental Suppliers

It should be apparent that the nonprofit sector is not isolated from the rest of the economy. Because of the interdependency of all sectors, public actions directed at nonprofits affect other parts of the economy as'well; conversely, actions directed at for-profit firms and governmental agencies affect nonprofits—frequently in quite unanticipated and even undesired ways.

Many nonprofits compete with for-profit firms or government, or both, in "mixed" industries. The nonprofit American Automobile Association (AAA) competes with the for-profit auto clubs run by Mobil Oil Company and Sears; the local nonprofit YMCA provides athletic facilities and exercise classes in competition with proprietary "health clubs" such as the Elaine Powers Fitness Club and Vic Tanny Health and Racquetball Club. Nursery schools operated by local churches and other nonprofit agencies compete with profit-making schools. Nonprofit hospitals face increasing competition from rapidly growing for-profit, "investor-owned" hospital chains such as Humana and Hospital Corporation of America. Elementary and secondary schools, although overwhelmingly run by government, exist alongside a sizable nonprofit component—mostly but not entirely run by church organizations; there is even a small for-profit component, which includes, for example, the American Renaissance School in White Plains, New York.[30]

The interaction of nonprofit organizations with the rest of the economy makes the task of policymaking complex. Every action taken to encourage, discourage, redirect, or otherwise regulate nonprofits brings side effects for the organizations with which they compete or from which they make purchases. Policy measures designed with the rest of the economy in mind (for example, changes in personal income tax or business property tax rates) can also have strong effects on nonprofits.

This interplay of nonprofit organizations with other institutions is particularly evident in mixed industries, especially those with a large nonprofit sector. More kidney dialysis stations are owned by nonprofit organizations than by either for-profits or government. Forty percent of children in formal day-care organizations are in nonprofits. Over 20 percent of spending on research and development is accounted for by nonprofits. Among libraries and information centers, nonprofit and governmental providers dominate overwhelmingly, but there is also a proprietary sector (Table A.22). Many industries are mixed—with for-profit, governmental, and private nonprofit organizations coexisting—but there has been little attention paid to why they are so, what the consequences are, and what public policy ought to be toward them. In the vast economics literature on industrial organization essentially no attention has been paid to the institutional dimension of industry structure and its implications for economic performance.

It is not surprising that in mixed industries that provide collective services the nonprofits, to a large extent, have tax-deductible status; indeed, the overwhelming majority of the nonprofits that operate libraries or research centers have this status. More generally, although slightly under half of all nonprofits filing tax returns (form 990) in the period 1971–1977 had tax-deductible status, the percentages were substantially greater in industries that appear to generate sizable external or collective benefits. For organizations in scientific research (activity codes 161, 162, 180, 181, and 199 in Figure 4.3), 72 percent of the 4,772 nonprofits had tax-deductible status, and 83 percent of the 1,122 nonprofit libraries (activity code 61) had tax-deductible status.[31]

The vast majority of nonprofits providing—or, at least, potentially providing—trust services had tax-deductible status, too. In the nursing home industry (activity code 152), all but one of the 89 nonprofits sampled were tax deductible; among day-care centers (activity code 574), only 12 of the 578 filers did not have tax-deductible status. (Dialysis stations are not covered by a specific activity code, so data could not be gathered.) As is the case with nonprofits providing collective services, these nonprofits are granted tax-deductible status because they are believed to contribute to the public interest.

The mixed-ownership industries include not only public-type nonprofits but also commercial or proprietary nonprofits—for example, health insurers and sporting and recreational camps (Table A.22). Whatever the justification may be for not taxing their net income, there would appear to be a social judgment that their activities do not convey broad public benefits and so do not deserve further subsidization through tax deductibility of contributions. In fact, few of these nonprofits are tax deductible. Among health insurance organizations (activity code 163), only one of 48 nonprofits was tax deductible and although the IRS data do not permit identification of sporting and recreational camps, among the broader class of nonprofits engaged in "sports, athletic, recreational and social activities" (activity codes 280–319) only 12 percent of the 17,804 tax-return filers in that larger category reported being tax deductible.

The nonprofit economy is clearly a complex part of the national economy. Its overall size, whether gauged by assets, revenues, employment, or contribution to the national income, fails utterly to convey its rich diversity. Among different industries, however, nonprofit organizations are of very unequal importance. They are essentially irrelevant in manufacturing, but they are a major factor, and in some instances the dominant factor, in the social services. Some nonprofits provide private goods; others, collective goods; and still others, trust goods. They engage in some activities, such as health care, that have grown rapidly in recent years, and in others, such as schools, that have been declining. Furthermore, they often compete with proprietary firms and even with governmental agencies.

Knowledge about the nonprofit economy is growing, yet major gaps remain. Not much is known about its changing composition, or about how effective nonprofits are in meeting society's wants as part of a pluralistic economy. The paucity of data has restricted serious examination of relations among nonprofit organizations, proprietary firms, and governmental agencies and has left us with a weak information base from which to design and implement public policy toward the nonprofit sector. (Even less is known about nonprofits in other countries. Appendix B offers a glimpse of nonprofit activity outside the United States.)

The nonprofit economy is heavily urban. Of the total of $61.5 billion of revenues of nonprofit, tax-exempt service organizations in 1982, 50 percent went to organizations in 20 of the nation's 300 metropolitan areas. Some 22 percent went to three—New York, Washington, D.C., and Los Angeles—and 9.5 percent went to the largest, New York.[32] How these funds were distributed geographically when spent by the organizations is unknown.

Inadequate data is not the only source of problems of understanding how and how well the nonprofit sector performs. A theory of institutional behavior is needed that will indicate what kinds of data are needed and how to interpret them. Is private enterprise being stifled excessively by expansion of the nonprofit sector? Alternatively, are nonprofits filling important gaps in markets where neither private firms nor governments are responding adequately to consumer wants? Answers to such questions require a combination of a theoretical framework, with which to define "excessive" expansion of nonprofits and "gaps" in markets, and quantitative testing.

Important policy issues are at stake. Should there continue to be unrestricted entry, exit, and size of individual nonprofits? How efficient are nonprofits? How innovative are they? And what is the increased competition from the growing nonprofit sector doing to the proprietary part of the economy? Although the answers are unknown, public policy proceeds apace, on the basis of an apparent faith in the virtue of competition—even for an economic sector that has been chosen explicitly to interfere with the ordinary competitive processes of the for-profit market. These are issues that have been largely disregarded by Congress, which writes the principal laws affecting nonprofits, by the IRS, which administers them, and by researchers, who seek to understand and evaluate the nonprofit economy.

FIVE

Charitable Donations

If the financing of nonprofits affected only nonprofits, the key public policy question would be how to design a system to generate sufficient revenues for the nonprofit sector. That would be complex enough. But nonprofits function in the economy alongside for-profit and governmental institutions—competing with them for markets and for revenues—and thus affect and are affected by these other segments of the economy. The question of support is therefore quite complicated. Public policy can be devised simply to permit nonprofit organizations to exist; to permit nonprofits to compete with for-profit firms; to provide for public subsidies for nonprofits; or to provide for specific forms of subsidies, such as deductibility of donations on individual and corporate income tax returns.

I have posed these policy choices on how to finance the nonprofit sector as if they were independent of decisions about the level and kinds of activities that should be undertaken by nonprofits, but those decisions cannot be disentangled from the question of finance. When, for example, President Reagan extols the social value of expanding the voluntary nonprofit sector as an alternative to government services, he implies that more economic output should be provided by nonprofit organizations and less by government. When he then proposes changes in tax laws that have the effect of contracting charitable donations by reducing marginal income tax rates and the incentive to itemize deductions on personal income tax returns, he seems to be saying that the nonprofit sector can expand as its revenues are falling. Unless nonprofits are able to offset the revenue loss resulting from changes in the tax law that reduce incentives to donate, however, the nonprofit charitable sector will contract, not expand. Moreover, not all nonprofit industries will contract and certainly not all will contract equally; the effect of reducing high marginal tax rates, for example, will be felt especially by educational and cultural organizations, which depend on higher-income donors.

The policy choices go beyond the matter of how much total revenues the nonprofit sector, or any of its component activities, can generate. They also involve the source of revenues; nonprofit organizations and society in general are not, and should not be, indifferent as to whether nonprofits raise a given sum through donations or through sales and fees. Because an organization's outputs reflect the sources of its revenues—and vice versa—deciding what society wants from the nonprofits and how the nonprofits should be financed requires joint decisions on activities and financing. Depending on precisely what outputs a nonprofit is providing, it will have greater or lesser success in its attempts to raise donations or to sell its services; conversely, depending on how it raises its funds, it will be constrained in different ways in what it may do with them.

Nonprofit organizations, unlike most proprietary firms, are limited by public policy in the kinds of activities they may engage in; at the same time, these restrictions enhance their ability to generate resources—particularly donations of money and labor. Thus, both the level and the form of outputs in the nonprofit sector depend critically on public decisions.

Correspondence between form of outputs and source of revenues is not limited to the nonprofit sector. Firms in the proprietary sector are financed, in the long run, through sales. This is the mechanism through which they are rewarded for their performance—for providing the kinds of products that consumers want and are willing to pay for. Other forms of institutions, including governments and the private nonprofits, exist, at least to some extent, precisely because the for-profit sector is unsuccessful in meeting some consumer wants. Profit-oriented firms will not provide what they cannot sell profitably. Their dependence on sales as their source of revenue dictates the level and kind of goods and services they provide.

Other forms of institutions, however, do not need to sell profitably—or at all. Governments depend little on their ability to sell services to individual consumers; they tax to finance their activities. Private nonprofit organizations confront a dilemma, able to rely neither on the principal financial mechanism used by governments (taxation) nor on the one used by proprietary firms (sales). If they provide only what they can sell profitably, they are unlikely to be able to overcome the shortcomings of the proprietary sector; if they do provide outputs that cannot be sold profitably, how are they to finance them? The answer lies substantially in donations, although other considerations also come into play.

The following table summarizes characteristic relations among an organization's institutional form, the type of its output, and its unique source of financing.

Type of Organization	Outputs	Source of Financing
For-profit	Private goods	Sales revenue
Governmental	Collective goods	Taxes
Nonprofit	Collective/trust goods	Donations

Donations are not necessarily cash payments. They may take the form of a variety of reduced prices for nonprofits, such as lower postal rates and, of great importance, subsidized interest rates on borrowing. In 1984 the tax-deductible 501(c)(3) nonprofits benefited from the sale of $10.1 billion of tax-exempt industrial development bonds—principally for nonprofit hospitals and educational facilities—up from $8.1 billion a year earlier. These sums, although only a small fraction of them constitute subsidies, exceeded the total of all corporate and foundation contributions to all charities. Industrial development bonds with their implicit subsidies were issued in every state except Alaska, Maine, Utah, and Wyoming.[1]

Private donations may also involve loans or sales to nonprofits at reduced prices. A nonprofit organization that considered establishing a loan fund for the poor, for example, found, through market research, that "a sizable number of people are willing to accept a lower interest rate if they are assured that their money will be used to promote housing for low-income people." And the IRS, making what amounted to an additional contribution of taxpayer money, ruled that lenders "will be taxed only on the interest they receive and not on any imputed interest."[2]

How successful a nonprofit organization is in obtaining donations (contributions, gifts, or grants, or CGG) depends on a variety of factors, including a number of public policy decisions. (Of course, many nonprofits, including hospitals, for example, depend little on CGG, relying instead primarily on user charges.) If, for example, nonprofits that solicit funds by mail did not receive a public subsidy for postal services, as they now do, they would face higher costs of fund raising and raise less funds.

When the Reagan administration submitted its budget to Congress in March 1981, it proposed to cut the subsidy for this third-class bulk mail of nonprofits by 37 percent. The resulting congressional action led the U.S. Postal Service to raise the rate that nonprofits pay for presorted third-class mail from 3.8 cents per piece to 5.9 cents, an increase of 55 percent. Particularly for those nonprofits that engage in substantial mail solicitation, the revenue-reducing effect of this measure could well have been large. The March of Dimes, for example, devotes about 8 percent of its total budget to postage; such a jump in postal rates was a severe blow to its budget.[3]

The ability of nonprofits to raise funds depends not only on governmental decisions to give subsidies but also on the form of subsidies. For example, should government specify, directly or indirectly, how its subsidies will be used? More concretely, should one nonprofit be subsidized more than another simply because it uses a particular form of communication to raise funds (in the example above, a letter campaign)? Or should public subsidies, whatever their total amount, be neutral, so that each nonprofit organization can determine what form its fund raising should take? Why should it be public policy to encourage nonprofits to use the mails—and, even more specifically, to use third-class rather than, say, first-class (more rapid) mail? Further, if nonprofits are to be subsidized, why should the subsidy be, in effect, earmarked for fund raising? Why not permit the organization to choose between using the subsidy for fund raising and for carrying out its principal, tax-exempt, purpose? These are matters that have received scant attention, if any. There is a presumptive case, though, for giving subsidies in ways that will not distort decisions by nonprofits on how their funds are used. There have been no studies of the degree to which the postal subsidy has increased mail solicitations, but we do know that the volume of subsidized nonprofit mail has grown steadily and substantially—from about 4 billion pieces of mail in 1972 the number has soared past 11 billion in 1985.[4]

Another policy matter regarding fund raising is whether there should be any restriction on the amount of fund raising that an organization does. Should there, for example, be an upper limit on the percentage of a nonprofit's revenues that is spent on fund raising? Many state and local laws have imposed such limits, and a great deal of controversy has resulted (leading to recent decisions by the United States Supreme Court), but neither the consequences nor the desirability of any such limit, let alone what that limit ought to be, are understood well. Legal and social constraints on fund raising by nonprofits obviously have important implications for the nonprofits themselves, but they also have important implications for the proprietary and governmental sectors of the economy. Nonprofit-sector fund raising is putting growing stress on the economic health of the proprietary sector, and pressure is increasing for public intervention to restrict nonprofits.

Fund-raising efforts by nonprofits, it must be noted, meet with considerable success. Donations—CGG—are the second largest revenue source for nonprofits (sales of goods and services are the largest). Lacking the government's power to tax, nonprofits depend a good deal on donations, and yet charitable donations are something of an enigma. To a small donor the connection between his or her contribution and the outputs it finances may seem rather remote. The resulting reluctance to donate—"free-rider" behavior—is doubtless a major obstacle to nonprofit organizations' reliance on voluntary giving. Nonetheless, the magnitude of charitable giving is impressive. Personal gifts to the approximately 320,000 tax-deductible nonprofits are estimated to have been over $66 billion in 1985. They have remained rather stable at close to 2 percent of personal income since data were first gathered in 1970. Gifts from philanthropic foundations and private corporations added $8.6 billion to this figure. (See Table C.1, in Appendix C, for details.)

Private contributions—individual and organizational—constituted an increasing share of the national income for fifteen years following 1955, when they were 2.3 percent. They rose to 2.7 percent in 1969, but they have been essentially stable since 1973, at about 2.3 percent (see Table C.2). At the same time, however, private contributions have declined steadily as a share of the total expenditures by nonprofits; donations brought 70 percent of charitable nonprofits' revenues in the mid-1950s, but this share decreased dramatically over the next quarter-century, to less than 33 percent in 1984. Still, voluntary contributions continue to be substantial, both absolutely and as a proportion of total nonprofit expenditures, notwithstanding the tendency for free-riding.

What Factors Influence Voluntary Giving?

Because donations to nonprofits are typically used to provide public-type services such as medical research and aid to the poor, the problem arises of how to generate voluntary giving—that is, how to overcome the tendency of people to free-ride on the contributions of others. Nevertheless, substantial donations are given (although possibly at a much lower level than individuals' true assessments of what the services are worth); it is clear that the "strong" version of free-rider behavior—namely, that people will not contribute at all—is incorrect.[5] Experimental studies have also confirmed that people will contribute to the provision of collective-type goods even when the opportunity for free-riding exists.[6] If more were known about why people donate to nonprofits, society would be in a stronger position to make appropriate changes in, say, tax laws or regulations on information about each nonprofit's activities, to bring about the desired effect on giving to nonprofits.

Social norms regarding appropriate levels of donations may help explain contributions. There may well be a "demonstration effect" of giving, such that each individual's willingness to contribute to a nonprofit increases with the amount contributed by others.[7] Although this seems quite likely to be important, the forces through which these norms are set and changed are poorly understood and are therefore not changeable through public policy measures.

Income tax deductibility also has an effect on giving, since the higher a taxpayer's marginal income tax bracket, the lower is the cost of giving, provided that the taxpayer can take advantage of the opportunity to itemize deductions or that contributions are deductible even for those who do not itemize, as they were, on a trial basis, between 1982 and 1986.[8] Even at the highest marginal tax rate—until 1987 50 percent—however, a $100 donation cost the giver $50, and so the question remains open as to why givers give.

Regardless of why people donate, that they give more when the after-tax cost of doing so is lower has policy implications that have received a great deal of attention. Income tax rates have been found repeatedly to have a strong effect—higher rates leading to increased giving—just as theory would suggest, since higher tax rates imply a smaller after-tax cost, to the donor, of giving. Quantitative findings, however, have ranged widely; 16 econometric studies have estimated price elasticities as low as -0.10 and as large as -2.54.[9] That is, if the "price" of donating a dollar is defined as 1 minus the marginal income tax rate, a reduction in tax rate from 40 percent to 30 percent, for example, would increase the price of donating a dollar from 60 cents to 70 cents; this increase in price, of about 15 percent, could result in a reduction in an individual's giving of as little as 1.5 percent (15 percent times 0.10) or as much as

38 percent (15 percent times 2.54). The mean price elasticity estimated from these studies is -1.24; thus, the apparent average responsiveness of individual charitable giving to changes in income tax rates is relatively great, a given percentage change in the "price" of donating results in a 24 percent greater percentage change in donations. In the example of a decrease in the marginal tax rate from 40 percent to 30 percent, this 15 percent increase in price of giving would reduce giving by some 18.6 percent (15 percent times 1.24).

The wide range of elasticity estimates is a basis for some concern as to the appropriateness of the models and data used to generate them. While every study included a tax rate variable, the studies varied greatly in the other explanatory variables and the range of donor incomes included; they also differed in their inclusion of characteristics of the donors—such as age, race, marital status, and education. Moreover, all of them disregarded characteristics of the recipient organizations—for example, its reputation, its level of fund-raising expenditures, and its efficiency in converting donations into final services rather than into administrative and fund-raising costs; we will see later in this chapter that these may be important determinants of giving, although whether they influence aggregate giving or only the distribution among competing charitable organizations is unclear.

The deduction for charitable giving was added to the federal income tax law in 1917, four years after the original law was enacted; in 1918 an estate tax deduction was added for charitable bequests, but it was 1935 before corporations were first allowed to make tax-deductible contributions.[10] These deductions presumably had only a small effect on giving prior to World War II, since income tax rates were tiny until then. Now, with far higher rates of personal and corporate taxation, tax rates are a major influence on charitable giving. In 1985, when the Reagan administration introduced its "Tax Proposals for Fairness, Growth, and Simplicity," the proposed reduction of the top-bracket personal income tax rate from 50 percent to 35 percent—later reduced further, to 28 percent by the Senate-House Conference Committee—was widely endorsed; still, the nonprofit sector's national organization, Independent Sector, noted its concern over the expected loss of $4 billion in gifts.[11]

Other features of Reagan's proposals would influence charitable giving, too, but the principal point is this: changes that were intended for very different purposes would affect charitable giving in ways that may well have been unforeseen and that almost certainly were unintended. A "flatter"—more proportional—income tax, with reduced top-bracket tax rates, as adopted in 1986 to take effect in 1987, has both supporters and opponents. Few from either group seemed eager to cut into charitable giving, yet reduced donations would be an outcome. Similarly, the administration's proposal to eliminate the deductibility of state and local taxes had nothing directly to do with charitable giving; however, that proposal, if enacted, would have substantially reduced the number of taxpayers who would itemize, and this, in turn, would have the side effect of diminishing the incentive to donate to nonprofits.[12] In short, the current dependence of charitable giving on tax deductibility has enormous and generally unfortunate consequences.[13] Incentives to donate are strengthened and weakened as incidental and often accidental results of changes in personal and corporate tax laws.

The same issues arise at the state level. In the spring of 1985, for example, the governor of Wisconsin proposed virtually to eliminate itemized deductions and to reduce the top-bracket state income tax rate from 10 percent to 8 percent. Jerald Schiff and I estimated that these changes would have increased the after-tax cost of donating to nonprofits to a degree that would lead to a 4 percent reduction in total giving; moreover, because giving by high-income donors would be reduced the most, the types of charities they favored—such as educational and cultural organizations—would suffer even larger reductions in donations.[14]

The fraction of an organization's revenues used for fund raising also influences donations to nonprofits. Both public policymakers and scholarly researchers have focused on this variable recently. The United States Supreme Court, for example, has issued two landmark decisions concerning the constitutionality of laws that limit an organization's fund-raising budget. In 1980, in *Village of Schaumburg v. Citizens For Better Environment* (444 U.S. 620), the Supreme Court ruled against a municipal ordinance by the village, a suburb of Chicago, that prohibited solicitation of contributions by any charitable organization that did not use at least 75 percent of its receipts for "charitable purposes." That is, not more than 25 percent could be devoted to fund raising. Four years later the Court struck down a Maryland state statute that imposed a like percentage limitation on fund-raising expenses, even though it was more flexible than the Schaumburg ordinance and included the possibility of administrative waivers of the 25 percent fund-raising limitation if the organization could explain its costs to the state's satisfaction (*Secretary of State of Maryland, Petitioner v. Joseph H. Munson Company, Inc.,*

467 U.S. 947). In this decision the Court found the magnitude of an organization's fund-raising costs an unconstitutional basis for a local or state government to restrict the organization's activities. The editor of the *Philanthropy Monthly* wrote in response to that decision that "Nothing could be more central to the future of the non-profit sector [than] . . . the meaning of high fund-raising costs and . . . the powers of government to control or influence charitable solicitation."[15]

Although the decisions striking down both laws rested on protection of First Amendment rights—the Court objecting to any "statute that creates an unnecessary risk of chilling free speech" *(Munson)*—a substantial body of public opinion apparently supports legislation that restricts an organization's fund-raising expenses. Indeed, as of mid-1984 there were laws limiting fund raising in all but 11 states. Laws that restricted fund raising in ways that appear to have been struck down by the Supreme Court still exist in Arkansas, Connecticut, Georgia, Hawaii, Illinois, Kansas, Kentucky, Massachusetts, Minnesota, New Hampshire, New Jersey, North Dakota, Oklahoma, Oregon, Pennsylvania, Rhode Island, South Carolina, and Tennessee.[16] Such widespread legislation suggests that prospective donors do care about the fund-raising percentage and take it into account, or at least attempt to do so, when deciding on the level and allocation of charitable donations.

The intention of these laws appears to be consumer protection. The "price" of donations—as reflected by the organization's fund-raising percentage—is presumed to be important to prospective donors. Whether 25 percent, or any other specific number, is critical to donors, however, is by no means clear. Thus, it is noteworthy that there are some states that, rather than restricting the fund-raising percentage, require only its disclosure. This is the case in California, Florida, Indiana, Louisiana, Maine, New Mexico, North Carolina, Virginia, and Washington.[17] Whether a state attempts to limit an organization's fund-raising percentage or merely to require its disclosure, these actions suggest strongly that voters care about an organization's fund-raising percentage. This concern is another illustration of the importance of informational inequalities—in this case between nonprofit organizations and prospective donors regarding what is done with donations.

The alternative regulatory approaches used by various states—some limiting the fund-raising percentage, others mandating its disclosure in some fashion, and some doing neither—points up another social choice. Whichever alternative is adopted, should the choice be made at the state or at the federal level? The case for federal action has not been made strenuously, but in this area as well as many others the increasingly mobile population of the United States is gradually bolstering the still-weak case for national standards. Whether a nonprofit organization's fund-raising percentage should be the subject of a legislative standard, an informational disclosure requirement, or some other regulation is a familiar problem in consumer-protection legislation. Generally such legislation has concentrated on providing information to consumers, although regulatory standards have been adopted in cases of great risk (such as the use of flammable material in children's pajamas) and where information is sufficiently complex that it is hard for consumers to assess (for example, Food and Drug Administration criteria for acceptable drugs).

One reason for requiring disclosure of fund-raising activities and fund-raising expenditures by nonprofits is that prospective donors are typically unable to assess the use to which their marginal donation would be put. Still, the case for mandatory disclosure is not overwhelming. After all, if donors do care, it will be in the interest of nonprofits seeking donations both to control the level of fund-raising expenses and to announce fund-raising percentages.

Do people actually regard a greater fund-raising percentage as objectionable, leading them to donate less? The conventional wisdom is that they do—witness the solicitations of many charitable organizations that emphasize the modest level of their fund-raising expenditures and administrative costs. A request for a contribution to the National Foundation for Cancer Research, for example, stated: "The cost of solicitation and administration is expected to be 31 percent of the gross amount collected. For each $1.00 donated, it is estimated that the amount devoted to research will be 69 cents." Even in cartoons the convention is honored: in one a derelict, hat in hand, wears a sign saying "No part of your contribution goes for administration,"[18] in another the sign reads "Only 35% of your contribution goes for booze."[19]

In a recent study, however, economist Richard Steinberg argues that it is irrational for donors to care about the fund-raising ratio. Each donor should assume, he argues, that the total amount of an organization's fund-raising cost, whatever it is, is set at the level that would maximize net donations and is not changed by one individual's relatively small donation. As a result, according to Steinberg, an individual donor could expect that all of his or her own contribution would go for the stated purpose, not for fund raising.[20]

An alternative behavioral model suggests that donors do care about an organization's fund-raising percentage. In this model donors assume that the marginal percentage of any contribution that goes into fund raising rather than into the provision of charitable activities will be the same as it was, on average, for that organization the previous year, and the larger that fund-raising percentage the less a donor will wish to give.[21] In effect the fund-raising percentage is a "price" of purchasing (providing) an additional dollar's worth of an organization's outputs.[22] If a prospective donor expected that 20 percent of a donation would be used for fund raising, and if the donor regarded such expenditures as not what his or her donation should be used for, then the price of providing $1.00 of the organization's output would be $1.25 ($1.00/[1.0 − 0.2]). If the fund-raising percentage were 50 percent, then the price would be $2.00.

In either of these models, donations are affected by a donor's marginal income tax rate. They differ with respect to the effect of the organization's fund-raising percentage. Quantitative findings are contradictory. Steinberg examined donations in four metropolitan areas (Philadelphia, Los Angeles, Houston/Galveston, and Minneapolis/St. Paul) and for six groups of nonprofits (involving social services, health, education, arts and culture, science and research, and miscellaneous). There was generally no statistically significant relation between the share of fund raising in an organization's budget in one year and the level of donations to it in the following year.[23] This is consistent with the view that donors simply do not care about the fund-raising percentage—a view that clashes, however, with the existence of widespread legislation limiting fund raising or requiring its disclosure (unless legislators are misinformed about consumer preferences).

A different conclusion was reached in the other study, which Nestor Dominguez and I recently carried out; we found that donations to a nonprofit organization depend not only on the fund-raising "price" and on the level of the organization's total fund raising, but also on two variables not included in Steinberg's model. These two additional variables are the age of the organization (a proxy for the extent to which donors trusted it) and the interaction between age and the level of fund raising (to reflect the possibility that the effectiveness of fund raising would itself differ with the organization's age).[24] The data analyzed included a considerably larger set of nonprofits than those counted in the other study—some 7,600 nonprofit, tax-deductible organizations from the entire country that filed IRS form 990 tax returns for all four years 1973–1976.[25]

Dominguez and I estimated "donations functions"—logarithmic relations between the level of donations a nonprofit received and each of the following—the price of donating, the level of fund raising, and age (years since tax-exempt status was granted by the IRS)—for the United States as a whole, for seven industries in four major areas of activity in which nonprofit organizations are prominent: health, education, welfare, and cultural activities.[26] Our statistical findings, summarized in Table 5.1 (and shown in more detail in Table C.3), are striking. Table 5.1 shows only the signs of the relationships (regression coefficients); an asterisk indicates that the relationship is significantly different from zero at the 10 percent level or better.[27] First, we found that donations do respond negatively to the fund-raising percentage; the estimated "price" elasticity—which reflects the sensitivity of donations (CGG) in one year to the

Table 5.1 Effect of price of donating, fund-raising expenditures, and age of organization on donations, by industry, 1973–1976

Industry (Activity Code)	Price of Donating	Total Fund-raising Expenditures	Age of Organization	Sample Size
Library (061)	− *	−	+ *	554
Art exhibit, museum, zoo, etc. (060, 091)	− *	−	+ *	283
Goods and services to the poor and aged (560, 575)	−	−	+	219
Hospital (150)[a]	− *	−	+ *	2,615
Aid to handicapped (160)	− *	−	+	1,411
Scientific research (diseases) (161)	− *	−	+ *	2,060
School, college, trade school (30)[b]	− *	−	−	572

Source: Burton A. Weisbrod and Nestor D. Dominguez, "Demand for Collective Goods in Private Nonprofit Markets: Can Fundraising Expenditures Help Overcome Free-Rider Behavior?" *Journal of Public Economics* 30 (June 1986), 83–95.

Note: Shown here are the signs of the regression coefficients of the "donations functions" calculated in the study cited above. A minus sign indicates that an increase in the independent variable—price of donating, fund-raising expenditures, or age of organization—is associated with a decrease in donations; a plus sign indicates that an increase in the independent variable is associated with an increase in donations.

a. 75 percent sample.

b. 20 percent sample.

* Significant at 0.10 level or better.

organization's fund-raising percentage in the preceding year—is negative for all seven industries, and statistically significant for six. Donors are sensitive to this measure of the after-tax price of contributing a dollar's worth of output. The negative responsiveness is particularly great for art exhibits, museums, and the like, for which a 1 percent increase in the "price" of giving results in an estimated 2.65 percent reduction in donations. For all the other industries, a given percent increase in price results in roughly an equal percent decrease in donations, as Table C.3 shows (that is, the elasticities are approximately equal to −1). Also as expected, an organization's age has a positive effect on the effectiveness of its fund raising, significantly so for four industries.

The conflicting findings of these two studies have not yet been resolved. Dominguez and I included some variables not found in Steinberg's work and used a larger and more comprehensive set of data. Nonetheless, only further research will resolve the matter.

Further research is also needed to interpret the results of these studies. Results indicating no effect of the fund-raising price on donations could mean that donors do not care about that price, but it could also mean that donors are unable to obtain information about fund raising. If donors do not care about the price of fund raising, then perhaps governmental actions to limit an organization's fund-raising percentage or to require its disclosure are inappropriate. On the other hand, if competition among nonprofits fails to result in adequate pressure on organizations to announce their fund-raising percentages, even though donors desire the information, a disclosure requirement might be in order. Our research results, which indicate that the fund-raising percentage does influence donations, imply that at least some significant fraction of donors are reasonably informed and that they respond to the information by giving less to the "higher-priced" nonprofits. This evidence could be interpreted to support governmental inaction—on the ground that donors are already obtaining the information they want—or, on the other hand, to support governmental prodding of nonprofits to elicit more "truth in advertising" about the fund-raising percentages of organizations soliciting donations. In short, the policy debate over just how much information is socially efficient cannot be resolved by such studies, but studies can at least narrow the terms of the debate.

Added fund-raising expenditures are likely to have two countervailing effects on donations: a positive direct effect of advertising and solicitation, but a negative effect of the associated increase in the price of donating.

The combined effects are shown in the second column of Table 5.1. In every one of the seven industries, the overall effect of added fund-raising expenditures on donations is not significantly different from zero. In other words, an increase in fund-raising expenditures would not be expected to lead to any increase in contributions; the negative effect of additional fund raising on the price of donating is just offset by the positive promotional effect. Nonprofits are acting, in effect, to maximize total donations, not to maximize donations exclusive of fund-raising costs.

These findings lead to a vexing question that underlies much of the policy analysis debate about the appropriate role for nonprofit organizations. If nonprofit organizations are not seeking to maximize profits, what are they seeking? One answer that has been proposed and widely accepted, even though it is essentially untested, is that nonprofits act as if they want to generate as large a total budget as possible.[28] This hypothesis is consistent with our evidence that each of the seven classes of nonprofits spent on fund raising up to the point at which the marginal contribution to gross organizational revenue is zero.[29]

Our findings that nonprofits are maximizing their gross revenues from donations contrast with Steinberg's findings that additional fund raising would increase donations. Steinberg concludes that nonprofit social service and arts and cultural organizations are spending too little on fund raising if their goal is to maximize output. The marginal return to an additional dollar spent on fund raising by a "welfare" organization he estimated at $1.21, whereas the return for a cultural organization would be $2.08. Health organizations, by contrast, were spending more on fund raising than would maximize their service activities. Steinberg estimated a return of only $0.13 to the marginal fund-raising dollar.[30] Such sharply contrasting findings across industries are surprising, for there is no theory to suggest that the various nonprofit industries should behave so differently. Our findings, by contrast, display far more consistency (see Table C.3). Clearly, though, research into these issues is in its infancy.

Dominguez and I hypothesized that another factor helping to explain the level of donations to a nonprofit is the organization's age, which serves as a proxy for its reputation for trustworthiness. Donors may use the age of the firm as a signal of the extent to which it actually provides the level and quality of output it purports to supply. Nonprofits that are perceived as untrustworthy in this respect will tend to be driven out. Our findings support this reasoning. For six of the seven industries, we find that older organizations received more donations, if we hold constant their levels of fund-raising and prices (fund-raising percentages), and in four of the industries the relationship is statistically significant. The "goodwill" effect is comparatively small, though; for example, a 10 percent increase in an organization's age (about 1–2 years, on average) is associated with an average increase of some 0.4 percent in donations.[31]

Fund raising by private nonprofit organizations is analogous to advertising by proprietary firms. Both are instruments for influencing consumers on how to spend their money. For nonprofits, as for proprietary firms, advertising and reputation increase revenues. Thus, the size of the nonprofit economy depends on the freedom and flexibility that public policies give to nonprofits to control their fund-raising efforts, and on the prices that nonprofits must pay for using the various fund-raising media, together with the effectiveness of the fund-raising methods. If legislation restricts the fund-raising percentage, there will be less fund raising; if postal rates for nonprofits are subsidized whereas newspaper solicitations are not, there will be more solicitations by mail and less by newspaper.

Another area needing more study is the source of donations. In addition to private donors, government also provides contributions, gifts, and grants to nonprofits. A specific breakdown of percentages is not available, though. Only in 1980 did the IRS amend its form 990 tax return for nonprofits to reflect how much of a nonprofit organization's donations came from government and how much from private sources; these data are not yet available from the IRS. A nonrandom sample of the 1980 returns (the best information currently available) reinforces the point that nonprofit organizations in different industries differ greatly both in their dependence on donations and in the relative importance of private and governmental donations.[32]

Religious organizations receive 93 percent of their total revenues from donations; all of it is from private sources (see Table C.4).[33] Civic and social action nonprofits receive 88 percent of their revenues as donations, split equally between government and private sources. Cultural organizations receive about half their revenues as contributions, gifts, and grants, with four-fifths coming from private sources, and health organizations, which also receive approximately equal amounts of revenue from contributions and from other sources, are relatively far more dependent on government than on private donors. The accuracy of these data is somewhat questionable, and, indeed, they are in some instances quite different from data reported in another source.[34] Still, it is clear that nonprofit-sector industries differ a great deal in their relative financial dependency on governmental and on private donations.

In the early 1980s there was a large decrease in grants by the federal government to nonprofit organizations. Research by the Nonprofit Sector Project at the Urban Institute projected a decrease of 22 percent in the real dollar value of federal support between fiscal years 1980 and 1986. The cuts, however, were expected to be very uneven across service sectors—66 percent for the arts, but only 9 percent for health care (see Table C.5). Government support is a "two-edged sword." Nonprofit organizations are typically pleased to have it, but when political considerations drive government to cut it, the nonprofits can suffer substantial reductions in revenues.[35] These cuts in government support triggered efforts by nonprofit organizations to find other sources of revenue. In addition to contributions, nonprofits obtain substantial sums through sales, dues, or other forms of user fees. As they have sought to supplement these income sources, nonprofits have come into increasing conflict with other organizations, governmental and proprietary.

If nonprofits obtained all their funding from private donations, if those donations were not affected by tax laws, and if government were a negligible provider of social services, the interaction between the nonprofit sector and the rest of the economy would be small. Changes in the level or composition of activity in the nonprofit sector would reflect the wants of donors, and increases or decreases in activity would not bring forth such policy questions as whether government should do more, given that nonprofits are doing less, or whether nonprofits should be allowed to expand into new product markets where they compete with proprietary firms. These conditions did hold substantially at the turn of this century and perhaps even until the mid-1930s. Then government involvement with social services began to expand significantly and, with the advent of World War II, income tax rates rose above a minute level. Today the interdependency of the nonprofit, governmental, and for-profit sectors is both important and complex, and understanding the various aspects of these ties is critical for designing public policy.

Does Governmental Spending "Crowd Out" Private Donations?

A number of attempts have been made to determine the relationship between government's provision of social services and nonprofit charitable activities. Generally the focus has been on the effect of changes in governmental spending on the level of private contributions. Using theoretical models in which governments and private nonprofits are seen as providing essentially identical goods and services—an assumption that I believe has some basis but that is incorrect in general—the authors of two recent articles have posited that increased governmental spending results in dollar-for-dollar crowding out of donations.[36] There has been little research on the reverse relationship—the effect of charitable donations on the level of government expenditures—or on the reciprocal effects,[37] but the general perspective of the theoretical literature suggests that any change in the level of public-type services provided in one institutional sector causes some crowding-out effect in another. There could, however, be a reverse effect—an increase in governmental spending could encourage private donations—if, for example, private donors saw increased governmental expenditures as a signal that a particular program area was more deserving of private support than had previously been recognized. (If the increased governmental spending was in the form of grants to nonprofits, that could serve as an indicator of governmental confidence in nonprofits, which might increase private donations.)[38] Quantitative studies have led to quite different conclusions than the extreme crowding-out theory implies. One study that estimated the relationship between welfare payments by the government and private charitable contributions found evidence of partial, but far from dollar-for-dollar, crowding out—a 10 percent increase in cash transfers to the needy or in spending on social services led to only about a 2 percent decrease in private charitable contributions;[39] another study found no evidence at all of crowding out.[40]

A more-recent examination helps to reconcile these conflicting findings, which range from complete crowding out to no effect of governmental activity on the public-type nonprofits. Jerald Schiff finds that governmental expenditures have very different effects on private charitable giving, depending on the type of governmental program.[41] The previous evidence that little or no crowding out occurs comes from studies in which governmental spending included an aggregate of many kinds of programs, some of which may cause an increase and others a decrease in private charitable giving. Schiff finds that cash transfers by government to the poor do exert a substantial and statistically significant negative effect on charitable giving; but spending on other social services—such as health services and housing—has the opposite effect, higher governmental spending leading to more, not less, private giving. When cash transfers and other social welfare spending are aggregated, their effects offset each other, so that total governmental spending on social welfare has no significant effect on donations to private social welfare charities.

The interrelations between governmental activities and donations to private nonprofit organizations may well vary considerably depending on what programs are involved, and they are probably more complex than research has recognized. Governmental activity and charitable giving to nonprofits could change in the same direction if, for example, increased media attention to the homeless brought expanded action by government as well as by private donors. Even so, however, governmental activity and charitable giving could be either substitutes or complements in the sense that an increase in one would cause a decrease (the substitute case) or an increase (the complementarity case) in the other. Moreover, the effects of governmental expenditures on private giving may depend not only on the level and program area, but also on the form of that expenditure. Specifically, the government's direct delivery of services may have a materially different effect from its grants to, or contracts with, private nonprofit organizations to provide those services.[42] The success or failure of the nonprofit sector in obtaining funds depends critically on its multidimensional interactions with government.

One of the key issues regarding the interdependency between government and nonprofits is the degree of similarity between the publicly and privately provided activities as well as the way they are funded. For example, if some people derive satisfaction from the individual act of donating, then they would presumably prefer such voluntary donations to equal compulsory tax payments used for the same purpose. More generally, services provided by government and those provided by the nonprofit sector are probably not perfect substitutes. Governments typically face constraints requiring them to provide goods and services to a more disparate group of people and the probable result is a different quality of output than a nonprofit would provide.

In theoretical research on crowding out it is generally assumed that the services provided by government and private charities are the same— simply the transfer of *money* to a poor person. Donors may well prefer to give voluntarily while recipients perhaps prefer to be aided more anonymously by government. But aside from those two issues, the assumption that private philanthropy and governmental transfers are perfect substitutes in providing *cash* aid to the poor is reasonable. Cash transfers, however, are far from the typical form of activity of either the public or nonprofit sectors. When other services are at issue, governments and nonprofits may provide differing outputs—both imperfect substitutes and complements for each other. Basic research on diseases, for example, is probably a close, if not perfect, substitute, whether it is produced by government or by nonprofits. In contrast, governmental support for higher education is probably complementary with private giving to non-profit colleges. Private giving can support construction of a college's physical plant and employment of additional teachers, both of which permit an increase in the number of students; government-sponsored student loans can make it possible for a larger number of students to afford to attend the college.

Whether the activities of government and nonprofit organizations are substitutes, complements, or unrelated, the effect of anything done in one sector on the activities in the other sector will differ. Taxes, subsidies, regulation, or any other policy measures that affect one sector of the economic system are likely also to have side effects on the others. This is a sobering generalization, for it implies that the interplay of economic sectors makes the development of public policy far more complex than it would be if the sectors were independent. Thus, recent changes in taxes and expenditures by the federal government have cut into revenues of the nonprofit sector. These cuts have led to the expansion of nonprofits into new activities that have brought them into competition with organizations in the proprietary sector.

SIX

Revenues from Sales

Nonprofit organizations rarely survive on donations alone. In fact few nonprofits even receive a substantial portion of revenues from donations. In 1973–1975, some 38 percent of tax-deductible nonprofits received 10 percent or less of their revenues from donations; half received less than 25 percent from donations. At the other end of the spectrum, 21 percent of the organizations depended very heavily on donations, receiving more than 90 percent of their revenues in this form. Nonprofits are typically involved in a variety of fund-raising markets to supplement revenues.[1]

Nonprofits increasingly encounter the proprietary sector of the economy as they pursue other sources of revenue. Small businesses particularly resent nonprofits' for-profit endeavors. Responding to numerous complaints from the small business community, Frank Swain, Chief Counsel for Advocacy for the Small Business Administration (SBA), said "Small private businesses are laboring under a tax code which taxes them but not some of their competitors—nonprofit organizations doing business for profit."[2] Increasingly the SBA and various industry groups representing small businesses refer to nonprofits as "unfair competition." They call for leashing the nonprofit sector to prevent its further expansion into activities that have heretofore been the domain of proprietary firms. Some small-business leaders are seeking legislative and administrative action to restrict what they see as a subsidized sector that competes with those who subsidize it (including private businesses).

This kind of criticism of nonprofits raises both factual and normative questions. Is there substantial competition between nonprofit organizations and proprietary firms? Is the competition growing? What forms is it taking? Is such competition "unfair"? What does "unfair" mean?

What should be the limits on what nonprofits may do to raise revenues? And even if the competition is unfair to the proprietary firms, is it inefficient or otherwise undesirable for promoting social welfare? In any event, should public actions be taken to restrict the inventiveness of nonprofits in their search for new activities, markets, and resources?

Competition with the Proprietary Sector

Supporters of both the nonprofits and the proprietary organizations agree that cutbacks in federal funding (beginning around 1980) have led an increasing number of nonprofits to seek new revenue by engaging in profit-making activities; as a result, the two forms of institutions have come into growing conflict.[3] A community group in Milwaukee, for example, has purchased a launderette in hopes of generating profits to be used for its community welfare activities.[4] Other for-profit endeavors of nonprofit organizations include a commercial weatherization and home improvement company, a food-management service for hospitals and schools, a restaurant,[5] a construction and home improvement company, a commercial greenhouse business,[6] and a national for-profit development company that builds festival marketplaces in smaller cities.[7] Even public television, its government funding having been sharply cut, has resorted to dramatically new measures for raising revenues.[8] A recent book with the intriguing title *Enterprise in the Nonprofit Sector* emphasizes the new links between two topics that many people have traditionally regarded as contradictory. "Enterprise," however, is no longer excluded from the nonprofit sector. "Sixty-nine percent of the organizations we surveyed have given birth to new [profit-making] enterprise within the past twelve years," the authors assert.[9]

Managers of nonprofits are apparently eager to learn as much as they can about new ways to maximize revenues. The 1983 annual conference of the Nonprofit Management Association, for example, included a "special day-long" seminar on "Profit-Making Business Ventures for Nonprofits."[10] Guidance for "executives and staff members of nonprofit institutions [on how] to use marketing techniques to increase the revenues of their organizations" is available through such mechanisms as the 1984 National Training Conference, sponsored by the Center for Responsive Governance—at $300 per attendee.[11] The Grantsmanship Center offers a three-day workshop—given 51 times, in dozens of cities, between June and December of 1984 alone—which, at a tuition price of $395, promises to "help [nonprofits] determine what kind of business venture is right for your agency and how to set it up . . . Your nonprofit agency can start a business—and generate dollars that aren't dependent on grants or contributions."[12]

Commercial activity by nonprofits is not entirely new; the data on revenue sources of nonprofits in the mid-1970s make it clear that even then there was substantial dependence on nondonated revenues—either from membership dues or from some form of sales. As early as 1908, the Metropolitan Museum of Art opened a sales shop; even before that it sold copies of photographs from its collections. College bookstores have long existed to sell course materials. One of the best-known examples of sales of goods to generate income for a nonprofit organization is the annual Girl Scouts cookie sale. In 1982 the Girl Scouts of America sold 125 million boxes of cookies for gross revenue of over $200 million.[13]

Some of the new activities that nonprofits are moving into will come to be questioned as sufficiently remote from the purpose for which tax exemption was granted that the net income is subject to taxation as "unrelated business income" (UBI). Some of these activities are so clearly unrelated to the organization's purpose that they are organized into separate for-profit entities.[14] Other new activities will be in the "gray" area; these cases are likely to constitute a growing administrative problem for the IRS, as financially hard-pressed nonprofits increasingly probe the outer limits of exempt-income activities. A 1985 report by the federal General Accounting Office (GAO) points out that UBI revenues already cause problems, for the "IRS does not have sufficient information on UBI tax noncompliance to fully understand the nature and magnitude of UBI noncompliance and develop profiles of high noncompliant tax-exempt organizations engaging in UBI activity." The GAO report notes the limited staff available to the IRS for investigations, the "increasing UBI activity," and the substantial rate of noncompliance that their audit disclosed. Measured in dollars, noncompliance with the tax on unrelated business income was estimated at 25 percent for social welfare organizations, but 58 percent for charitable and educational organizations, and 61 percent for business leagues.[15]

It is commonly believed that if a nonprofit organization uses the profit from an activity to finance its tax-exempt activities it does not owe tax on the profit. Under present law, however, the way the income is used is not relevant. Whether earnings of a nonprofit are taxable as ordinary corporate profits depends on whether the activity that *generated* the income is substantially "related" to the organization's exempt purpose, not on what is done with that income.[16]

When nonprofits seek profitable enterprises they almost inevitably move away from charitable and collective-type services and into the sale of private-type goods—and into competition with private-sector enterprises. Recent research supports the expectation that when the budgets of nonprofit organizations are squeezed, the nonprofits respond by shifting to sales of goods in private markets. Jerald Schiff and I hypothesized that nonprofits pursue the goal of maximizing their output of a "charitable" service, subject to the necessity of at least breaking even financially.[17] We see the nonprofit organization as a potential provider of two kinds of goods or services—charitable and "private"; the organization's managers and directors prefer to produce the charitable good, which is financed by private donations and by governmental support, but they may resort to selling private output to "cross-subsidize" their charitable activities. This model of behavior, to the extent it is correct, implies that private businesses do, indeed, have reason to fear that reductions in governmental support prompt nonprofits to extend their activities into markets for private goods.

In this framework, a change in governmental expenditures can have a number of effects on nonprofits: (1) the direct effect on revenue; (2) a "crowding out" effect; (3) a revenue-source substitution effect (as, for example, when nonprofits switch to sales of less preferred, private-type outputs); (4) fund-raising effects (changes in governmental spending can affect the optimal level of nonprofits' expenditures on solicitation of private donations); and (5) exit/entry effects (governmental budget cuts can affect the number of nonprofit organizations).

Utilizing data from tax returns of the more than 11,000 social welfare nonprofits in the United States between 1973 and 1976, Schiff and I estimated the effects of changes in various types of governmental welfare spending—cash transfers, purchases from nonprofits, and direct governmental provision of services—on the variables listed above. Because of data limitations, which prevented us from distinguishing, for example, between private and governmental donations, we estimated the effect of changes in spending by the government on only four measures: total donations to a nonprofit organization, total sales by each nonprofit, total solicitation expenses by each, and the total number of nonprofit organizations providing social welfare services in the state.[18] Among the factors that determine these four relationships (regression equations), we hypothesized, are the forms of welfare expenditures in the state in which the nonprofit is based; the characteristics of the state, including the incentive to donate (which depends on the proportion of taxpayers who itemize and the per capita income in the state); the characteristics of the nonprofit organization, including its age (to take into account the effect of reputation) and whether donations to it are tax deductible; and the level of each nonprofit's fund-raising (solicitation) expenditures.

Our study allowed for interactive effects whereby, for example, a cut in governmental purchases from nonprofits could affect the level of an average nonprofit organization's revenue in a number of ways—directly decreasing it and indirectly either increasing it or diminishing it further as nonprofits then changed their fund-raising expenditures and their efforts to sell private goods. Moreover, insofar as some nonprofits cease activity because of such cuts, with the result that total contributions are shared among fewer nonprofits, contributions per nonprofit would be affected.[19]

Schiff and I found that most of the expected effects in fact occurred. Changes in welfare expenditures do exert a statistically significant impact on the level and composition of revenues—as between donations and sales—for nonprofit welfare organizations, but the magnitude and even the direction of effect differs depending on whether the change is in the cash transfers, direct provision of welfare services, or purchases of services from nonprofits by government. When governments reduce their direct provision of social services, the nonprofit sector responds by increasing its sales activities. A 10 percent cut in social service spending by government would cause nonprofits to increase their sales by an estimated 1.3 percent.

This finding—that reduced governmental spending, by adversely affecting nonprofits' ability to finance their preferred charitable activities, leads to increased sales efforts by nonprofits—is derived from study of welfare organizations only. The general question, though, of how nonprofits' sales activities respond to changes in the availability of various forms of public and private revenue, remains open; Schiff and I also found, for example, that cuts in other forms of governmental welfare spending—cuts in cash transfers—do not result in an increase in nonprofits' sales revenues.

The question of whether nonprofits should be restricted, taxed, or even prohibited from competing with the proprietary sector is moving increasingly into the policy arena. A growing number of nonprofits see access to profit-making activities as indispensable, but an increasing variety of proprietary firms are challenging the proposition that competition from nonprofits is wise public policy. A recent survey by the Congressional General Accounting Office found, for example, that 84 percent of private research firms and 90 percent of racket-sport firms claim that nonprofit, tax-exempt universities and fitness groups compete unfairly with them.[20]

Much of the anecdotal evidence of complaints from the private sector about competition from nonprofits involves educational and health organizations. The National Audio-Visual Association, for example, has criticized the Education Media Center of the University of Colorado, Boulder, which rents over 5,700 films "to both schools and the general public (including private businesses) in direct competition with local for-profit firms engaged in the same business."[21] The Minnesota Education Computing Consortium (MECC) is a nonprofit organization that develops, produces, and sells educational computer software nationally. According to a critic from its private-sector competitors, it sells the software at prices "that for-profit producers of these materials cannot match . . . [and it] controls approximately 20 percent of the marketplace of classroom computer software outside of Minnesota."[22]

Travel agencies, too, are increasingly concerned about the growing competition from on-campus travel centers operated by colleges and universities. Organizations such as the International Study and Travel Association (ISTA) at the University of Minnesota are being accused of selling airline tickets, tours, and so forth for uses that are unrelated to the educational purposes of the university. "Yet the center enjoys tax-exempt treatment of all its income and accumulated reserves, as well as subsidized rent and support facilities from the university," according to a private travel agent.[23]

A critic of university-based research sales claimed that "colleges and universities and independent nonprofit organizations offer [research] services in competition with for-profit firms as a by-product of tax-exempt 'basic' research and education functions . . . faculty entrepreneurs are able to underprice local firms because they do not have to factor equipment and other capital costs into their prices."[24]

Nonprofit hospitals are expanding "vertically" into a growing number of for-profit activities that either provide services to hospitals or that provide services on the recommendation of hospitals. For example, nonprofit hospitals and clinics are increasingly moving into the retail end of the hearing aid industry.[25] They have also begun marketing laundry services, in direct competition with local private laundries, and three nonprofit hospitals in the Philadelphia area have begun manufacturing prosthetic devices, in competition with private manufacturers of artificial limbs.[26]

One overall indicator of competition between proprietary and nonprofit organizations in various industries is the importance of sales revenues to the nonprofits. When nonprofits generate the bulk of their revenues through sales, they are probably providing outputs in competition with proprietary firms, whereas when their funds come mainly from donations they are probably providing outputs that differ in type from what the proprietary market provides.[27] Thus, the average nonprofit in the legal aid industry is not very competitive with its proprietary counterparts, for these nonprofits receive only 3 percent of their revenues from "sales." In scientific research, by contrast, the average nonprofit appears to be much more like its proprietary counterparts, for it receives 86 percent of its revenues from sales (see Table C.7 in Appendix C).

Another overall indicator of competition between proprietary and nonprofit sellers is the relative size of the nonprofit component of mixed industries. The larger the nonprofits' share of sales in an industry, the greater is its impact on the for-profit component. Among blood banks, nonprofit facilities in the mid-1970s were only one-tenth as numerous as proprietaries; in nursing homes there were fewer than one-third as many beds in nonprofits as in proprietary homes. By contrast, in child day care, nonprofits supervised 80 percent as many children as proprietaries did; among renal dialysis centers nonprofits were nearly three times as numerous as proprietaries; and among family planning clinics, nonprofit facilities were thirty times more numerous than proprietaries (Table C.8).

When a nonprofit seeks to sell some outputs profitably in order to fund other activities (that is, to cross-subsidize), it must find outputs that are both salable and profitable. The position that public policy should take concerning these activities depends on the side effects of permitting or restricting them. Should there be any constraints on the type or level of profit-making activities by nonprofits? One issue to be concerned about is what kinds of money-generating activities nonprofits are likely to engage in, if they were unconstrained. Another is whether it is both economically efficient and equitable that those activities be pursued. Finally, does the tax system deal appropriately with the expansion of nonprofits into the new areas? Currently, government taxes nonprofits' "unrelated business income" as ordinary corporate profit, and for some classes of nonprofits it limits the proportion of total revenue that may arise from activities that are unrelated to the organization's exempt purpose.

Whether a nonprofit expands into markets that are "related" to its exempt purpose or into other, unrelated, areas, the competition with proprietary firms affects nonprofits in important ways. Some are favorable: competition with proprietaries should stimulate efficient production, diversify revenue sources, and perhaps provide a stimulus to greater creativity. But some are unfavorable: becoming a multipurpose organization is likely to pose new administrative and managerial problems and, most important, the pressure to perform profitably in the competitive marketplace can divert resources and energy from the organization's principal public-type purposes even while total resources are being expanded.

All these possible consequences are speculative; hard evidence does not exist. My conjecture, though, is that as a nonprofit branches out from its central mission, the quality of its principal, tax-exempt activities will decline. If so, an increase in financial dependence on market sales relative to donations—holding other things, including total revenue, constant—will diminish the contribution of nonprofits to social welfare. When the shift in revenue sources, however, simultaneously expands total revenue, the overall outcome is not clear. Increased resources bring added outputs, but at the cost of the distraction of the nonprofit from its declared mission.

The policy choices are (a) having fewer, "purer" nonprofits that are financed by donations and that are less constrained in their activities, and (b) having a larger nonprofit sector that receives more revenue from sales of private-type goods or from those governmental and private contributions that come with tighter "strings" attached. In my judgment, it is impossible to adopt tax or other measures that drive nonprofits into private-goods markets—that is, toward option (b)—without compromising their principal rationale for existing—their contribution to social welfare.

The cries of unfair competition, by the private sector, result partly from judgments about how to define a nonprofit's unrelated business income. That income is fully taxable; in that sense nonprofits are somewhat discouraged from engaging in the activities that generate it. Under the law, net income for a nonprofit is taxable if it resulted from an activity that is not "substantially" related to the "charitable, educational, or other purpose which fixes the basis for its exemption under Internal Revenue Code Section 501."[28] Depending on how broadly or narrowly the IRS interprets the "exempt purpose" of the organization, the nonprofit will have a larger or a smaller domain in which it can compete with proprietary firms at a tax advantage.

The tax law did not always restrict, tax, or otherwise handicap nonprofits' revenues, as it now does. In 1948, when a group of alumni donated the Mueller Macaroni Company to the New York University (NYU) Law School, Mueller's profits were given tax-exempt status because NYU was a nonprofit organization.[29] But two years later, in an apparent attempt to deal with the charge of unfair competition, Congress amended the Internal Revenue Code to exempt from taxation only the "related" business ventures of nonprofits.[30] Concerns about "unfair" competition by nonprofits somehow became translated into concerns about business activity that was not "substantially related" to the exempt purpose.

Administrators and courts have found it very difficult to apply the "substantially related" concept. One Circuit Court judge referred to "hair-splitting" decisions in a case involving whether sales by a nonprofit hospital's pharmacy to private nonhospitalized patients of physicians on the hospital staff were tax exempt.[31] A former commissioner of the Internal Revenue Service, Sheldon Cohen, expressed the frustrating complexity of distinguishing taxable from nontaxable income of nonprofit organizations: "Nonprofits are a whole can of worms that Congress has yet to look at in a broad way. I have been blowing the trumpet for years to get lawmakers to spell out clearly what should be tax-exempt and what should not be."[32]

In 1983 another official of the Internal Revenue Service reiterated the complexity of administering the tax laws as they relate to nonprofits. He noted that virtually no federal tax revenue is collected from the nonprofits—only $24.6 million on the total unrelated business income of $557 million in fiscal year 1982.[33] Although this revenue from nonprofits was less than one two-hundredth of one percent of the $600 billion of federal budget receipts, nearly one percent of the IRS staff has been involved with the nonprofits. The IRS handles the more than 50,000 annual applications for tax-exempt status; it must deal with constitutional issues such as whether a university that practices racial discrimination should retain tax-exempt status (for example, the 1983 U.S. Supreme Court decision involving Bob Jones University); it must determine whether some income of nonprofits is taxable as unrelated business income; and so forth. Collecting revenues from the nonprofit sector is, on average, thousands of times as costly per dollar as collecting from individuals and private firms.

Some of this ambiguity could be avoided, of course, by a change in the law and its administration. Nonprofits could be required to define more precisely and narrowly the activities for which they request tax exemption. Currently, nonprofits are granted exempt status for such broad purposes as "education" or "community development." How broad should the definition of a nonprofit's exempt purpose be? Proprietary firms would like it to be narrower, so that nonprofit organizations would be more restricted. Nonprofits would like it to be broader, giving greater flexibility. Weighing such conflicting arguments is very difficult, and the perspective of a tax-collection agency—such as the IRS—is not the most appropriate one for balancing the claims of the two groups.

Another question—seemingly technical, but of considerable import— is how a nonprofit organization's costs should be allocated between its exempt and nonexempt ("unrelated") activities. When a nonprofit is producing both kinds of output, it is in a position to exercise discretion in the way it allocates certain costs—such as the cost of capital equipment, office space, and salaries—that apply to both. It will want to allocate as much of these joint costs as possible to the otherwise profitable unrelated business activities, so as to minimize reported taxable net income and hence tax payments. Nonprofits that may appear to make little profit on the unrelated business activities, where they compete with proprietary firms, may actually make substantially greater profits than are shown on the bottom line. This is an additional administrative headache for the IRS, and, it seems, an additional source of unfair competition to proprietary firms.

Determining the amount of a nonprofit's unrelated business income is squarely in the hands of the IRS, but when it comes to the problem of competition between nonprofits and proprietary firms other administrative agencies of government, having other perspectives, are also making important decisions affecting the ability of nonprofits to compete. Public policy is less than consistent in its treatment of nonprofits.

Through a variety of tax laws and subsidy programs, nonprofits are treated as worthy of explicit encouragement. At the same time actions have been taken that effectively reverse such institutional encouragement. A recent decision by the Office of Management and Budget (OMB), for example, resolves, at least for now, one element of the debate over unfair competition, competitive bidding between nonprofit and for-profit firms for federal government contracts. Proprietary firms have argued that their bids are higher simply because they must pay federal, state, and local taxes that their nonprofit competitors do not. In August 1983, the OMB altered its rules on bidding. Federal agencies are now required to take into account, in awarding a contract, an estimate of the tax revenue forgone if the contract is awarded to a nonprofit: "If the apparent low bidder or offeror is a tax-exempt organization, the contract price must be adjusted by an amount equal to the Federal, state and local income taxes that would be paid by the lowest non-tax-exempt bidder or offeror. This adjustment is necessary to determine which bidder or offeror has the lower overall cost to the Government." The rules also specify how the federal government is to choose in the case of a tie between a nonprofit, tax-exempt organization and a nonexempt bidder. If the tax-adjusted price is identical to the nonexempt organization's price, the nonexempt organization is the winner.[34]

If garnering revenue through sales of private goods does have an adverse effect on the public-serving quality of nonprofits' activities—and the matter is by no means resolved—then the objections of private firms to competition from nonprofits must be viewed as part of a larger problem. Even though the basic institutional-choice problem—what is the efficient and equitable role for nonprofits relative to proprietary and governmental organizations—is unresolved, nonprofits are subject to the prescriptions of a variety of governmental agencies: IRS administration and interpretation of tax laws have proceeded, OMB directives and court decisions have been made. Intentionally or not, wisely or not, these agencies are influencing not only the size, scope, and financial resources of the nonprofit economy but, in the process, the proprietary and government sectors as well.

This is a paradox. Society seems to have an unarticulated but *de facto* policy that sees an important difference between the social desirability of activities engaged in by nonprofits when they are supported by donations (most of which are contributed indirectly, through the tax system, by taxpayers in general) and when they are supported by sales of goods in private competitive markets. We obviously find it difficult to set the limits for entry by nonprofits into competition with proprietaries. At the same time we draw the line at competition for government contracts. The apparently conflicting policies of both encouraging and discouraging nonprofits may reflect the belief that the type of activity an organization engages in depends on the source of revenue to finance it—that is, that public-type goods are produced by organizations funded by donations, private-type goods by those funded by sales. Social policy may represent, then, a preference for those nonprofit activities that are likely to be supported by donated funds over those that are supported by the profits from sales of goods in competitive markets. If this is the basis, even in part, of the patchwork public policy toward nonprofits, it is important to learn more about the validity of the proposition that the source of revenue affects the nature of output. This is one more example of the weak analytic and factual base that now underlies policy toward nonprofits.

Do Nonprofits Have a Net Advantage?

However the nonprofits use the funds generated from competitive sales, another important factual question is just how great is the alleged advantage that nonprofits have when they compete with proprietary firms. This advantage, after all, is presumably the basis of the "unfair competition" complaint. That complaint rests on more than simply the exemption from profit tax and the deductibility of donations to some nonprofits. Beyond the tax deductibility of donations for some nonprofits, and the exemption from corporate-profit taxation for all, nonprofits have both advantages and disadvantages in any potential competition with proprietary firms. Numerous legal rules define what can be done with the resources commanded by nonprofits, some of which are more restrictive than those confronting for-profit firms, others less so.

On one hand, nonprofits may not pay out any surplus or profit to anyone associated with the organization; they are effectively cut off from the market for equity capital. This nondistribution constraint means that the organization must serve a public interest; according to the IRS, the "prohibition of inurement, in its simplest terms, means that a private shareholder or individual cannot pocket the organization's funds except as reasonable payment for goods and services."[35] Excessive wages or salary, rental charges, or purchase price of property would be evidence of private inurement, although the cost of determining what is "excessive" serves as a clear obstacle to IRS enforcement. In April of 1987, for example, in the midst of the scandal over the PTL television ministry, it was reported that the IRS was attempting to revoke PTL's tax-exempt status "because a substantial portion of PTL's net earnings [in 1981–1983] went to benefit former PTL President Jim Bakker, his relatives and other PTL officers"; the confidential IRS report, apparently written in 1985, contends that Bakker was paid "nearly $1 million more than was *reasonable* those three years."[36]

Competition between for-profit and nonprofit organizations is continually in flux. Either form of institution may expand into a traditional domain of the other. In the product safety testing industry, the overwhelming domination by a single nonprofit organization, Underwriters Laboratories, Inc.—identified by the ubiquitous UL symbol—is being challenged by a growing number of commercial testing laboratories. Charges and countercharges are made, each form of organization claiming its superiority. The problem with the private laboratories, according to the UL president, Jack Bono, is that they could certify products as safe without fully understanding safety standards that they have not been involved with developing. The problem with UL, according to private firms' representatives, is that its service is too slow.[37] Both parties may be right. The fact is that in this industry, as well as in every other one in which for-profit and nonprofit organizations compete, public policy is unclear. This, in turn, reflects the fact that the research base—the body of theory about competition among forms of institutions and the body of empirical evidence—is so thin.

Charitable nonprofits—those that may accept tax-deductible donations—are also severely limited in their freedom to engage in lobbying or in other political activities to support or oppose a particular candidate or to influence legislation. These constraints are comparatively recent. The prohibition on participation in political campaigns originated in a Senate floor amendment added by Lyndon Johnson in 1954. Johnson apparently believed that a foundation in Texas had provided financial support for his opponent in an election.[38] The limitation on attempts to influence legislation originated earlier, though, in a 1934 Senate floor amendment; the sponsor indicated irritation with the activities of one specific nonprofit organization, the National Economy League.[39]

The limitation on legislative lobbying—which does not apply to proprietary firms—has posed enforcement problems that attenuate its effectiveness. Internal Revenue Code section 501(c)(3) states that "no substantial part of the activities" of a charitable organization may be used for "carrying on propaganda, or otherwise attempting, to influence legislation." The term *substantial* is obviously imprecise. It has been interpreted to mean more than 5 percent of an organization's time and effort;[40] under the Tax Reform Act of 1976, however, most charitable organizations (although not churches and some others) have the option of electing to hold to specific expenditure limitations rather than the vague "substantial" criterion. Under this option, an organization is permitted to spend on lobbying up to 20 percent of the first $500,000 of its expenditures (exclusive of fund-raising expenditures), 15 percent of the next $500,000, and 5 percent beyond that, for a total of $1 million per year. Expenditures aimed at influencing the public on legislative matters are limited to 25 percent of these amounts.[41] Even now, charities are under increasing pressure to restrict lobbying and, indeed, the definition of *lobbying* continues to be a source of contention. (See Appendix D.) As of mid-1987 the IRS is still revising the administrative rules it developed in November 1986, rules that would, according to sixteen members of the Senate Finance Committee, "severely limit the rights of charities to communicate with legislators and public officials."[42] At the same time, the *ways* that nonprofits may try to influence public opinion are being questioned and restricted. In 1986 the IRS began to require by its Revenue Procedure 86-43, that an "educational" organization, to retain its tax exemption, must provide "full and fair" information, not "significant" unsupported views or "substantial use of inflammatory and disparaging terms" or conclusions derived more from "emotional feelings" than from "objective evaluations."[43]

Another constraint faced by charitable nonprofits is that they may not commit, encourage, or induce acts that are illegal or are contrary to public policy. Thus, for example, the IRS maintained that an organization formed to promote world peace and disarmament was not a charitable organization because it encouraged civil disobedience at protest demonstrations.[44]

The laws and regulations that restrict nonprofits' activities can, however, be violated. Jim Bakker and the PTL, the IRS charged, violated the nondistribution constraint—paying to an officer of the nonprofit organization what would otherwise have been deemed profit but was disguised as wages. The nonprofit National Endowment for the Preservation of Liberty, which collected funds for the Nicaraguan "contras," allegedly violated the restriction on the kinds of activities in which the organization could engage. This tax-deductible, 501(c)(3) organization, "purported to be an educational and charitable organization devoted to the study, analysis and evaluation of the American socio-economic and political systems." Legally it could spend funds only for these purposes, yet a professional fund raiser, Carl R. Channell, admitted that he conspired with Lieutenant Colonel Oliver L. North of the National Security Council staff to defraud the government by raising more than $2 million in tax-exempt contributions "to purchase military and other types of non-humanitarian aid for the contras."[45]

The nonprofits, however, are not subject to some constraints that are commonly believed to exist. Most notably, they are not restricted in the amount of profit they may make, only on what they may do with the profits—essentially being constrained to use them to purchase more resources for the organization. This is true whether the nonprofit is a charitable organization or a private-type organization, such as a sporting club or hobby group.

The freedom of a nonprofit to reap substantial profits was affirmed in a recent case before the Third Circuit Court of Appeals. Presbyterian and Reformed Publishing Co., a 501(c)(3) religious publisher founded in 1939, had seen its profits grow dramatically, because of the popularity of books written by one of its authors, from $20,000 in 1969 to $300,000 in 1979. The appeals court, overturning an IRS ruling that had been upheld by the Tax Court, ruled that the success of an organization should not jeopardize its exempt status; the organization should not be forced to choose between expanding its audience and maintaining its tax-exempt status.[46]

Neither are nonprofits prohibited from engaging in activities, commercial or other, that are totally unrelated to the purpose for which they were granted exemption from the corporate income tax; rather, if tax-deductible nonprofits do engage in such activities they must pay ordinary corporate-profits taxes on the unrelated business income—that is, on the profits from these unrelated activities—except that the first $1,000 of such income is not subject to tax.[47] Restrictions on nondeductible organizations' UBI are somewhat more stringent.

Nonprofits also have a number of tax and subsidy advantages over proprietary firms. Governmental subsidies extend beyond the corporate income tax exemption and, for some, deductibility of donations to them. Other areas of special treatment or exemption include Social Security, unemployment insurance, the minimum wage, securities regulations, bankruptcy and antitrust laws, unfair competition, copyright, and postal rates.[48] But even this impressive list is incomplete. On August 27, 1982, a law was signed requiring large firms that are granted patents to pay a user fee equal to 100 percent of the costs incurred by the federal government in awarding the patent; nonprofit organizations (as well as small firms and independent inventors) need pay only 50 percent.[49] In addition, certain nonprofits—those charitable-type organizations that are tax-exempt under section 501(c)(3) of the Internal Revenue Code—are exempted from the section of the Organized Crime Control Act that prohibits gambling businesses.[50]

Many nonprofit organizations also benefit from favored tax treatment by the individual states in which they operate. Most states exempt them from paying sales taxes on their purchases and from paying property taxes. The property tax exemption has often been the source of considerable hostility between large nonprofit institutions, such as universities, and local governments that are obliged to provide police, fire, and other public services to the nonprofits but receive no property taxes in return. Sometimes the nonprofits make voluntary payments in lieu of property taxes, but even in those cases the amount of the payment is frequently debated. Furthermore, the exemption from property taxation may induce nonprofits to utilize more capital-intensive and land-intensive production processes than do proprietary firms, which must pay such taxes.

In light of all these differences between nonprofit and proprietary organizations, what is the net effect on competition between them? In one sense the answer is clear: nonprofits enter into competition with proprietaries only when they expect to be able to compete effectively and, when it is revenue they are seeking, to do so profitably. They compete with travel agencies, testing laboratories, and distributors of hearing aids, but not with mining companies, steel mills, and department stores.

Only a little is known about the quantitative importance of the various subsidies that are provided to nonprofits. Because these subsidies differ from state to state—even though the federal portion is the same across all states—it is possible to determine whether there is a systematic relationship between the magnitude of a state's subsidy to nonprofit organization's and the size of the nonprofit sector relative to the proprietary sector in that state. This information is vital; it helps ascertain the effect various public subsidies have on the ability of nonprofit organizations to survive and to compete with proprietary firms.

Economist and lawyer Henry Hansmann examined the relative importance, among the states, of nonprofits relative to proprietary organizations in a number of industries in which they compete—hospitals, nursing homes, primary and secondary schools, and postsecondary vocational schools. In these industries competition with proprietaries generally comes from nonprofits that engage in the principal activity for which they were granted tax-exempt status, not in unrelated business activities. Still, the findings shed light on the question of whether nonprofits have a competitive advantage.

The higher the level of a state's taxation of private business, the greater the competitive value to a nonprofit of exemption from those taxes. Thus, in states that have higher property tax, sales tax, and corporate income tax rates, nonprofit organizations receive, in effect, a greater subsidy than do nonprofits in states with lower tax rates. Nonprofits can be expected to have a larger market share in the higher-tax states, and they do.[51] In the competition between nonprofit and proprietary firms, tax exemption of nonprofits makes a difference—particularly the exemption from sales and corporate income taxes. Exemption from property taxation gives nonprofits a particular incentive to locate in city centers, where property tax rates are usually high.

Granted that tax and other subsidies to nonprofits enhance the ability of nonprofits to compete, is there something "unfair" about this arrangement? Should laws or their administration be changed so as to reverse the inroads of nonprofits into proprietary markets? Two separate issues are of concern to us here: competition in the specific industry for which the nonprofit has been given exempt status, and competition in industries or activities unrelated to those for which exempt status was given. There is also a considerable gray area between the two.

The first arena of competition might seem to be uncontroversial. Congress has determined that the nonprofit form of organization should be encouraged—that is, subsidized—to engage in certain activities. If those subsidies give the nonprofits a competitive advantage, that is the intent. If proprietary firms are handicapped or even driven from the market, so be it.

However, this model of the legislative process is too simple. It assumes that government has determined that the nonprofit form of institution is socially preferred on grounds either of efficiency or of equity, but that nonprofits would not exist to an appropriate degree without subsidization. Government is credited with considerable knowledge and a decision process that leads to maximization of "social welfare." But the facts are far from clear. Evidence that nonprofit hospitals serve the public better than proprietary hospitals do, for example, or that nonprofit schools, nursing homes, day-care centers, or publishers deserve encouragement not forthcoming to their proprietary counterparts is by no means overwhelming. It is fair to say that serious attempts to detect the social rationale for encouraging nonprofits in particular areas of economic activity have been scant and indecisive, at least in industries other than health care.[52]

The potential advantage the nonprofit form of institution has over proprietary firms in meeting the needs of poorly informed consumers implies that neither the nonprofit form nor the proprietary is likely to be preferred by all consumers. Poorly informed consumers may prefer dealing with a nonprofit insofar as the organization's constraint on the distribution of profit reduces its incentive to act opportunistically. For these consumers, the public subsidies to the nonprofits are valuable. Other, better-informed consumers have no such institutional preference; they will prefer to deal with any organization, regardless of ownership form, that provides the wanted outputs at the lowest price. Since public subsidies to the nonprofit sector may reduce the number of proprietary firms, for these consumers the competitive advantage granted to nonprofits may seem counterproductive, inefficient, and unfair.

The second arena for competition is the market for unrelated outputs—where nonprofit organizations seek to reap profits for use in their "primary," exempt activities. Here the issue of fairness, as the affected proprietary firms see it, or of economic efficiency, as an analyst taking the perspective of economic welfare might view it, is cloudy at best. An analytic framework for informing public policy on how far nonprofits should be permitted to reach out to compete with proprietary firms must take into account two sorts of interdependencies: in costs, between a nonprofit's costs of producing its primary outputs and its costs of producing other, unrelated outputs, and in revenues, between a nonprofit's ability to generate revenues from its primary activities and its ability to obtain revenues from other sources.

If there were no such interdependencies—that is, if both production costs and revenues for a tax-exempt commodity, x_1, and another, unrelated, commodity that is not tax-exempt, x_2, were independent of each other—a nonprofit producer of x_1 would have no advantage in the market for x_2; it would have to compete with for-profit firms in the latter market, where consumers would patronize the more-efficient suppliers, regardless of ownership type. But the assumption of independence is not likely to hold. Nonprofits that seek new product markets where they can make profit to augment their receipts of donations will select precisely those products and services where their initial, subsidized production of x_1 provides a competitive advantage.

The advantage could be one of costs. Consider a proprietary firm engaged in product testing or archeological work that complains about competition from a nonprofit university because the university can employ graduate students at lower wages than the proprietary firm must pay. The firm is arguing, in effect, that graduate students are joint inputs to the production of both their own education and these other research activities. It should come as no surprise that the university would find it efficient and profitable to make use of just such cost-saving opportunities, rather than to engage in any of a myriad of other production activities—such as mining or automobile production—in which the resources utilized in its educational activities would give it no advantage.

Such joint-cost economies, representing real efficiencies, are also the basis of a public policy dilemma. Given that an organization—in this case, a university—is producing tax-exempt outputs, x_1 (education), it can be economically efficient for it also to produce certain other, nonexempt, outputs, x_2 (research). At the same time, expansion into the latter markets brings the subsidized organization into direct competition with unsubsidized firms in the proprietary sector of the economy. For-profit firms may claim unfair competition; yet that competition is efficient, given the initial judgment that there are type-x_1 commodities that merit subsidization through nonprofit organizations.

Joint costs may seem to be a technical matter that can be handled by accountants and that involves no major policy choices, but such a view is wrong. When costs are truly joint—the same resource being used to produce two (or more) outputs—there is no correct way to divide the costs; any division would be arbitrary. Yet the choice has important policy implications when the various outputs are subject to differing regulatory and subsidy standards, some being tax exempt, others not.

The joint-cost problem is not hypothetical. It has already led to Supreme Court decisions, such as *Secretary of State of Maryland, Petitioner v. Joseph H. Munson Company, Inc.* (467 U.S. 947). In this case the Court had to consider how to treat costs that are incurred jointly for fund raising and for other purposes, such as the education of the public about matters that are well within an organization's area of tax-exempt activities, when a nonprofit's fund-raising expenditures are restricted to a set fraction. Consider, for example, a mailing that includes both a solicitation of funds and an explanation of the important problem that the nonprofit organization addresses. The United States Supreme Court, in the landmark *Munson* decision, was clearly concerned about the potential for abridging freedom of speech if a regulatory agency could decide how to allocate the joint cost of such a mailing in the process of determining whether the nonprofit exceeded the 25 percent limit on fund-raising expenditures. The Court apparently saw "no basis for allocating expenses between fund-raising and protected speech (which could reasonably include all activities of a charity) because 'solicitation is characteristically intertwined with information and perhaps persuasive speech.' "[53] Not only are the two intertwined but, said the Court, "without solicitation the flow of such information and activity would likely cease."[54]

The controversy over joint costs is indeed "a collision of . . . law and accounting." The issue, at one level, centers on the extent to which nonprofits can obtain revenues, but at another level it involves fundamental constitutional rights. Accountants routinely allocate joint costs (including "fixed" costs) according to customary rules, but the historical context of their procedures—carried over from private-sector accounting—is quite remote from the issues of constitutionality and the role of the nonprofit sector, which arise here. As one analyst, focusing directly on public policy choices, put it, "As pure accounting, this [joint-cost matter] is dealt with routinely. The reason it has not been a routine matter here is that government regulators, who are lawyers, want to use accounting as a control device in their oversight activities."[55]

The Supreme Court, while striking down laws that place limits on fund raising, has not objected to laws that require nonprofits to provide information about their fund-raising percentage. Yet the problem of how to allocate joint costs remains; there is no "correct" division of truly joint costs. Pressure from regulatory agencies for release of such information—regulation of which implies that higher fund-raising costs are undesirable—will cause nonprofits to search with their accountants for ever more "creative" ways to show that their fund-raising costs are small. More stringent requirements may lead to redefinition of terms and changes in accounting practices that may provide donors with less information. This could lead to even greater regulatory involvement, with increasingly detailed specification and monitoring of nonprofits' accounting practices.

The same problems arise as nonprofits expand into activities that generate unrelated business income. By charging much of the joint costs to the for-profit enterprise, the nonprofit can reduce, if not eliminate, its

UBI, which is taxable, even though the activity is actually quite profitable. By the same token, private or public contributions for the nonprofit's main (exempt) activities permit purchase of resources that can be used jointly in both its exempt and nonexempt activities; thus, if nonprofits are permitted to extend their activities, donors' contributions constitute a joint subsidy for all of the organization's activities—whether intended or not—including those that are substantially unrelated to its exempt purposes.

Nonprofits seeking additional revenues can be attracted to new activities not only because of interdependencies in cost but also because of interdependencies in demand. Consumers who are obtaining x_1 from a nonprofit organization may also prefer to purchase other, x_2, goods and services from it. Indeed, a nonprofit organization in search of profits will seek out just such relationships. For example, patients leaving a hospital may prefer to buy prescription drugs from a pharmacy at the hospital rather than from another down the block. Similar complementarities seem to be at the root of a number of claims of unfair competition, such as hospitals selling hearing aids and universities providing travel services. If consumers do prefer to purchase a variety of goods and services from the same source, then to restrict a nonprofit's outputs would hurt consumers. Yet to permit the nonprofit to expand its activities would hurt proprietary producers.[56]

A number of proposals are now being considered to reduce competition from nonprofit organizations with proprietary firms. The interdependencies in production costs and in consumer demands make it very complex to evaluate the proposals from an overall societal perspective. One of the current plans to limit nonprofit business activities would increase the tax rate on the first dollar of UBI of the nonprofits, setting it at the highest marginal corporate tax rate, 46 percent, rather than at the lowest, 16 percent. Another would totally prohibit unrelated business activities. Still another would alter the criteria for determining what is an "unrelated trade or business," so that the IRS would consider not only whether an activity is "substantially related" to the organization's exempt purpose, as it does now, but also its impact on proprietary firms. There is also a proposal to amend the Federal Trade Commission (FTC) Act, which exempts nonprofits from the restrictions on unfair competition.[57]

Recent litigation over the meaning of unrelated business income highlights the complexity of the issues. A decade elapsed while the Internal Revenue Service, the United States Claims Court, and the United States

Supreme Court considered whether the income, in 1975, from advertising in the *Annals of Internal Medicine*—published by the nonprofit American College of Physicians, a 501(c)(3) organization—is taxable as unrelated business income.[58] The sum of tax involved in this case was only $55,965—which may seem trivial to occupy the time and energy of the IRS, which initially ruled the income of $153,388 taxable; the Claims Court, which reversed that ruling; and the United States Supreme Court, which reversed the Claims Court in 1986. The long-term impact of the case, however, may be substantial.

This decision plus a subsequent one in which the Supreme Court defined as unrelated business income the revenues from life insurance sold by the American Bar Association's endowment to lawyer members— the first unanimous and the other six to one—raise the broad question, "Is 'fund raising' an unrelated business activity?"[59] The answer is neither a clear yes nor a clear no; in the Supreme Court decision on the *Annals* case, however, Chief Justice Burger, with Justice Powell concurring, called for explicit regulation of fund-raising activities: "Such regulations, of course, are for the Executive Branch and the Congress, not the courts."[60] What is quite clear is that the greater the latitude permitted for nonprofits' fund-raising activities, the louder will be the charges of unfair competition coming from the private sector.

Complaints of unfair competition do not come only from the private sector. Nonprofits, too, claim that "business has entered customarily nonprofit fields as health and child care."[61] There may well be a tendency for each form of organization to argue that incursion of the other form into an activity dominated by it is "unfair," but surely the appropriate social roles for the private and the nonprofit sectors cannot be determined by which form of organization was "first"—even if that were clear.

Congress continues to struggle with the problem of competition between nonprofit and for-profit organizations and the related role and application of the UBI tax. For several days in June of 1987, hearings were held by the oversight subcommittee of the House Ways and Means Committee. Focusing on the broad issue of the appropriate roles of the public, private, and nonprofit sectors, the hearings dealt with such questions as how the nature and extent of nonprofits' income-producing activities changed since 1950; to what extent taxable (private) and tax-exempt (nonprofit) organizations are competing; whether the goals— whatever they are—of the UBI tax are being realized; and whether the IRS has a satisfactory enforcement program in this area.[62]

In competing for the consumer's dollar, nonprofit organizations and proprietary firms each have their own disadvantages. Nonprofits may not raise capital by issuing stock and, insofar as they provide public-type goods, they face the problem of free-rider behavior. By contrast, for-profit firms find it costly, if not impossible, to obtain donations. Subject to these constraints, both types of organizations have available to them various means of increasing revenues. A proprietary firm can increase sales by changing the level and quality of output, as well as price, assuming it does not operate in a perfectly competitive market. A nonprofit organization can raise the amount of donations it receives by undertaking fund-raising activities; it can also produce goods and services that can be sold at a profit to finance the activities for which it was granted tax exemption.

When nonprofits move into these "secondary" markets they act more and more like proprietary firms, and they become increasingly competitive with the proprietaries. Proprietary firms now claim, with growing stridency, "unfair" competition from the subsidized nonprofits that are expanding into the traditional markets of private enterprise. This truly poses a dilemma for public policy.

SEVEN

Volunteer Labor

Financing nonprofit organizations is not a matter of money alone. Volunteer labor is a substantial resource, too, but rarely do discussions of public policy toward nonprofits encompass it. There is evidence, though, that governmental actions that appear to have nothing at all to do with volunteer labor actually do affect its supply and, hence, the strength of the nonprofit sector. Regrettably, the U.S. Bureau of Labor Statistics (BLS) disregards volunteer labor in its surveys of the labor force, and so we know little about its magnitude, changes over time, and the forces influencing its supply and demand. Even the National Commission on Employment and Unemployment, which in 1978–1980 examined statistics on the labor force, failed to recommend inclusion of volunteers in BLS surveys, although the matter was debated.

In recent years nonprofits adopted a number of strategies to adjust to cutbacks in federal support. Nonprofits not only sought new sources of money; they also increased their search for volunteer labor. Indeed, a 1982 survey disclosed that "the single most frequently reported coping strategy is to place greater reliance on volunteers. Nearly a third of all [nonprofit] agencies surveyed indicated they had increased their use of volunteers over the past year."[1]

In the private market economy, it is customary to equate the amount of paid labor with the total amount of labor that is used. Since little or no labor services are volunteered without pay to General Motors, United States Steel, or the A&P food stores, the omission of volunteer labor is of scant significance. Less than 3 percent of volunteers reported in 1985 providing their services to for-profit firms.[2]

For the rest of the economy the tendency to disregard unpaid labor is a major oversight. By not counting volunteer labor in national statistics on the labor force, we understate both the total number of persons who are engaged in productive activity outside the home and the number of employed persons. In the process we understate the proportion of the labor supply that is "employed" productively outside the home. Moreover, individuals do shift from one type of activity to another—paid employment, volunteer work, housework and other productive activities, formal and informal; by not counting volunteers, we record such shifting as changes in the size of the labor force and in the number of persons "employed" and "unemployed."

Data on volunteer labor, although they are improving, remain sketchy. They show that volunteers constitute a major resource to the economy as a whole and that they are enormously important in health, education, and social services, areas that are overwhelmingly in the private nonprofit sector. No attempt to understand the nonprofit sector would be even reasonably complete if it did not underscore the role of volunteer labor.

In 1980 52 percent of persons aged 14 years or older volunteered time to organizations; the total hours were the equivalent of 5.9 million full-time equivalent (FTE) workers (assuming 1,700 hours per year)—5.4 percent of the nation's employed labor force.[3] Some 79 percent of all volunteer labor—4.6 million FTE workers—was supplied to the nonprofit sector (with 18 percent going to governmental organizations).[4] This volume of unpaid labor in the nonprofit sector is nearly as large as the lower-bound estimate I proposed in Chapter 4 of total *paid* labor in the nonprofit sector, 4.95 million FTE workers. The latest Gallup survey, in 1985, disclosed a substantial increase in total hours volunteered, especially to nonprofits—48 percent of persons 14 and over volunteering nearly 14 percent more hours, amounting to 6.7 million FTE workers, with 80 percent of this labor going to nonprofits (see Table E.1 in Appendix E).[5]

Volunteers are an enormously important resource within the nonprofit economy. Indeed, the value of volunteered time is probably some 70–90 percent as great as the amount of paid labor; in 1984 it was estimated at $80 billion, compared with $102 billion of paid wages and salaries (including fringe benefits).[6] The total amount of labor—paid and unpaid—utilized by the nonprofit sector is, in short, close to twice as large as data on paid labor alone would suggest. Volunteer time may equal only some 6 percent of the entire labor force, but it is more like 40 percent of the labor force in social service nonprofits, where it is concentrated.

The best evidence available indicates that not only has the absolute volume of volunteer labor continued to grow, but it is growing more rapidly than the volume of paid labor employed in the nonprofit sector. Between 1974 and 1985 volunteering to charitable, social welfare, nonprofits—the organizations that are tax exempt under section 501(c)(3) of the Internal Revenue Code—grew by 60 percent in terms of FTE workers while the number of FTE paid employees increased 44 percent. In the mid-1970s the FTE amount of labor volunteered to charitable nonprofits was 60–62 percent of the number of paid workers (full time and part time); a decade later it had risen sharply to 70 percent (Table 7.1).[7]

The market value of this volunteer labor has been estimated by assuming—quite simplistically—that each volunteer could earn, in the marketplace, a wage equal to the average hourly wage of nonagricultural workers, plus 12 percent for fringe benefits. This method, although it is questionable and needs improvement, produced an estimated market value of volunteer labor in 1980 of $74 billion.[8] This value of donated time—which was the equivalent of some 5 percent of total wages paid in the economy in 1980[9]—is 50 percent greater than the total contributions of money to these organizations from all sources, some $48 billion

Table 7.1 Full-time equivalent (FTE) volunteers (14 years old and older) and paid employment in the charitable sector,[a] 1974–1985

Year	Total	FTE Volunteers (millions) Working in Nonprofits	Working in Charitable Sector	Paid Employees in Charitable Sector (millions)	FTE Volunteers as a Percent of Paid Employees in Charitable Sector
1985	6.7	5.3	4.8	6.9	69.6
1984	6.6	5.2	4.7	6.7	70.2
1983	6.4	5.0	4.6	6.6	69.7
1982	6.3	5.0	4.5	6.5	69.2
1981	6.1	4.7	4.3	6.4	67.2
1980	5.9	4.7	4.2	6.2	67.7
1977	4.6	3.6	3.3	5.5	60.0
1974	4.2	3.3	3.0	4.8	62.5

Source: Unpublished table supplied by Independent Sector (Washington, D.C.), November 1986.

a. "Charitable sector" refers to all nonprofit organizations that may receive tax-deductible contributions. The organization that supplied the data for this table, Independent Sector, refers to these nonprofits as the "independent sector."

in 1980.[10] In 1985, by this method, a total of $110 billion of labor was volunteered by persons at least 14 years of age—60 percent more than the $68 billion of money contributions in 1984, the latest year for which information is available.[11]

Services are volunteered to a wide variety of nonprofits. Some 84 percent of all charitable nonprofits report using volunteers.[12] About half of the value-weighted hours of volunteer time are devoted to religious, health, or educational organizations (see Table E.2 in Appendix E). Volunteers are quantitatively more important than paid workers in religious and in cultural organizations, and are about half as important in both education and social welfare groups (Table E.3). In the health sector—largely hospitals—which employs 47 percent of all paid workers in charitable nonprofits, the estimated value of volunteer labor is close to one-fourth of paid wages and salaries. The method of valuing volunteer labor that I described above may well overstate its value: people may be less productive as volunteers, and, in addition, those who actually volunteer may be less productive in the marketplace than the average person who chooses paid work. In any event, it is clear that the level of activity of nonprofit organizations—and, hence, their effects on other parts of the economy—would be substantially lower were it not for volunteers. (Data about volunteer labor in other countries are even more limited than they are for the United States, but its relevance is clearly worldwide, as Appendix B shows.)

Supply and Demand

The reasons for volunteering are many; they include wanting to help the needy, religious concerns, and the desire to obtain work experience.[13] Both economic theory and recent statistical research suggest, though, that the amount of labor that people are willing to donate depends partly on economic forces, including tax laws and programs undertaken by government that substitute for, or are complementary with, activities in the nonprofit sector.[14]

Some of the forces influencing the supply of volunteer labor are not susceptible to change through public policy; there is little, if anything, that can be done to change the desire an individual has to help others or to alter the tendency of parents of young children to volunteer less than do parents of older children. The life-cycle pattern of volunteering is for volunteering to increase with age, other things being equal, up to around age forty-three and to decrease thereafter.[15] But public policy can and does affect the amount of volunteer work that is offered by individuals with particular attitudes and preferences. Policies on taxes and public expenditures affect individuals' perceptions of the benefits and costs to them of volunteering. The amount of donated time is influenced by the same governmental policies that influence private donations of money, but the effects of changes in governmental activity on the supply of volunteer labor are more complex because the goals of people who supply labor are more varied than are those of people who donate money.

Individuals who volunteer in order to gain work experience are not likely to volunteer more merely because government cuts back on social services. Indeed, the contrary is likely, since reductions in government spending are likely to reduce the demand for the kinds of paying positions that these volunteers hope to obtain eventually. Still, the state of the economy affects the supply of volunteer labor to nonprofits; the stronger the economy the easier it will be for a worker to get a paid job and, hence, the less attractive a volunteer job will be. Between the 1981 and 1985 Gallup surveys of volunteers, the percentage of volunteers who gave as a reason for volunteering their desire "to learn and get experience," or to help "get a job"—in short, as preparation for entering the labor market—dropped slightly, from 11 percent to 10 percent.[16] The age pattern of these responses is noteworthy; while 17 percent of volunteers under age 35 gave these reasons for volunteering, only 5 percent of volunteers 35–64 did so, and no one age 65 and over gave such reasons.[17] This decrease with age is expected, since investment in learning and experience is likely to be more profitable for younger people who can expect a longer working life.

Paul Menchik and I found that the after-tax wage rate that a person receives has a significant negative effect on the amount of time that he or she volunteers. For the people in our sample, whose average after-tax hourly wage was $4.17 in 1973—the data are regrettably old but are the latest available—an increase of that wage by one dollar, other things equal, resulted in a decrease of 4.8 hours per year from the mean of 49.7 hours.[18] This negative effect was expected. The larger the market wage one can obtain, the greater is the opportunity cost of volunteering and the less of it can be expected.

Government policies affect the supply of volunteer labor through their effects on the after-tax wage in two ways: (1) through actions that influence the before-tax wage rates (for example, by affecting the overall level of economic activity or through other mechanisms such as laws prohibiting discrimination against women or minorities); and (2) through the personal income tax system (which determines how much of any gross wage is left with the earner after tax). A reduction in marginal income tax rates, such as was enacted by Congress in 1986, will have the effect of increasing the after-tax wage. This will diminish the amount of volunteering—just as it will diminish donations of money.

Some people report that their motivation for volunteering is "to do something useful to help others." This reason was given by 45 percent of volunteers in 1981 and by 52 percent in 1985. Such people may well increase their volunteering if government does less to help the needy. The age pattern of the volunteers who gave such "helping" reasons is in sharp contrast with the pattern of volunteers seeking experience; there was little variation across age groups in the reported relevance of being useful to others—some 50–55 percent of volunteers gave that reason in every age class except for the group between 25 and 34 years of age, of which 45 percent gave this reason.[19]

The effect of governmental social service spending on the supply of volunteer labor is not readily apparent. Some research on it has been done.[20] Menchik and I found that there is not a negative relationship—as both the "crowding out" and "helping" models would predict—between the level of governmental expenditures on social services and the amount of volunteering; rather, there is a small positive association. We found that an increase in spending by local governments on social services by $50 per capita per year (the national average being $260 for the year studied, 1973) would result in some, albeit a small, increase in volunteering—by an average of one hour annually.[21] This aggregate relationship, however, masks considerable differences across specific program areas. We found that increased governmental spending exerts a negative effect on the supply of volunteer time in the areas of "higher education" and "social welfare," but not in the areas of "lower education" or "natural resources."[22]

The amount of volunteer labor utilized is a result of both supply factors, which influence the willingness of individuals to donate their time, and demand factors, which reflect the willingness of organizations to use volunteers rather than paid workers or capital equipment. Governmental actions affect both. It is assumed in quantitative research on the market for volunteer labor, however, that demand is essentially unlimited—that organizations will accept any amount of volunteer labor that is offered to them—so that the only effective limit to the utilization of volunteer workers is its supply.

Whether or not it is valid to assume that the volume of volunteer labor depends only on supply-side factors, it is clear that public policies can affect the willingness of people to donate their time. I have already noted that any governmental action that increases the opportunities for workers to find a well-paying job or a job that provides better work experience will increase the relative attractiveness of paid labor and so will decrease the supply of volunteer labor. By contrast, any action that increases marginal tax rates on earnings or that permits tax deductibility (or a tax credit) for volunteer work will increase the relative attractiveness of volunteering and so will increase the willingness of individuals to supply volunteer labor.

The assumption that the demand for volunteers is unlimited, which leads to the assumption that public policy can affect only the supply, is plausible but not really valid. The part-time and intermittent nature of most volunteers' willingness to work is a limitation for many organizations. Thus, it is quite likely that only limited numbers and types of volunteers will be accepted even at a wage of zero. As a result, the number and types of volunteers demanded can be changed through public actions. For example, an organization's use of volunteer labor could be subsidized (or taxed), and the greater the subsidy (or tax), the more (or less) volunteer time organizations would accept, all else being equal.

Subsidization of organizations that use volunteers has not been a subject of policy debate, but it has merit. Private employers who hire—for pay—disadvantaged and long-term unemployed workers are now eligible for federal subsidies, under the Targeted Jobs Tax Credit Program. Such a program, involving credits of as much as $3,000 per year per worker, is designed to encourage employment of particular groups of workers. It could be extended to volunteers as well; that is, nonprofit (or other) organizations that use volunteers—of all types or of special types such as the disadvantaged and long-term unemployed—could become eligible for a payment from government. Monitoring problems would have to be surmounted lest unscrupulous organizations simply claim to be using volunteers and giving them job experience while actually doing nothing but collecting the subsidy. Restricting such a subsidy to the use of volunteers in nonprofit or government organizations could simplify enforcement, since the nondistribution constraint limits these organizations' ability to turn the subsidy into payments to managers or entrepreneurs.

In 1982 the Senate of the state of New York passed a law that would have allowed a subsidy in the form of a tax deduction for people who volunteered their time to charitable organizations; it provided an incentive for people to volunteer and, in the process, to shift resources into the nonprofit sector, but neither the magnitude of effects nor the overall desirability were well understood.[23] Perhaps this is why the State Assembly did not pass the bill.[24]

The alternative to subsidizing volunteers—namely, taxing them—might seem foolish. One basis for it, though, would be not to discourage volunteering but to encourage it by bringing volunteers into the Social Security System. Taxation has not been proposed, to the best of my knowledge, but it has merit. Including volunteer work under Social Security would present a tax cost for organizations (and also for volunteers themselves, if they were also taxed, as paid workers now are), and depending on how coverage for volunteers was phased in, there would be added burdens on paid workers. There would also be some real advantages. The status of volunteers would be raised and their social contribution would be explicitly acknowledged by their inclusion in the Social Security program along with paid workers. Thus, inclusion of volunteers under Social Security would increase the supply of volunteer labor. Although the direct effect of the tax would be to decrease the amount of volunteer labor demanded, because its cost to the organization would increase, there would be a countervailing increase in demand if the elevated social status of volunteers led them to be more productive.

This is not the place to develop a complete benefit-cost analysis of the inclusion of volunteer labor under Social Security. There would be, of course, practical problems of implementation, such as how much to tax an hour of unpaid labor, but these do not seem to be insurmountable; the tax could be based on an imputed value of the labor, or, more simply, there could be a fixed dollar amount of tax for an hour's worth of volunteered labor. There would be added costs of bookkeeping for the recipient organization, and there would be regulatory problems of ensuring that the volunteering actually occurred, as well as problems of defining "volunteer work" for purposes of receiving Social Security coverage.

The argument that the demand for volunteer labor is limited and, hence, that it can be influenced by public policy is supported by evidence from a 1984 report on the use of volunteers by large national agencies. It showed heavy use of volunteers in one particular way, for fund raising, particularly by health-related organizations (Table E.4); this is an activity in which volunteers can work rather independently and at flexible hours. Although an older but more comprehensive survey showed greater diversity of activities by volunteer workers (Table E.5), the types of activities suggest that volunteer labor is not a close substitute for paid labor in all uses. A 1982 survey of how nonprofits were adjusting to diminished federal funding found that although most were increasing their use of volunteers, they at the same time stressed the limits of volunteerism; in particular they expressed reservations about the extensive replacement of paid professionals with volunteers.[25]

Current U.S. tax law includes a number of provisions that affect—explicitly or implicitly—the supply of volunteer time. At present, contributions of money, but not of volunteered time, are deductible from taxable income—although only for itemizers.[26] If volunteered time were deductible, more of it would be supplied. Recently there have been legislative proposals and actions to allow volunteers to deduct some portion of the "value" of their donation of time. The 1982 New York State bill would have allowed volunteers who give at least 100 hours a year to deduct from their taxable income 5 percent of the value of their services, up to $500; organizations receiving these volunteer services would have been required to keep records of hours worked by each volunteer, and "the value" of that time to the organization. The federal government recently passed a law raising the automobile expenses that a volunteer may deduct, from 9 cents to 12 cents per mile traveled while volunteering, but the value of time itself remains nondeductible.

A goal of subsidies to individuals who volunteer is to increase the supply of volunteers. Little is known, however, either about the magnitude of the effect that tax subsidies for volunteering have on the supply of volunteer labor or about the extent to which any positive effects will come at the expense of reduced donations of money; donors may choose to cut back on contributions of money as they increase donations of time. Some research evidence indicates, though, that such switching will not occur. On the contrary, it appears that reducing the cost of volunteering leads to an increase in both hours and dollars donated.[27]

Existing law, by allowing deductibility of donations of money but not of time, may seem to bias donors' choices in favor of giving money, but it does not. The value of volunteered time cannot be deducted; at the same time, a volunteer does not pay income tax that would be required if, rather than volunteering time, a person worked those hours and donated the earnings to charity. In short, regardless of whether an individual volunteers an hour of time that could be devoted to earning a wage—say, $8—or works that hour, receives the pay, pays the income tax on it, and gives the balance to a charity, the donor has worked one hour and has forgone the opportunity to obtain $8 minus the marginal income tax for personal consumption. Donors may or may not prefer to help an organization by volunteering services to it rather than by giving cash, which can then be used to purchase services; and recipient organizations may or may not prefer receiving an hour of a person's time to the amount of money, after tax, that the person can earn in an added hour of work—but the cost to the donor is the same. The tax system is "neutral," providing equal incentives for donating time and money, at least for tax-payers who itemize their donations of money.[28]

The opportunity cost of volunteering has an important implication: the tax rate on money income affects the supply of unpaid volunteer labor. Reduced income tax rates, by increasing the after-tax income from work, do have a "substitution effect"—shifting incentives in favor of money-making activities and away from volunteering (as well as from donating money). At the same time, reduced tax rates also increase taxpayers' after-tax money income, and this "income effect" increases volunteering (and money donations); higher-income people can be expected to vol-unteer more, other things being equal. Research shows that, controlling for a number of variables likely to affect volunteering—including the in-dividual's after-tax wage rate, age, sex, number and ages of children, and community size—a 10 percent increase in income—perhaps from dividends, rents, interest, or transfer payments—leads to a 6.5 percent increase in the number of hours volunteered.[29]

Thus, when income tax rates fall, the income effect increases vol-unteering while the substitution effect decreases it. The net effect is not clear; it is likely, though, that substitution effects will dominate and so reductions in income tax rates will diminish volunteering, while increases in rates will augment it.

Tax laws affect incentives to volunteer time in other ways. If, as seems likely, decisions to volunteer are related to decisions to donate money, then any provision of the tax law that alters incentives to give money will affect voluntarism as well. If donors regard donating money and time as alternative ways of helping an organization, then changes in tax laws that have a direct effect on contributions of money to nonprofits will have an offsetting effect on contributions of time. Alternatively, if individuals regard donating money and time as complementary ways of helping, so that they prefer to give both in some particular relationship, then any provisions of tax laws that affect the incentive either to donate money or to volunteer time will affect the amounts of both in the same direction. The degree of complementarity or substitutability of donations of money and time has received only scant attention. A 1985 survey of volunteers, conducted by Yankelovich, Skelly and White, did determine, though, that people who volunteer are likely to donate more money than are non-volunteers. This finding did not, however, control for other differences between volunteers and nonvolunteers, and, indeed, volunteers, while making mean contributions of $830 in the past year, compared with $510 for nonvolunteers, did have greater household income, $29,500 versus $25,400.[30]

Changes in an individual's pretax income, average tax rate, marginal tax rate, and deductibility status—each of which affects after-tax income—all affect both the amount of money donated and the amount of time volunteered. A 1985 Treasury Department proposal that would have limited deductions to monetary contributions in excess of 2 percent of adjusted gross income, for example, would affect both voluntarism and money donations. Tax-law changes that appear to be unrelated even to money contributions may nonetheless affect the two forms of giving. A reduction or elimination of deductibility for state and local taxes would reduce the number of itemizers, for example, thereby cutting the incentive to donate money, which would be deductible only to itemizers, and at the same time would affect the incentive to volunteer in various ways.

If, as seems likely, giving of money and time are related, any change in tax laws that affects the incentive to volunteer will also influence donations of money. Thus, a change in the sum that a volunteer can deduct for automobile miles traveled in the course of volunteering would affect directly the amount of time volunteered and indirectly the volume of money donations. Any change in tax laws or in IRS administrative rulings, such as those affecting the deductibility of other expenses incurred in the process of volunteering to nonprofit organizations, will affect volunteering but may also affect contributions of money.

Parade magazine in a recent article titled "How to Enjoy Your Vacation . . . and Get a Tax Break Too!" highlighted the potential tax consequences of volunteering to a tax-deductible nonprofit.[31] By volunteering services, the article points out, an individual can "sign on for a tax-deductible vacation . . . in Florida, atop a mountain peak in Colorado or in Alaska . . . or exotic places like Borneo, Polynesia or Australia." Although the tax-law requirement is that the volunteer must actually work, the problems of enforcing such requirements are severe. Even so, an IRS official warns, in the same article, that "we strongly suggest you seek tax counsel before incurring any expenses if you anticipate taking a deduction [for such travel] on your tax return."[32] Sound tax policy cannot be constructed unless we recognize the multiple and interdependent ways through which both the law and its administration affect contributions of time as well as money, and thereby the strength and vitality of the nonprofit economy.

EIGHT

Are Nonprofits Really Different?

If nonprofit organizations perform a useful role, they must provide outputs that cannot be provided profitably by private enterprise. The lure of profit does not lead to a socially efficient allocation of resources when there are socially valuable forms of outputs that are not rewarded financially—either because they are costly for buyers to evaluate or because they go to persons with little ability to pay. Do for-profit and nonprofit organizations act differently in providing outputs that are hard for consumers to monitor and in the manner in which outputs are distributed? In particular, do both nonprofits and proprietary firms take advantage of opportunities to reap profits at the expense of underinformed consumers, or are there differences between the two on this very important matter?

To answer these questions, I propose that we examine industries in which nonprofit and proprietary firms coexist.[1] Systematic differences in organizational behavior would provide evidence that institutional form does matter. Whether any differences are offset by other dimensions of economic behavior is another issue. Even if nonprofits were found to provide more complete information to consumers, for example, they might also be less cost efficient.[2] Because profitability and social welfare often conflict in regard to the distribution of outputs and the dissemination of information, I will focus on these aspects of economic behavior.

Distribution of Outputs

A profit-motivated firm sells its outputs to the highest bidders. What do nonprofits do?

Evidence on the ways that organizations distribute outputs is hard to find. Consider, though, the use of waiting lists. A profit-maximizing firm has little incentive to keep a waiting list, apart from uncertainties associated with fluctuating, unpredictable, demand. If there is excess demand for the services of a private hospital, school, or any other firm, profit can normally be increased by raising price.[3] Thus, proprietary firms seldom use waiting lists on a sustained basis.

What about nonprofits? If they are largely for-profits in disguise—as they might be if the nondistribution constraint is so costly to enforce that it is of no real importance—there will be no difference on the matter of waiting lists. To the extent, though, that nonprofits are "bonoficers"— organizations whose goals include distributing outputs to "needy" or to "deserving" persons regardless of ability to pay, as well as treating underinformed consumers "fairly," even at the expense of profit—they will act quite unlike profit-motivated firms. Nonprofits will be more likely to use waiting lists and they will take less advantage of underinformed consumers.[4] Even if nonprofits are not bonoficers, however, they might use waiting lists simply because they are inefficiently rigid in pricing their services as market conditions change. Such inefficiency could occur because managers and directors are restricted from sharing in organizational profit.

I have examined the use of waiting lists in three industries to see whether nonprofits and proprietary sellers differ. The industries, all within the medical care sector, are nursing homes, psychiatric care facilities, and facilities for the mentally handicapped.[5] The data come from a national random sample survey, carried out by the U.S. Bureau of the Census, of over 500 such long-term-care facilities in 1976, the most recent survey of this kind undertaken. My econometric analyses of the rich set of data from this survey, called the Survey of Institutionalized Persons (SIP), take a variety of forms. The analyses employ statistical regression techniques that estimate the quantitative relationships between the institutional form of a provider organization—church-related nonprofit, other nonprofit, governmental, proprietary (for-profit)—and each of a number of dimensions of organizational behavior, including the use of waiting lists to allocate services, and other aspects of behavior discussed below. The regression estimates control for differences among organizations in such terms as size, price charged, and staff-patient ratio. Technical detail is presented in Appendix F. (Tables in Appendix F also include data on governmental facilities, but they will not be discussed, since our focus is on the comparison of for-profit and nonprofit organizations.)

With respect to whether there are systematic differences among institutions in the use of waiting lists, I controlled statistically for the effects of extraneous factors that vary with institutional form and influence the use of waiting lists—the organization's age, number of beds, price per patient-month, ratios of physicians and nurses to beds, and revenue sources (the proportions of patients whose costs were being paid by private sources, by Medicaid, and by Medicare).

I found that there *are* differences between nonprofits and for-profits. First, proprietary firms were markedly less likely to maintain a waiting list than were church-owned nonprofits. In nursing homes and in facilities for the mentally handicapped, proprietary organizations were significantly less likely than either church-owned[6] or other nonprofits to have a waiting list. Nonprofits not owned by churches used waiting lists less than the church-owned nonprofits but more than proprietaries (see Table F.1 in Appendix F).[7] The magnitude of differences can be large. Among nursing homes, for example, although proprietary homes may well have a waiting list—I estimated that this probability is 0.70 at the mean values of all the other independent variables—a church-owned nursing home has a 0.95 probability of having a waiting list, other things equal.[8]

Second, for those organizations that did have a waiting list, the number of names on it was also systematically lower for proprietary firms, if organization size and other variables mentioned above are held constant. Church-owned organizations were likely to have the longest waiting lists—significantly so, however, only among nursing homes[9]—and, again, the other nonprofits were less distinguishable from proprietaries (Table F.2).

Evidence from three long-term-care industries is not enough for reaching a sweeping conclusion; we need evidence for other industries. At this point, however, there are two tentative conclusions. (1) In general, nonprofits are less likely than proprietary firms to use prices to ration output and more likely to use waiting lists. (2) There are differences within the nonprofit sector—church-owned and other nonprofits behaving somewhat differently; the bonoficing model seems to apply more to the church-owned organizations.

Dissemination of Information

Consumers who are well informed should be indifferent about the institutional form of a seller. All that should count is how satisfied the consumer would be with a particular seller's output and its price.

When consumers are underinformed relative to producers, however, they may turn to nonprofit organizations. Do nonprofits in fact act differently from proprietary firms, and if they do, do they take less or more advantage of their informational superiorities? Do consumers of complex services, such as nursing home care for the elderly or day care for young children, gain something from knowing they are doing business with a nonprofit rather than with a proprietary seller? Which form is preferable from the standpoints of efficient allocation of resources and equity? Is it or is it not true that nonprofits are more "trustworthy" as agents for underinformed consumers?

We can learn something about these questions by comparing the behavior of nonprofit and proprietary organizations in markets where consumers are underinformed and learning is difficult. Underinformed consumers are generally not totally ignorant about a commodity—only about some attributes that they find costly to judge. Easily assessed (type-1) attributes of various goods and services include the size of a nursing home, the color, year, and model of a used car, the taste of canned tuna, and the mailing address of a charity that claims to aid overseas poor. Attributes that are costly to assess (type-2 attributes) include the sensitivity of care in a nursing home, how quickly the used car starts on a cold day (given that it is being assessed in the summer), whether the tuna was caught in an area believed to have been a dumping ground for mercury, and how much of one's charitable donation gets to the poor and in what form.

The problem with hard-to-monitor attributes is, in effect, the cost of developing and enforcing a contract that specifies these characteristics of the product. If, moreover, consumer mobility in these markets is limited, because of the high costs of switching providers, another avenue of consumer adjustment is, if not foreclosed, at least severely limited. Thus, even if consumers eventually gain information, as they learn from experience, the costs of searching for alternatives and of moving have the effect of limiting consumers' ability to adjust. Competition—if it involves only profit-seeking firms—may not overcome consumers' informational handicaps in the markets for nursing home services, basic medical research, charity to the poor, and other high-information-cost services.

Can nonprofit institutions succeed where private markets fail? Can the scandals in proprietary day-care centers and nursing homes be prevented by greater reliance on nonprofits? Is the blunting of incentives to seek profit desirable? The answer to these questions depends partly on whether nonprofits are more likely to provide certain socially valuable but privately unprofitable services than are proprietaries.

If there are systematic differences in type-2 attributes of goods provided by for-profit and nonprofit sellers, consumers can use institutional form as a source of information. The type-2 attributes are, after all, the dimensions of service that consumers have the most difficulty monitoring.[10] These are the dimensions of service for which a private firm has the greatest incentive to "shave" quality because detection is costly—to reuse "disposable" hospital syringes and kidney dialysis filters,[11] to reduce the quality of efforts to teach young children in a preschool day-care center, or to decrease marginally the quality of commercial aircraft maintenance. Nonprofits are not a major force in all these industries, but some forms of restrictions on unbridled maximization of profit are.[12]

If nonprofits do act less opportunistically than do proprietaries, if they take less advantage of informational superiorities, then there are two answers to the question, Do consumers gain by knowing an organization's form of ownership? Yes, for poorly informed consumers—they will know they are less likely to be taken advantage of by a nonprofit. No, for well-informed consumers; they are not at an informational handicap, and so they have no reason to prefer dealing with a nonprofit. The interesting result is that proprietary firms and nonprofits can coexist in an industry, each catering to a different subset of consumers.[13]

A Test Case: Long-Term Care

We can compare nonprofit and proprietary sellers in a sector of the economy that involves substantial type-2 attributes: long-term care for the aged, ill, and handicapped. Buyers of the services of a psychiatric facility, a facility for the mentally handicapped, or a nursing home are often poorly informed about critical aspects of service. Beyond that, patient mobility is low (though not zero)—especially, it seems, for residents of nursing homes and the mentally handicapped. Evidence on mobility is very limited, but it does appear to be less restricted for psychiatric patients, who are often in and out of various facilities. These differences in consumer mobility will become significant when we analyze the differences in information available to consumers across industries.

The interplay of poor information and limited patient mobility is clearest in nursing home services. First, these services are seldom purchased more than once in a person's lifetime; as a result, consumers—patients or family members—gain little information from their own experience.

Second, the services involve a complex set of attributes, including subtle relations between patients and attending staff—the quality of "tender loving care"—that are very difficult to assess prior to admission and are difficult to specify in a contract. Third, a specific consumer often has unusual needs, which means that there are limits to what can be learned from other consumers' experiences. Fourth, the frail physical or mental condition of the patient makes relocation difficult even if and when a patient learns from experience that services are not satisfactory; the "exit" option therefore has limited value. As a result of immobility, evidence on consumer information about and satisfaction with nursing homes poses far less of a statistical selection-bias problem than it does in markets where consumers are more mobile. When switching sellers is easy, consumers gravitate to providers who are satisfactory. Patients who cannot easily opt out of facilities with which they become dissatisfied, therefore, may have something to tell us about differences in proprietary and nonprofit facilities. In the rest of this chapter I will review the results of studies of long-term care from the past decade in an attempt to analyze these informational differences and their effects.

Gathering data is difficult. If differences in type-2 dimensions of behavior persist across institutions, they must be difficult to discern—for analysts as well as for consumers. Not one of the pieces of evidence presented here is a definitive test of differences in interinstitutional behavior. Together, though, they present a noteworthy pattern.

My data come from several sources—principally from the Survey of Institutionalized Persons (SIP), but also from two other studies of nursing homes. In the Census Bureau's SIP survey of long-term-care facilities, families were asked a variety of questions that disclose how well informed consumers are at nonprofit and proprietary facilities and what consumers *learn* at the different types of institutions about the hard-to-monitor attributes of service.[14] The key question, once again, is whether there are differences in type-2 attributes that are related systematically to form of ownership. If there are, public policy might be designed to encourage or to discourage nonprofit organizations—depending on the nature of the differences—in markets where consumer information is particularly poor.[15]

PERIODIC REVIEW OF PATIENTS' NEEDS

How well informed are family members kept about the quality of services being provided to their relatives? Do nonprofits provide more complete information?

The SIP survey provides evidence on how well informed consumers are about one element of the care being provided at each facility. Family members were asked: "Does this facility conduct a periodic review to determine a patient's suitability for continued residence?"[16] In fact, virtually every facility, regardless of ownership type, did undertake such a review. Focusing on those that did, I asked whether consumers (assumed to be the patients' family members) at nonprofit facilities were better informed about this aspect of service than were their counterparts at proprietary facilities.

The bonoficing model of nonprofits predicts that consumers will be kept better informed by nonprofits—simply because doing so is socially desirable, even if not profitable. There is, after all, a cost to providing the information, but with a poorly informed, immobile clientele, there may be scant profit to be realized by incurring the costs. A profit-oriented firm thus has little incentive for a high-quality, costly, review process—which would entail topics that consumers would find hard to understand and assess—and so an organization that is actually not undertaking careful reviews has little incentive to raise the matter of review with family members. A nonprofit that was a for-profit firm in disguise would act no differently from a proprietary firm.

A nonprofit might be neither a bonoficer nor a profit maximizer. If its objectives did not include the social goals of the bonoficers, and yet the nondistribution constraint was binding on it, it would pursue the narrow interests of the manager or directors, who might wish simply not to be bothered. If so, the nonprofit would also have little interest in taking the trouble and incurring the cost of keeping consumers informed. Such nonprofits would provide no more information than would proprietary firms—perhaps even less.

To isolate the effect of institutional form on consumer information, I controlled for a number of variables that might affect the flow of information and at the same time be correlated with ownership type. These variables included not only (a) the size of the facility (number of beds)—on the assumption that communication problems might be more severe in larger facilities, but also (b) the length of time the patient had been at the facility, and (c) the frequency of the family members' visits. The latter two were held constant on the belief that how well informed a family member was might depend on the opportunities to obtain information, quite apart from the organization's efforts to provide it. If, however, the frequency of visits was itself influenced by the form of institution—for example, if consumers were more trusting of one type of institution and, hence, felt less need to visit it—then it would be inappropriate to hold constant the frequency of visits; the resulting estimates would be biased. This possibility cannot be ruled out.

I found that in all three industries—nursing homes, psychiatric care facilities, and facilities for the mentally handicapped—family members of residents at for-profit institutions were less likely to know that the facility made periodic reviews of each patient's needs, other things equal. They were less likely to know this than their counterparts at church-owned nonprofit facilities and at other nonprofits.[17] Again, as the distribution of waiting lists at different kinds of institutions showed, the church-owned nonprofits in all three industries were most unlike the proprietaries and the other nonprofits were intermediate between the church-owned institutions and the proprietaries, although the differences are statistically significant only for facilities for the mentally handicapped (Table F.3).[18]

USE OF SEDATIVES IN NURSING HOMES

Another test of opportunistic responses by proprietary and nonprofit sellers to consumers' lack of information is a comparison of the use of sedatives in nursing homes. Sedatives have a medically useful role to play, but they can also be used simply to cut costs; they are less expensive than, say, giving special attention to more active patients who need to be kept busy. Consumers—patients or their family members—have little ability to determine whether medical needs or cost cutting explains the amount of sedation. Nursing home managers are far better informed.

What is involved here is not a significant amount of intentional and medically inappropriate sedating of otherwise active patients. At most, the decisions are marginal. Given the difficulty consumers have in knowing when it is medically justified to use sedatives, the issue is this: do the different incentives faced by proprietaries and nonprofits, and perhaps the differences in goals, cause that margin to be shifted?

A fragment of information can be gleaned from a study of the use of sedatives—actually hypnotic drugs—at church-affiliated nonprofit and proprietary nursing homes.[19] During a 12-month period in 1982–1983, all of the 338 newly admitted patients at 9 nursing homes in south central Wisconsin were followed for 90 days to determine differences in use of sedatives across homes. About one-third of the patients, 121, received prescriptions permitting use of these drugs, and they were followed to determine whether the drugs were administered.

Two major findings came out of this study. First, there was no significant difference between the percentages of patients in proprietary and nonprofit homes who received a hypnotic *prescription* at the time of admission—36.7 percent versus 33.3 percent. This is important as an indicator of the medically determined "need" for sedation, for it reflects a physician's judgment of whether attending nurses should be authorized to use sedatives "as required." (Few nursing homes have a physician always present; the examining physician determines whether to permit a nurse to exercise discretion, in which case a prescription is written.) Although the data are imperfect, it appears that there was no material difference in the medically determined need for sedation among patients in proprietary and nonprofit homes.

The second finding was in sharp contrast to this conclusion. The number of dosage units actually *administered* to those patients who had received a prescription varied a great deal between the proprietaries and the nonprofits. Patients in nonprofit homes received an average of 3.0 units per month of sleeping medication, whereas patients in proprietary homes received more than four times as much—12.5 units, a highly significant difference.

Many factors could explain these differences, including differences in medical needs that were not indicated by the proportion of patients for whom an enabling prescription was written. The findings, however, are consistent once again with the interplay of incentives and hard-to-measure attributes of output. If incentives led the proprietary homes to be more concerned with increasing profit than were the nonprofits—either because organizational goals differed or because the nondistribution constraint dulled nonprofits' eagerness to increase profits—we would expect for-profit homes to use more drugs in order to economize.

The fact that we find such a relationship does not prove that the proprietaries do, in fact, take greater advantage of their informational superiority on the "true need" for medication, but it is consistent with that interpretation. I would add, however, that it is also consistent with the argument that proprietaries are more efficient; the nonprofits may be underutilizing the drugs relative to what "best" medical practice, or some other measure of appropriate behavior, would dictate.

If sedatives were being used to save costs and thereby augment profits, the greater utilization of sedatives in proprietary homes should show up as lower utilization of other resources. Data to test this implication were not available from the study of sedatives, but they were available from the national Survey of Institutionalized Persons. This survey disclosed that—holding constant a nursing home's size, age of facility, and price—church-affiliated nursing homes, compared with proprietaries, did have (a) more full-time registered nurses,[20] (b) more full-time maintenance workers,[21] (c) more volunteer workers,[22] and (d) fewer full-time administrators (Table F.4).[23] These are not all of the types of resources used in a nursing home (part-time workers are not accounted for, for example), the quality of the labor could not be controlled, many of the differences are not statistically significant, and there are no explicit controls for the medical "needs" of patients. Still, there is a pattern here: proprietaries appear to use less labor of the types required for active patients—nurses, maintenance workers, and volunteers—and more labor of the type required to manage the organization and make it "efficient"—administrators. These findings are all consistent with the interpretation that differences in use of sedatives reflect differences in the pursuit of profit.

"SATISFACTION" WITH SERVICES

How can we determine whether there are differences in the provision of type-2 services by nonprofit and proprietary organizations? I propose an indirect test. Suppose that we had data on consumer satisfaction with a particular service and could observe how it changes as consumers gain more experience with the commodity. For example, a patient's length of stay in an institution is a measure of the opportunity to gain information about even the hard-to-monitor characteristics of services. As length of stay increases, the patient may or may not gain more information; for a pure type-1 attribute, quality could be fully assessed prior to admission or purchase, and so satisfaction with it would not vary greatly with experience. For type-2 attributes of service, though, which the consumer is unable to evaluate prior to admission, satisfaction will vary with experience, as consumers accumulate information.[24]

Suppose we found that satisfaction with a particular attribute of service varied with experience and varied in a different way for nonprofit and proprietary providers. For example, suppose we found that consumers dealing with a nonprofit seller might become less dissatisfied (or more satisfied) with the quality of service rendered than did consumers who bought from a proprietary seller—after controlling for the initial level of satisfaction. This would suggest that consumers who dealt with nonprofits received less adverse news, as they learned from experience about type-2 attributes, than did customers of proprietary firms. This finding would support the view that institutional type is related to the provision of the hard-to-monitor aspects of service. (An alternative explanation, though, is that consumers buying from nonprofits—especially church-affiliated nonprofits—were simply less willing to admit or express dissatisfaction.) A systematic difference in level of satisfaction over time would be consistent with the view that proprietary firms exploit their informational advantages more fully and provide lower levels of the type-2 attributes than consumers had anticipated at the time of purchase or admission.[25] If there are such systematic differences across institutions, an organization's institutional form would be an important factor for consumers to consider when choosing among organizations. If no such differences are found, this would constitute evidence contrary to the hypothesis that nonprofits take less advantage of their informational superiority.

Living in a long-term-care facility provides information to patients and their family members about attributes that could not be judged at the time of purchase; experience discloses information. Even if the consumer cannot utilize the information—perhaps because it is too complex to have been included in a contract that could be claimed to have been breached, or because the consumer is too immobile to respond by shifting to another seller—it will affect the consumer's appraisal of "satisfaction" with the service.

Does learning occur at different rates at proprietary and at nonprofit facilities? If so, is the experience relatively more favorable (or less unfavorable) to nonprofits or to proprietaries?

In the Survey of Institutionalized Persons, family members were asked whether they were satisfied with the services being provided to their relatives: "Do you feel this facility has provided the kind of services and care your family member needs?" Family members were also asked whether they like or dislike each of five specific attributes of the facility—buildings and grounds, rooms and furnishings, treatment services, relations with staff, and social activities. I interpret all these as questions about "satisfaction"—overall and with particular components of service—although I make no presumption that the five attributes are the only ones to be considered in determining overall satisfaction.

Satisfaction can be thought of as a measure of the correspondence between the level of service expected and the level actually provided. It is less likely that consumers will be dissatisfied with type-1 attributes than with type-2 attributes, because type-1 attributes are observable (although not necessarily fully apparent) prior to admission. We want to know whether satisfaction or dissatisfaction with type-2 attributes changes at different rates at nonprofit and proprietary facilities, as consumers learn through experience. Whatever the level of consumer satisfaction is at admission, does it change differently among customers of nonprofit and proprietary institutions; is it, for example, similar to the curves shown in Figure 8.1? If satisfaction is systematically related to length of stay, we can make inferences about whether the patient has obtained bad news (as portrayed in the figure) or good news (upward-sloping lines) about the services provided, relative to initial expectations; we can also determine whether the pattern is different between nonprofits and proprietaries.[26]

In analyzing the relationship between satisfaction and length of stay, I controlled for the "price" charged—specifically, for the average revenue per patient per month in each institution. I then estimated the influence of length of stay on the probability that the consumer reports being satisfied.[27] This was to account for the possibility that reported satisfaction is affected by the price, whether paid by the consumer or by a govern-

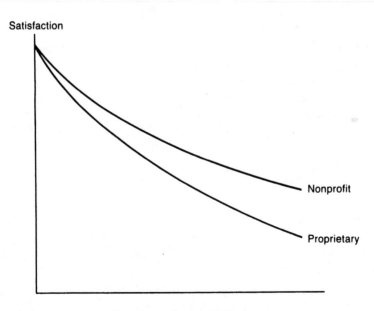

Figure 8.1 Hypothetical relationship between experience (length of stay) and satisfaction with long-term-care facilities

mental or private insurer, for price does vary somewhat among ownership forms.

The evidence is impressively, although not 100 percent, consistent across all types of institution. In all three industries—nursing homes, facilities for the mentally handicapped, and psychiatric institutions—overall satisfaction with church-owned nonprofits was greater than it was with proprietary organizations,[28] and for two of the industries—nursing homes and facilities for the mentally handicapped—customers (actually family members of patients) of other, non-church-related nonprofits reported greater satisfaction than did the customers of proprietary sellers (Table F.5). This is true not only for overall satisfaction but also for each of five components of service—buildings and grounds, rooms and furnishings, treatment services, relations with staff, and social activities (Tables F.6–F.11). Most of the differences are statistically significant.[29]

For psychiatric facilities, a more cloudy picture emerges. Satisfaction with religious nonprofits is, again, higher than satisfaction with proprietary firms, overall and in four of the five individual dimensions, but none of the differences is significant. In striking contrast are the findings for the nonreligious nonprofits; consumers are less satisfied with them than with proprietaries, although significantly so only for rooms and furnishings (Tables F.6–F.10)! Once again we find evidence of differences between religious and other nonprofits.[30]

Consumer satisfaction depends on both type-1 and type-2 attributes. Although attributes such as relations with staff and the quality of treatment services might seem to have the largest type-2 component, even buildings, grounds, rooms, and furnishings can have attributes that are difficult to evaluate prior to admission or to specify in a service contract. The distance of a building from the street is surely easy to observe, but how well the facilities are maintained and how suitable the layout of the building is for the particular, evolving needs of the patient are more difficult to observe.

Experience provides information about these evolving needs, too. In all three industries, consumers' experience led to greater satisfaction even with buildings and grounds at nonprofit facilities than at proprietaries; in other words, the information disclosed by living at a facility was more favorable at both church-owned and other nonprofits than at proprietary facilities. The same pattern—less satisfaction with proprietaries—was found for each of the other service components in nursing homes and facilities for the mentally handicapped.

CONSUMER COMPLAINTS

Yet another source of evidence is data on formal complaints about care provided at different facilities. Complaining to a state agency can be interpreted as a reflection of dissatisfaction; hence, we can learn about consumers' acquisition of information by examining complaints. Do consumers who take the trouble to complain to a government agency about the services of a long-term-care facility complain more about nonprofit or proprietary organizations?

In a study of some 500 nursing homes in Wisconsin, the answer was clear; holding constant a number of important variables other than form of institution, which might affect proclivity to complain, Mark Schlesinger and I found that there were significantly more complaints against proprietary than against either religious or other nonprofit nursing homes.[31] People may complain or not complain, of course, for a variety of reasons. Insofar as complaints reflect dissatisfaction, these findings add one more piece of evidence that institutional form matters when informational problems are severe. The evidence is again favorable to nonprofits, and somewhat more so to the church-related institutions, which had even fewer complaints, other things equal, than did the other nonprofits.

Review of the Evidence

Table 8.1 summarizes the conclusions reached in my examinations of long-term-care facilities. Evidence for the three industries—nursing homes and facilities for the mentally handicapped and for psychiatric patients—does not permit broad generalization about systematic differences between for-profit and nonprofit organizations throughout the economy. It does, however, support my emphasis on distribution of output and dissemination of information. The latter, in particular, is an attribute of behavior that is typically overlooked in research on comparative institutional behavior.

No single interpretation follows unambiguously from the evidence, yet these findings are more consistent with a model of nonprofits as bonoficers rather than as for-profits in disguise. There are, to be sure, other models of behavior that would also predict such behavior. For example, the objectives of nonprofit and of proprietary organizations might be the same—to maximize the income or some other measure of managers' and directors' well-being. The nondistribution constraint, though, would blunt the incentives for nonprofit managers to take advantage of infor-

Table 8.1 Differences in behavior between nonprofits and proprietary organizations in three long-term-care industries

	Nursing Homes		Facilities for Care of the Mentally Handicapped		Facilities for Psychiatric Care	
	Religious Nonprofits	Other Nonprofits	Religious Nonprofits	Other Nonprofits	Religious Nonprofits	Other Nonprofits
Distribution of Outputs						
1. Are nonprofits more likely to maintain a waiting list?	Yes*	Yes	Yes*	Yes*	Yes	No
2. Are nonprofits' waiting lists longer?	Yes*	Yes	Yes	No	Yes	Yes
Dissemination of Information						
3. Are consumers at nonprofits better informed about periodic reviews of each patient's needs?	Yes	Yes	Yes*	Yes*	Yes	Yes
4. Do nonprofits make less use of sedatives?	Yes*	n.a.	n.a.	n.a.	n.a.	n.a.
5. Are consumers more likely to be "satisfied" with nonprofits?	Yes	Yes	Yes	Yes	Yes	No

6. Are consumers more likely to be satisfied with nonprofits in each of the following areas?

Buildings and grounds	Yes*	Yes*	Yes*	Yes*	Yes	Yes
Rooms and furnishings	—	Yes*	Yes*	Yes*	No	No*
Treatment services	Yes*	Yes*	Yes	Yes*	Yes	No*
Relations with staff	Yes*	Yes*	Yes*	Yes	Yes	No
Social activities	Yes*	Yes*	Yes	Yes	Yes	No
7. Are consumers less likely to complain formally about nonprofits?	Yes*	Yes*	n.a.	n.a.	n.a.	n.a.

Sources: Multiple regression analysis of the following sets of data. Rows 1–3, 5, 6: U.S. Bureau of the Census, 1976 Survey of Institutionalized Persons, Current Populations Reports, Special Studies, Series P-23, no. 69 (Washington, D.C.: Government Printing Office, 1978). Row 4: Bonnie L. Svarstad and Chester A. Bond, "The Use of Hypnotics in Proprietary and Church-Related Nursing Homes," School of Pharmacy, University of Wisconsin—Madison, October 1984. Row 7: Burton A. Weisbrod and Mark Schlesinger, "Public, Private, Nonprofit Ownership and the Response to Asymmetric Information: The Case of Nursing Homes," in The Economics of Nonprofit Institutions, ed. Susan Rose-Ackerman (New York: Oxford University Press, 1986), 133–151. Also see Tables F.1–F.3 and F.5–F.10 in Appendix F.

* Differences from proprietary firms is statistically significant at the 0.10 level or better.

n.a. = Data are not available.

— = Regression equation could not be estimated because of technical problems.

mational superiorities, since any additional profit obtained by capitalizing on such superiorities could not increase the income of nonprofit managers and directors. By the same token, a nonprofit manager would be more likely to use a mechanism other than price—such as a waiting list—to ration access, because he or she could not benefit from the added profit that increased prices would generate when excess demand existed.

Whether the explanation is differences in organizational objectives, differences in regulatory constraints, or a combination of the two, there do appear to be different institutional adjustments to informational advantages. Confronted by the choice of providing more or less information to patients and family members—confronted, that is, by the choice between taking more advantage or less of its informational superiority, between incurring or not incurring the costs of providing added information—proprietary and nonprofit institutions do appear to act differently. By this test, nonprofits do take less advantage of their informational superiority. My findings also suggest, though, that there is diversity among nonprofits; church-affiliated nonprofits seem to be more unlike proprietary firms than are other nonprofits.

Theoretic considerations suggest that nonprofit and proprietary organizations will respond differently to opportunities to use their advantages over poorly informed consumers; they also suggest that the two kinds of organizations will choose different mechanisms for distributing their resources. The reason in both cases is the same—the effect, direct and indirect, of the nondistribution constraint on nonprofits. This restriction on the right of managers and directors to share in their organization's profits blunts their incentives to seek profits, which decreases their incentives to take advantage of underinformed consumers and to sell outputs to the highest bidders.

The nondistribution constraint likely has an indirect effect as well. Because managers differ in their own preferences, they may sort themselves systematically between the proprietary firms, whose freedom to allow managers to share in profits they generate is unrestricted, and nonprofits, for which this freedom is restricted. If some managers are willing to forgo monetary rewards in order to realize satisfaction from providing certain types of outputs—such as social welfare services— then they will gravitate to the nonprofit sector, whereas managers who are less interested in providing benefits to others join proprietary firms. If this sorting occurs, nonprofit and proprietary organizations will come to serve different goals, the nonprofits being more aptly characterized as bonoficers—providers of socially desirable but privately unprofitable services.

Why nonprofit and proprietary sellers might be expected to behave differently—whether it is because of differences in restrictions alone, or also because of differences in goals—is less important than whether they actually do behave differently in their distribution of output and in their treatment of underinformed consumers. Evidence on both these dimensions of behavior is difficult to obtain and assess.

Data for several industries in which consumers are often poorly informed, and in which access by the needy may be important, have disclosed a striking—albeit not entirely consistent—pattern. Nonprofit and proprietary suppliers of nursing home and long-term psychiatric care and long-term care for the mentally handicapped do differ from their proprietary counterparts. They are more likely to rely on waiting lists to ration access, and they are more likely to provide information to consumers about hard-to-monitor dimensions of service. Data for industries outside health care should be examined to see whether these patterns also show up in such industries as education, legal services, and others that combine informational inequalities with important social welfare attributes.

Social decisions to grant the tax and other advantages of nonprofit status have potential for abuse. If the nondistribution constraint is sufficiently difficult to enforce, nonprofits might actually perform no socially useful role; yet at the same time they might distort the allocation of resources as they compete with the private sector. Under those conditions, nonprofits would be found to behave no differently from private firms in response to either distributional choices or informational opportunities. On the whole, the evidence for three industries provided no support for the view that nonprofits act essentially like private firms. At the same time, there are enough differences between church-owned and other nonprofits to make us cautious about generalizing about nonprofits as a whole. Institutional form does seem to matter, but some nonprofits are more "nonprofit" than others.

NINE

Recommendations for Public Policy

The nonprofit sector of the economy is large overall, massive in the social service area, and growing. Far from isolated from the mainstream of the economy, nonprofit organizations interact vigorously with the private and governmental sectors, both competing with them and supplementing their activities. Nonprofits confront constraints on their activities and on how they may finance them, but they also receive subsidies.

This book is basically an analysis of how the nonprofit economy functions within a modern mixed economic system. That system encompasses private, public, nonprofit, and hybrid institutional forms. The interdependencies among institutions imply that any measure that expands the domain of one form of institution affects all other forms. As a result, there can be no such thing as sound public policy toward nonprofits alone—policy can be wisely constructed only if it recognizes the ways that nonprofits interact with other elements of the economic system.

Speaking from this perspective, I offer in this chapter recommendations for policies that take into account some of the conclusions I have reached in my analysis of how the nonprofit economy works. I offer these recommendations to stimulate a much-needed public-policy debate on the appropriate activities, financing, and regulation of nonprofit organizations.

Developing a coherent and consistent policy toward nonprofits is no easier than determining what government should be doing or deciding how the private sector should be regulated, taxed, or subsidized; indeed, all of these "separate" problems are elements of overall economic policy. Because of the dynamic interaction between institutional choices and informational problems, there is no permanent answer to the question, What is the proper role of nonprofits relative to other forms of institutions? Through time, policy toward each form of institution must be adjusted as changes occur in technology and in patterns of demand. A more homogeneous population has less need for nonprofits than does one with more heterogeneous demands. A better-informed population has less need for nonprofit organizations than do ill-informed consumers. What public policy requires is a procedure for continued reappraisal of the social rules that constrain and encourage the nonprofit economy relative to the other components of the economic system.

The nonprofit form of institution is more than a component of a mixed economy. It is also an example of the vast array of institutional hybrids—forms of institutions that combine elements of private enterprise and government. These two perspectives on nonprofits imply two rather different reasons for focusing attention on them: one, to understand the nonprofit sector itself, and the other to see why, and under what circumstances, one or another form of institutional hybrid will serve society's needs in a modern economic system.

Under present law, Congress legislates the types of organizations that qualify for tax-exempt, nonprofit status and those that may be classified as tax deductible, and the Internal Revenue Service makes administrative decisions on whether individual organizations will be, or are, engaged in the approved activities. Substantial revenue loss is one result; the Office of Management and Budget estimated that in 1982 tax deductibility of charitable contributions resulted in a tax loss of $9.7 billion.[1]

Each year tens of thousands of new nonprofits begin operation. The consequences of this essentially free entry of nonprofits and of access to the subsidies attached to nonprofit status are not known. Although unrestricted entry into the private market economy has a great deal to commend it on grounds of competition, the same can not be said for the nonprofit economy, given the public subsidies it receives and given that this special treatment attests to the belief that there are important differences between the nonprofit economy and the private enterprise economy. Under existing law, however, the IRS, as the principal regulatory body for nonprofits, has no authority to deny entry on grounds of "excessive" competition; neither, for that matter, is it authorized to encourage new entrants by relaxing its rules if, for example, increased competition were deemed desirable. The IRS is not even authorized to inquire into the effects of the massive rate of entry of nonprofit organizations, such as the effect on the rate of exit of existing nonprofits.

Nonprofits engage in hundreds of activities, but most nonprofits are not the type that we, as citizens, identify with charitable, tax-deductible activities. They are, in one form or another, groups of like-minded people pursuing their own self-interest—operating clubs, union pension funds, trade associations, and the like—with little reason for special treatment. Many are engaged in legislative lobbying—some on behalf of the narrow interests of the organization's members, such as the firms in an industry seeking protection from imports, and some on behalf of vast numbers of citizens, most of whom are not associated with the organization and are not contributing to its revenues, such as people who wish to see a cleaner environment but are free-riding on the contributions of others.

Most nonprofits are denied the subsidies that we typically think of as accruing to nonprofits—tax deductibility of donations, exemption from property taxes, and postal subsidies. Trade associations and the various other forms of "clubs" are in this position, but so are most social welfare organizations that would receive these subsidies except for their "excessive" lobbying. Two thirds of the nearly one million nonprofits in the United States do not qualify for tax deductibility of contributions, nor for subsidized postal rates, and they are not given free "public service" advertising by commercial radio and television stations.

Nonprofits are also enormously varied in the ways they obtain resources. The two principal sources of revenues are donations and sales, with some nonprofit charities, for example, receiving all, or nearly all, of their revenues from donations, while others receive essentially all from some form of "sales" or user charges and still others rely on various combinations. Even the nonprofits that are eligible for tax-deductible donations receive, on average, more of their revenues from sales than from donations; nonprofit hospitals, for example, obtain over 95 percent of their revenues from payment for services rendered.

This wide diversity in the nonprofit sector is both what makes it difficult to formulate consistent and appropriate public policy and an effect of existing public policy. Given the size of the nonprofit sector and its extensive interplay with the rest of the economy, however, it is time that we, as a society, make some clear and consistent policy decisions. The policy proposals I favor are on a variety of levels; they address the kinds of activities that nonprofits may and may not engage in, what nonprofits may and may not do to raise funds, how and by what kind of agency the nonprofit sector should be regulated, by what means nonprofits should be subsidized by government—if they are subsidized at all—and how and whether nonprofits should be permitted to compete with proprietary firms.

I feel that the policy process should address three major issues concerning the nonprofit economy. The kinds of outputs nonprofits should and should not produce should be determined. The methods nonprofits may use to generate resources (their funding sources) should be regulated. Finally, the administrative mechanism through which the first two decisions are made should be monitored.

My proposals reflect two goals: (1) to insulate nonprofits from pressures to deviate from the social role they can and should play in a modern, mixed economy, and (2) to help move the economy to a better balance of institutional responsibilities among private enterprises, governments, and nonprofits. I believe nonprofits should be more restricted in some ways, more encouraged in other ways. I intend neither to attack nor to defend nonprofits. They deserve neither implacable foes nor unswerving defenders.

In previous chapters I have made the proposition that when private markets fail to allocate revenues efficiently, other forms of institution may be needed to fill the gap. Government can and does play a major role in regulating market forces but the political and legal constraints on government make this form of institution an imperfect provider of collective goods, including consumer information. Government tends to meet the demands of the majority for collective goods, leaving demands by some minority groups unsatisfied. Because nonprofits are free of this political constraint, they may complement government's activities to overcome limitations of private enterprise.

1. Nonprofits should be encouraged to provide collective goods, and not otherwise. They deserve support for engaging in activities that benefit many people other than their financial supporters, particularly for disseminating information to underinformed consumers and for supplementing direct public financing of collective-type services.

2. Nonprofits should be far more restricted from engaging in "unrelated business activities" that lie outside the range of their tax-exempt activities, and the scope of exempt purposes should be defined in more limited ways. Going into profit-making ventures—"related" or not—may generate revenues for a nonprofit, but in doing so it diverts the organization from its primary social purpose. "Diversification" poses the same problems for nonprofits as it does for private firms. Running a spaghetti factory— as New York University once did—may well strain a university's management even as it adds to its revenues.

As was pointed out in Chapter 6, the expansion of nonprofits' ordinary business activities has presented a growing set of problems, highlighting the fact that the nonprofit economy is far from independent of the private market. This interdependence is the basis for private firms' claims of unfair competition, and, although there remains much to learn about competition between nonprofits and proprietaries, it is likely that to a significant extent nonprofits are choosing to enter markets in which they can employ the same resources that are subsidized for tax-exempt activities. In addition, it is plausible—although, again, knowledge is extremely limited—that the expansion of nonprofit activities into business ventures has an adverse influence on nonprofits' effectiveness. Additional revenues may be generated, but a price is paid in the dissipation of organizational energies; the real costs of such fund raising thus exceed the budgetary costs.

3. *Interlocking control of nonprofits and proprietary firms should be abolished.* Nonprofits should not be permitted to have for-profit subsidiaries. Neither should for-profit firms be allowed to have nonprofit subsidiaries. More generally, interlocking managements of nonprofits and for-profit firms should be prohibited. All of these arrangements now occur and they all provide opportunities for abuse of the nonprofit form of institution, as the examples in Chapter 1 showed. When the two forms of organization are jointly controlled, there are simply too many opportunities for using the nonprofit form to enhance the profit of the proprietary partner. When men or women who are associated with private firms sit on boards of directors of nonprofits, they can and often do see to it that the organization purchases services from the proprietary firms they represent. When nonprofit and proprietary organizations are controlled by the same people, inputs that are used jointly by the two organizations can be accounted for in ways that load costs onto the taxed firm and revenues onto the nonprofit, thus permitting higher aggregate salaries to be paid, at the expense of tax collections.

4. *Tax deductibility should be dropped as the primary public encouragement for contributions.* The shortcomings of this means of stimulating donations are enormous. Any change in the tax system that alters the incentive to itemize tax returns or that changes marginal tax rates affects the incentive of the taxpayer to donate—even when these effects are neither intended nor desired. I reviewed some of these effects in Chapter 5. When income tax rates are cut, for example, the side effect is to shift resources away from nonprofits, since lower tax rates increase the after-tax cost of donating. Similarly, legislation designed to simplify tax returns by reducing the proportion of taxpayers who itemize—as enacted in

1986—has the side effect of increasing the cost to many taxpayers of donating. The Reagan administration's proposal in 1985 to abolish deductibility of state and local property tax payments would have cut further the number of taxpayers who itemized and, in the process, cut donations; whatever the desirability of such a change, its effects on the nonprofit economy would have been adverse—and unintended.

Deductibility has other disadvantages. It distorts nonprofits' activities. Taxpayers in high tax brackets and itemizers receive more tax advantages than other citizens from donating to nonprofits. Since the specific activities of nonprofits depend on their ability to raise funds, the existing system causes high-income persons and itemizers at all income levels to have the principal influence on nonprofit activities. Though not entirely bad, this arrangement is not consistent with the goal of nonprofits serving the broad public interest.

5. To offset the effects of eliminating deductibility, tax credits should be adopted for contributions to approved nonprofits. By contrast with tax deductibility, tax credits—a reduction of the donor's tax bill by a percentage of the donation—would make the after-tax cost of donating the same for all donors, regardless of income tax bracket and itemization status.[2] The credit need not be a 100 percent credit,[3] but it should be the same for all givers, although it could be made to vary among classes of recipient organizations. Furthermore, it could be extended to persons who had no tax liability at all; in that case, government would rebate to the donor a portion of his or her contribution.

6. Special postal subsidies for nonprofits should be abolished and replaced by broader, less restrictive subsidies. When government encourages nonprofits, it should be neutral with regard to the inputs nonprofits employ; there is little if any justification for providing more aid to organizations that use the mails to raise funds or otherwise to carry out their activities than to nonprofits that use telephones, newspapers, radio, or television. Moreover, such special-purpose subsidies pose continuing administrative and legal challenges, as, for example, how to determine whether a postal subsidy for fund raising by mail applies to "informational" material that accompanies the request for funds. Public subsidies should encourage the desired activities without distorting the means of carrying them out.

7. The IRS should be replaced as the principal regulator of the nonprofit sector. Nonprofit organizations are instruments through which social goals of efficiency and equity are pursued, but their principal regulator, the IRS, is basically a tax collection agency, although its Exempt Organizations Branch recognizes its wider responsibilities. Tax revenues certainly are relevant to public policy toward nonprofits—for example, nonprofits accrue a tax liability for "unrelated business income" (profit from activities other than those for which it was granted tax-exempt status)—and so the IRS should retain some responsibility; the administration of broad social policy, however, including determining the appropriate role for nonprofits, belongs elsewhere.[4]

The prospect of collecting additional tax revenue from nonprofits should be a trivial consideration relative to all the effects of nonprofits on the socioeconomic system. For the IRS, a government agency collecting hundreds of billions of dollars in taxes annually, the few millions it collects from nonprofits is insignificant. At the same time, the "watchdog" role over nonprofits involves the IRS in costly and time-consuming litigation, for example, over the constitutional issue of separation of church and state. Only a few years ago the IRS found itself in the middle of such a battle when it sought to withdraw nonprofit status from a church-affiliated college that discriminated against blacks.[5] Tax revenue was a minuscule concern; social policy issues were overriding.

IRS surveillance of the tax liabilities of nonprofits should continue, but much of the IRS's current responsibility should be transferred to another agency having broader responsibilities. This agency should have a regular role in monitoring both the output and financing of nonprofits as they relate to the private and public sectors of the economic system. Moreover, just as the U.S. Departments of Commerce, Labor, and Agriculture have become advocates of private industry, workers, and farmers, and just as the Small Business Administration has defended business groups from "unfair" competition from nonprofits, so too the nonprofits deserve an advocate within government. Current law relating to nonprofits is too vague and not founded on a coherent theoretic or statistical base. To alter that situation society needs an agency whose responsibility is directed specifically to the nonprofit economy—unencumbered by preoccupation with governmental tax revenues. It could play a socially valuable role in building understanding and strengthening legislation defining the appropriate activities of the nonprofit economy.

Establishment of any new agency of government should not be recommended casually. Is yet another bureaucratic arm of government really needed? Caution is more than appropriate; yet the considerable size of the nonprofit economy, its heterogeneity, growth, and expansion into competition with both government and private enterprise make an increasingly powerful rationale for focusing public attention on this part of the economy.

8. *A comprehensive statistical program should be developed to provide data about the nonprofit sector—its size, composition, outputs, fund-raising activities, and interactions with the private market economy.* It is startling how little is known about this large and growing segment of the economy. Its overall contribution to national product remains largely a mystery, as are the detailed sources of its funding through private donations, government grants, sales, dues, and so forth. A major form of resources to nonprofits—volunteer labor—is another mystery, in large part because official labor force statistics disregard it; given the evidence, set out in Chapter 7, that the market value of volunteer labor actually exceeds nonprofits' revenues from donations, the inattention to volunteerism handicaps our understanding of how the nonprofit sector—and, indeed, the labor market as a whole—functions.

Abuses of the special status given to nonprofits are a perennial problem, but we cannot monitor activities we know so little about. An expanded statistical program could be carried out by existing agencies that are experienced at keeping statistics, such as the Census Bureau and the Bureau of Labor Statistics. The agency proposed in recommendation 7, above, could be instrumental in funding and planning for a comprehensive statistical analysis of the nonprofit economy.

Each of these recommendations is offered in the spirit of constructive dialogue. My twin social goal is to take advantage of the unique role that nonprofit organizations can play in a mixed economy, while avoiding their incursion into domains better served by private firms or government. The recommendations all grow out of the work on this book, but I am quick to add that the preceding chapters, while laying the foundation for my policy recommendations, do not justify them fully. Discussion and debate are needed.

Some of these proposals would limit the activities of nonprofits; others would relax existing constraints on them. As we struggle to develop the mechanisms of social-economic policy in this area, we should bear in mind the ever-present danger of abuse of any form of institution. Exemption from taxation on corporate profits and other "tax-expenditure" subsidies, including deductibility of contributions by donors, helps nonprofits provide collective-type services to parts of the population that private markets and government might overlook, yet this same privileged status permits—even encourages—socially inefficient and inequitable action. All laws and regulations, including those applying to the nonprofit economy, are inevitably imperfectly enforced; organizations performing no socially useful purpose, seeking only to take private advantage of imperfectly enforced rules, can enter the nonprofit sector and, in the process, reduce public confidence in the sector—with unfortunate effects on legislation, fund raising, volunteering, and so on. As a result, it is in the interest of society, but also of the vast majority of nonprofits whose activities are socially valuable, to restrict the fund-raising and service activities of all nonprofits in order to maintain and enhance the reputation of the sector as a whole.

By focusing attention on nonprofit organizations, I have sought to direct attention to this "hidden" part of the economy; it is part of our daily lives, but at the same time it is an enigma. I have also tried to highlight the economic-political-social problem of institutional choice—the continuing process of developing institutions to meet changing needs. The search for the comparative advantage of each form of institution is the problem of institutional choice.

As with all kinds of hybrids, the nonprofit institution is in some respects quite strange. It is private, yet it is restricted in its ability to reward organizers and managers by distributing among them the organization's profit or surplus. In the process, incentives to be efficient are reduced. But the lure of profit, although powerful, is not the only, nor necessarily the best, motivator, particularly when informational handicaps beset consumers.

A major function of any economy is to encourage—that is, to reward—those who contribute to the public interest. When that contribution is difficult to monitor, it cannot be rewarded. Trade-offs are inevitable. We cannot simultaneously have institutions that have strong incentives to be efficient and also expect those institutions to have strong incentives to share information with consumers and to distribute outputs to other than the highest bidders. What we can do is to search for institutional mechanisms that contribute to an optimal balancing of incentives. The nonprofit institution—"warts and all"—has a great deal to offer a society working toward that goal.

Characteristics of the Nonprofit Economy

Table A.1 Number of nonprofit and for-profit corporations, 1967–1985 (thousands)

| Year (as of June 30) | Nonprofit Organizations[a] | | For-profit Corporations |
	Total	Tax Deductible[b]	
1967	309	*	1,534
1968	358	*	1,542
1969	416	138	1,659
1970	*	*	1,665
1971	*	*	1,733
1972	535	*	1,813
1973	630	*	1,905
1974	673	*	1,966
1975	692	*	2,024
1976	763	260	2,105
1977	790	276	2,242
1978	810	294	2,377
1979	825	304	2,557
1980	846	320	2,711
1981	851	328	2,812
1982	841	323	2,926
1983	845	336	2,999
1984	871	353	*
1985	887	366	*

Source: Nonprofit organizations: U.S. Internal Revenue Service, *Annual Report: Commissioner of Internal Revenue* (Washington, D.C.: Internal Revenue Service), 1968, p. 9; 1969, p. 14; 1972, p. 13; 1974, p. 32; 1977, p. 141; 1978, p. 101; 1979, p. 70; 1980, p. 76; U.S. Internal Revenue Service, *Annual Report: Commissioner of Internal Revenue and Chief Counsel for the Internal Revenue Service* (Washington, D.C.: Internal Revenue Service), 1981, p. 54; 1982, p. 60; 1984, p. 70; 1985, p. 70. For-profit corporations: U.S. Bureau of the Census, *Statistical Abstract of the United States: 1971* (Washington, D.C.: Government Printing Office), p. 459; *1975*, p. 490; *1979*, p. 553; *1982–83*, p. 528; *1985*, p. 516; *1986*, p. 517; *1987*, p. 503.

a. Data for nonprofits are not available prior to 1967.

b. An organization is counted as tax deductible here if it meets the requirements of Section 501(c)(3) of the Internal Revenue Code. There is a small number of organizations that are tax deductible under other 501(c) subsections.

* Data not available.

Table A.2 Number and disposition of applications for nonprofit status, 1956–1985

Year	Approved[a]	Disapproved	Other[b]	Percent Approved
1956	5,373	342	1,482	75
1957	5,015	371	1,723	71
1958	4,865	311	1,855	69
1959	4,920	317	1,557	72
1960	4,907	330	1,433	74
1961	4,780	362	1,439	73
1962	4,554	416	1,359	72
1963	4,871	328	1,102	77
1964	6,936	463	1,436	79
1965	11,929	717	1,668	83
1966	13,445	885	1,972	82
1967	13,672	814	2,136	82
1968	14,640	935	2,429	81
1969–76		Not available		
1977	36,017	2,389	8,661	77
1978	35,214	2,192	10,354	74
1979	35,342	2,536	10,637	73
1980	36,980	1,914	10,640	75
1981	36,854	1,639	13,853	70
1982	38,434	1,510	12,260	74
1983	38,604	1,180	14,163	72
1984	44,173	1,389	19,006	68
1985	44,205	1,076	14,216	74

Source: U.S. Internal Revenue Service, *Annual Report: Commissioner of Internal Revenue* (Washington, D.C.: Internal Revenue Service), 1956, p. 48; 1957, p. 45; 1958, p. 49; 1959, p. 52; 1960, p. 12; 1961, p. 16; 1962, p. 11; 1963, p. 7; 1964, p. 5; 1965, p. 6; 1966, p. 6; 1967, p. 10; 1968, p. 9; 1977, p. 141; 1978, p. 101; 1979, p. 70; 1980, p. 76; U.S. Internal Revenue Service, *Annual Report: Commissioner of Internal Revenue and Chief Counsel for the Internal Revenue Service* (Washington, D.C.: Internal Revenue Service), 1981, p. 54; 1982, p. 60; 1983, p. 64; 1984, p. 70; 1985, p. 70.

a. Breakdowns by Internal Revenue Code subsection are available since 1977.

b. Application withdrawn by taxpayer or not acted upon because of lack of required information.

Table A.3 Percent of all assets in the United States owned by government and nonprofit organizations, 1953 and 1975

| Year | Government | | | Nonprofit Organizations |
	Federal	State/Local	Total	
1953	7.5	5.6	13.1	1.5
1975	3.9	8.5	12.4	1.8

Source: Data in Raymond W. Goldsmith, *The National Balance Sheet of the United States, 1953–1980* (Chicago: University of Chicago Press, 1982), table 62, p. 146, table 76, p. 169, table 78, p. 172. For details on what is counted as an asset, see especially p. 23.

Table A.4 Assets of nonprofit organizations, selected years, 1953–1975

| Year | Total Assets (billion dollars) | | Percent of GNP | Percent of National Assets |
	Current	1972		
1953	42	72	11.5	1.5
1958	64	101	13.7	1.6
1963	90	135	14.6	1.7
1968	133	164	14.7	1.7
1973	210	181	15.4	1.8
1975	243	176	15.1	1.8

Source: Data in Raymond W. Goldsmith, *The National Balance Sheet of the United States, 1953–1980* (Chicago: University of Chicago Press, 1982), table 62, p. 147.

Table A.5 Percent of national income originating in the nonprofit sector, 1929–1985

Year	Percent	Year	Percent	Year	Percent
1929	3.3	1948	2.5	1967	3.5
1930	3.6	1949	2.7	1968	3.6
1931	3.9	1950	2.7	1969	3.5
1932	4.4	1951	2.5	1970	4.0
1933	4.2	1952	2.5	1971	3.9
1934	3.6	1953	2.6	1972	3.9
1935	3.3	1954	2.7	1973	3.8
1936	3.1	1955	2.8	1974	3.9
1937	3.1	1956	2.8	1975	4.1
1938	3.3	1957	2.9	1976	4.0
1939	3.2	1958	3.1	1977	3.9
1940	3.0	1959	3.1	1978	3.9
1941	2.4	1960	3.3	1979	3.8
1942	2.1	1961	3.3	1980	4.0
1943	1.9	1962	3.3	1981	4.1
1944	2.0	1963	3.3	1982	4.4
1945	2.3	1964	3.3	1983	4.4
1946	2.5	1965	3.4	1984	4.3
1947	2.6	1966	3.3	1985	4.4

Source: U.S. Bureau of the Census, *Statistical Abstract of the United States, 1982–83* (Washington, D.C.: Government Printing Office, 1982), 423; *1985,* p. 436; U.S. Bureau of the Census, *Historical Statistics of the United States, Part 1* (Washington, D.C.: Government Printing Office, 1976), 237.

Note: Income from the nonprofit sector includes compensation of employees in private households; social and athletic clubs; labor organizations; nonprofit schools and hospitals; religious, charitable, and welfare organizations; and all other nonprofit organizations serving individuals.

Table A.6 Ratio of full-time equivalent (FTE) workers to revenues and to assets, selected sectors, 1976

Sector, Industry, or Ownership Type	No. of FTE Workers per $1 Million Revenues	No. of FTE Workers per $1 Million Assets
Economy as a whole	5.50	
Service sector	7.19	
Government enterprises	6.31	
Health	6.33	
Hospitals		4.85
Government		5.92
For-profit		4.78
Nonprofit		4.38
Nursing homes	9.29	
Government	9.42	
For-profit	8.71	
Nonprofit	10.10	
Education	5.03	
Government	5.35	
Private	3.69	
Social Services	12.16	
Legal Services	11.22	
Art Museums	5.73	
Government	5.91	
Nonprofit	5.41	

Source: Burton A. Weisbrod, "Assets and Employment in the Nonprofit Sector," *Public Finance Quarterly* 10 (October 1982), 403–426.

Table A.7 Percent of hours of labor donated, by type of recipient organization, 1973

Type of Organization	Percent
Religious	18
Health	3
Educational	4
Cultural	1
Social services and welfare	1
Community action	3
Combined appeal	2
Environmental	2
Public affairs	1
Private foundation	10
International	3
Noncharitable (political)	*
Other noncharitable	29
Other charitable	*
Unknown	24
Total	100[a]

Source: University of Michigan Survey Research Center, *Survey of Giving* (Ann Arbor, Mich.: Survey Research Center, 1974).

a. The estimated total number of hours donated is 5.66 billion.

* Less than 0.5 percent.

Table A.8 Percent of persons age 14 and over reporting donations of labor in the past twelve months, by type of recipient organization, 1981 and 1985

	Percent	
Type of Organization	1981	1985
Religious	19	23
Health	12	9
Educational	12	13
Arts and cultural	3	4
Social services and welfare	5	7
Recreational	7	10
Civic, social, and fraternal	6	8
Political	6	4
Community action	6	4
Justice-related	1	1
Work-related	5	4
General fund raiser	6	11
Informal (no organization involved)	23	19
Other	1	*
Total	112[a]	117[a]
None	48	52

Source: The Gallup Organization, *Americans Volunteer 1985* (Princeton, N.J.: The Gallup Organization, February 1986), 9.

a. Totals come to more than 100 percent because some people volunteer time to more than one type of organization. Since 48 percent of persons in 1981 and 52 percent in 1985 reportedly gave no volunteer labor, the remaining half averaged donations of time to more than two types of organizations.

* Less than 0.5 percent.

Table A.9 Number of active entities on exempt organization master file, by Internal Revenue Code (IRC) section, 1969–1985[a]

IRC Section		1969	1976	1978	1980	1982	1984	1985
501(c)(1)	Corporations organized under Act of Congress[b]	961	1,067	25	42	24	24	24
501(c)(2)	Title holding corporations	3,992	5,114	5,272	5,358	5,522	5,679	5,758
501(c)(3)	Religious, charitable, etc.[c]	137,487	259,523	293,947	319,842	322,826	352,884	366,071
501(c)(4)	Social welfare	104,546	125,415	125,317	129,553	131,578	130,344	131,250
501(c)(5)	Labor, agriculture	77,737	87,412	87,531	85,774	86,322	76,753	75,632
501(c)(6)	Business leagues	27,594	42,120	45,325	48,717	51,065	53,303	54,217
501(c)(7)	Social, recreation clubs	36,189	47,820	49,964	51,922	54,036	55,666	57,343
501(c)(8)	Fraternal beneficiary societies	989	141,725	140,963	137,449	116,549	92,431	94,435
501(c)(9)	Voluntary employee's beneficiary societies	4,330	6,271	6,827	7,738	8,703	10,145	10,668
501(c)(10)	Domestic fraternal beneficiary societies	467	11,612	12,199	16,178	18,570	16,116	15,924
501(c)(11)	Teacher's retirement funds	14	14	11	12	13	11	11
501(c)(12)	Benevolent life insurance associations	4,211	4,685	4,863	4,945	5,071	5,200	5,244
501(c)(13)	Cemetery companies	3,809	4,959	5,529	5,997	6,290	6,845	7,239
501(c)(14)	Credit unions	5,022	4,686	5,118	5,639	6,074	6,053	6,032
501(c)(15)	Mutual insurance companies	1,728	1,454	1,408	1,140	1,073	998	967
501(c)(16)	Corporations for financing crop operations	39	30	28	22	22	19	18

501(c)(17)	Supplemental unemployment benefit trusts	674	790	807	806	784	747	726
501(c)(18)	Employee-funded pension trusts	—[a]	4	4	4	3	3	3
501(c)(19)	War veterans' organizations	—	13,960	21,233	22,247	23,851	22,100	23,062
501(c)(20)	Legal service organizations	—	0	4	46	90	140	167
501(c)(21)	Black lung trusts	—	—	0	0	9	14	15
501(d)	Religious and apostolic organizations	40	59	67	67	68	81	82
521	Farmer's cooperatives	6,462	3,969	3,606	2,985	2,791	2,673	2,542
	Totals[e]	416,291	762,689	810,048	846,433	841,334	871,224	886,658

Source: U.S. Internal Revenue Service. Annual Report: Commissioner of Internal Revenue (Washington, D.C.: Internal Revenue Service), 1969, p. 14; 1978, p. 101; 1980, p. 76; U.S. Internal Revenue Service, Annual Report: Commissioner of Internal Revenue and Chief Counsel for the Internal Revenue Service (Washington, D.C.: Internal Revenue Service), 1982, p. 60; 1984, p. 70; 1985, p. 70.

a. Data are not available prior to 1969 or for the years 1970–1975. Tax-deductible organizations are those in IRC section 501(c), subsections (3), (10), (13), and (19).

b. The decrease after 1976 resulted from a reclassification.

c. All organizations exempt under IRC Section 501(c)(3) are not included here because certain organizations, such as churches and integrated auxiliaries, need not apply for recognition of exemption unless they desire a ruling.

d. — indicates that the category did not exist in that year.

e. Totals may exceed the sum of the numbers in the columns because they include cooperative hospitals and educational organizations.

Table A.10 Gross receipts of nonprofit social welfare organizations, for fiscal years 1973–1982 (billion dollars)

Type of Organization	1973	1975	1977	1979	1980	1982
501(c)(3)	57.0	65.5	95.5	141.3	158.5	234.2
501(c)(4)	15.0	19.5	30.5	45.3	51.0	58.5
Total	72.0	85.0	136.0	186.8	209.5	292.7
As percent of GNP	5.4	5.5	6.6	7.7	8.0	9.5

Source: Receipts: 1973–80—Nelson Rosenbaum and Bruce L. R. Smith, "The Fiscal Capacity of the Voluntary Sector," Brookings Institution, Washington, D.C., December 1981, 13; 1982—Internal Revenue Service, *Statistics of Income* data as reported in United States General Accounting Office, *Tax Policy: Competition between Taxable Businesses and Tax-exempt Organizations* (GAO/GGD-87-40BR), February 1987, 57 and 59; GNP—U.S. Bureau of the Census, *Statistical Abstract of the United States: 1986*, 106th ed. (Washington, D.C.: Government Printing Office, 1985), 431.

Table A.11   Tax-exempt service industries in the United States, 1977

Industry	Number of Establishments	Expenses (billion dollars)	Payroll (billion dollars)	Paid Employees (thousands)
All tax-exempt service industries	165,614	85.37	41.69	4,950
Public-type				
Health services (all)	12,307	43.96	22.85	2,431
Nursing and personal care facilities	2,331	2.22	1.20	202
Hospitals	3,624	39.20	20.33	2,098
Outpatient facilities	4,178	1.80	0.92	85
Other	2,174	0.74	0.39	46
Educational services (all)	9,160	14.03	7.22	932
Elementary/secondary schools (not church-related)	3,297	1.30	0.74	99
Colleges, universities, professional schools, and junior colleges	1,755	12.03	6.16	784
Libraries and information centers	1,386	0.18	0.91	13
Correspondence and vocational schools	790	0.16	0.07	11
Other schools and educational services	1,932	0.36	0.16	25

(continued)

Table A.11 (continued)

Industry	Number of Establishments	Expenses (billion dollars)	Payroll (billion dollars)	Paid Employees (thousands)
Public-type (continued)				
Social services (all)	40,983	8.29	4.12	676
Individual and family social services	12,440	2.24	1.14	167
Job training and vocational rehabilitation	3,396	1.05	0.61	138
Child day care	10,641	0.83	0.49	102
Residential care	5,603	1.86	0.88	135
Other social services	8,903	2.32	0.99	133
Legal aid organizations	1,101	0.26	0.15	12
Museums, art galleries, and botanical and zoological gardens	2,252	0.61	0.27	32
Noncommercial	1,832	0.48	0.21	25
Commercial	420	0.13	0.06	7
Proprietary-type				
Membership organizations, except religious	82,666	12.07	4.41	600
Business associations	11,748	2.31	0.82	69
Professional membership organizations	4,870	1.28	0.43	35
Labor unions	23,418	3.47	1.30	179

Civic, social, and fraternal organizations	34,121	3.61	1.34	256
Political organizations	1,123	0.11	0.03	4
Other	7,366	1.29	0.48	58
Organization-owned hotels and lodging houses, for use on membership basis	3,096	2.20	0.05	13
Commercial laboratories	446	1.21	0.59	36
Amusement and recreational organizations	7,138	2.13	0.94	122
Producers, orchestras and entertainers	1,228	0.52	0.24	27
Membership sports and recreation clubs	5,910	1.60	0.69	94
Other: sporting and recreational camps and noncommercial educational, scientific, and research organizations	6,465	3.33	1.08	95

Source: U.S. Bureau of the Census, *1977 Census of Service Industries: Other Service Industries* (Washington, D.C.: Government Printing Office, 1979), x.

Table A.12 Growth of selected nonprofit service industries, 1977–1982

Industry	Number of Establishments (thousands)	
	1982	1977
Public-type		
Selected health services	10.0	8.7
Nursing facilities	3.0	2.3
Outpatient-care facilities	4.7	4.2
Health/allied services	2.2	2.2
Legal aid	1.3	1.1
Social services	52.6	41.0
Child day-care facilities	12.7	10.6
Proprietary-type		
Selected membership organizations	61.3	58.1
Business associations	12.1	11.7
Civic, social, and fraternal associations	35.4	34.1

Source: Adapted from *Non-profit Service Organizations: 1982,* as Assembled by the National Center for Charitable Statistics, from the 1982 Census of Service Industries Conducted by the U.S. Bureau of the Census (Washington, D.C.: National Center for Charitable Statistics, May 1985), 6.

Table A.13 Percent distribution of collectiveness index values within selected industries, for tax-deductible nonprofits, 1976

Industry (Activity Code)	Collectiveness Index				Number of Organizations
	0–24	25–49	50–74	75–100	
Schools (030)	69	11	8	12	613
Nursing homes (152)	76	3	6	15	88
Blood banks (156)	92	4	0	4	26
Scientific research (diseases) (161)	54	7	8	31	3,077
Civil rights (430)	30	2	3	65	299
Helping the poor (560)	51	6	4	39	476
Day-care centers (574)	56	7	6	31	566

Source: IRS form 990 data tapes.

Table A.14 Mean age of organizations by industry and Internal Revenue Code subsection, 1977[a]

Industry (Activity Code)[b]	Mean Age[c] (years)		
	501(c)(3) Organizations	501(c)(4) Organizations	Other Organizations
Education[d]			
School (030)	13	28	38
Nursery school (032)	9	7	28
Alumni group (034)	17	17	26
PTA (035)	11	20	17
Fraternity/sorority (036)	13	25	21
Scholarships (040)	8	15	19
Culture			
Library (061)	17	20	15
Historical site (062)	12	11	21
Commemorative event (064)	11	10	26
Fair (065)	16	20	18
Other instruction or training			
Publishing (120)	10	9	18
Discussion groups, etc. (123)	2	2	4
Study and research (124)	2	10	12
Health			
Hospital (150)	23	22	17
Health clinic (154)	13	21	21
Aid to handicapped (160)	11	23	30
Scientific research (diseases) (161)	14	20	18
Business and professions			
Business promotion (200)	13	13	12
Real estate association (201)	10	11	15
Professional association (205)	15	11	11
Employee or membership benefit			
Association of employees (263)	19	16	22
Employee and member welfare (264)	21	19	17
Youth activities			
Camp (325)	18	27	26
Juvenile delinquency programs (328)	9	19	19
Conservation and environment			
Preservation of natural resources (350)	26	19	22
Garden club (356)	12	11	13

(continued)

Table A.14 (continued)

	Mean Age[c] (years)		
Industry (Activity Code)[b]	501(c)(3) Organizations	501(c)(4) Organizations	Other Organizations
Housing			
Housing for the aged (382)	17	8	19
Inner city or community development			
Area development/renewal (400)	4	3	9
Attracting industry (403)	7	10	16
Volunteer firemen (407)	5	16	26
Political action and legislation			
Propose, support, or oppose legislation (480)	42	40	59
Activities directed to other organizations			
Community chest (600)	16	24	26
Gifts, grants, loans (602)	11	23	25
Nonfinancial services to other organizations (603)	3	2	5

Source: IRS form 990 data tapes.

a. Data from all organizations filing at least one tax return between 1971 and 1977. All such organizations were assumed to continue to exist as of 1977.

b. Industries included are those whose first activity code listed are codes for which there were at least ten organizations reporting positive gross receipts in each subsection group, except that organizations engaged in religious activities and activities referred to as "other" have been excluded.

c. An organization's age is the difference between 1977 and the year in which it received nonprofit status.

d. Data for the education sector are taken from a 20 percent sample of all education-related nonprofits.

Table A.15 Age distribution of nonprofits, 1977

Industry[a]	Percent Receiving Exempt Status[b]		
	1971–77	1965–70	Pre-1965
Education	33	23	44
Health	39	16	45
Culture	43	18	39
Welfare	56	16	28
Mutuals	79	2	19
Inner city and community development	54	16	30
Scientific research	77	2	21
Advocacy	18	76	6
Business and professions	42	26	32
Legislative and political action	44	22	34
Employee or membership benefit	22	21	57
Sports, athletic, and social clubs	37	22	41
Conservation and environment	26	14	60
Civil rights	38	16	46
Youth	40	16	44
Housing	43	21	36
Litigation and legal aid	96	3	1

Source: IRS form 990 data tapes.

a. An organization is classified according to the first activity code it listed.

b. Year of receipt of exempt status is the year of the IRS ruling, even though in some cases exempt status is granted retroactively.

Table A.16 Size distribution of nonprofits, for selected industries and cities, 1976

| | Industry | | | | | | | | |
| | Health | | | Education | | | Environment | | |
City	Percent Small	Percent Large	Number	Percent Small	Percent Large	Number	Percent Small	Percent Large	Number
Newark	39	4	157	36	6	123	36	0	14
Cleveland	32	5	219	45	5	176	59	3	39
Boston	26	7	243	26	10	220	49	5	39
Milwaukee	48	4	183	39	6	142	69	0	52
Seattle	29	4	203	42	3	121	60	0	30
San Jose	40	2	121	56	4	79	100	0	5
Phoenix	30	3	142	37	7	90	68	0	25
Houston	32	7	117	46	6	106	65	0	17

Source: IRS Form 990 data tapes.

Note: Small organizations are those whose gross annual receipts are less than $10,000. Large organizations are those whose gross annual receipts are over $1 million.

Table A.17 Four-organization concentration ratios, by industry group and city, 1976

| City | Industry Group | | | |
	Health	Welfare	Advocacy	Culture
Boston	.33	.36	.64	.39
Newark	.50	.51	.60	.65
Atlanta	.43	.46	.32	.57
Cleveland	.22	.25	.84	.67
Milwaukee	.93	.94	.62	.46
Houston	.38	.38	.63	.45
Phoenix	.34	.35	.90	.34
Seattle	.20	.20	.92	.47
San Jose	.25	.26	.91	.77

Source: IRS form 990 data tapes.

Note: The concentration ratio is the proportion of total revenues of all the nonprofits in the given industry group and city that is accounted for by the largest four nonprofits.

Table A.18 Number of establishments and expenditures, selected nonprofit service industries, 1977 and 1982

Industry	Number of Establishments		Expenditures (billion dollars)		Elasticity[b]
	1977	Percent Change 1977–82	1977	Percent Change 1977–82[a]	
Nursing and personal care	2,331	31	2.2	55	1.8
Outpatient health care	4,178	13	1.8	60	4.6
Legal aid	1,101	18	0.26	3	0.3
Child care	10,641	19	0.83	21	1.1
Business associations	11,748	3	2.3	43	14.3
Education, science, and research	1,914	2	1.4	31	15.5

Source: Non-profit Service Organizations: 1982, as Assembled by the National Center for Charitable Statistics, from the 1982 Census of Service Industries Conducted by the U.S. Bureau of the Census (Washington, D.C.: National Center for Charitable Statistics, May 1985), 6. Calculations of percent changes and elasticities are my own. The consumer price index was 181.5 in 1977 (1967 = 100) and 289.1 for 1982, according to *Economic Indicators,* Prepared for the Joint Economic Committee by the Council of Economic Advisers (Washington, D.C.: Government Printing Office, September 1985), 23.

a. Increase in real expenditures, measured as the increase in nominal expenditures minus the increase in the Consumer Price Index, 59 percent.

b. Percent change in real expenditures divided by percent change in number of establishments—that is, column 4 divided by column 2.

Table A.19 Regional variation in nonprofit-sector activity, 1977

Region	Nonprofit Organizations per 100,000 Population	Nonprofit Expenditures per Capita (dollars)
Northeast	58.2	522
North Central	50.2	348
West	48.4	262
South	36.8	208
United States	47.1	323

Source: Lester Salamon, *The Nonprofit Sector and the Rise of Third Party Government: The Scope, Character and Consequences of Government Support of Nonprofit Organizations* (Washington, D.C.: The Urban Institute Press, 1983), 18, as computed from U.S. Bureau of the Census, *1977 Census of Service Industries.*

Table A.20 Share of beds in nonprofit nursing homes, by geographic region, 1980

Type of Ownership	Percent of All Beds				
	United States	Northeast	North Central	South	West
All types	100	21	34	27	18
Nonprofit	22	27	41	19	13

Source: A. Sirrocco, "Nursing and Related Care Homes as Reported from the 1980 NMFI Survey," *Vital and Health Statistics*, Series 14, No. 29, DHHS Publication No. (PHS) 84–1824 (Washington, D.C.: Government Printing Office, December 1983), table 6, p. 11.

Table A.21 Distribution of short-term community hospital beds, by census region, 1984

Region	Total Number of Beds	Percent Distribution		
		Nonprofit	For-profit	Government
New England	50,963	93	1	6
Middle Atlantic	168,307	88	3	10
South Atlantic	165,969	59	17	24
East North Central	193,670	85	1	14
East South Central	75,546	49	18	34
West North Central	97,738	72	4	24
West South Central	111,789	48	22	30
Mountain	44,001	66	10	25
Pacific	109,074	64	17	19

Source: American Hospital Association, *Hospital Statistics, 1985 Edition* (Chicago, 1985), table 5B. (Excludes federal hospitals.)

Table A.22 Distribution of ownership in selected industries[a]

| Industry | Percent of Output | | | Unit of Measure |
	Government	Nonprofit	For-profit	
1. Nursing homes	8	22	70	Beds
2. General hospitals	26	65	9	Beds
3. Kidney dialysis	12	48	40	Stations
4. Day care	9	40	51	Children
5. Post-secondary education (includes vocational schools)	47	20	34	Revenues
6. Research and development	12	15	73	Spending
7. Health insurance	12	43	45	Persons served
8. Sporting and recreational camps	[b]	26	74	Expenses/receipts
9. Commercial research and development	[b]	36	64	Expenses/receipts
10. Libraries and information centers	[b]	95	5	Expenses/receipts
11. Bands, orchestras, dance groups, actors and other entertainers and groups	[b]	27	73	Expenses/receipts

Source: Row 1: A. Sirrocco, "Nursing and Related Care Homes as Reported from the 1980 NMFI Survey," *Vital and Health Statistics,* Series 14, No. 29, DHHS Publication No. (PHS) 84–1824 (Washington, D.C.: Government Printing Office, December 1983), table 6, p. 11.

Row 2: American Hospital Association, *Hospital Statistics, 1985 Edition* (Chicago, 1985), table 2A, p. 8; 1984 data for short-term hospitals.

Row 3: "National Listing of Providers Furnishing Kidney Dialysis and Transplant Services," U.S. Department of Health and Human Services, Health Care Finance Agency, June 1981.

Row 4: Mary Keyserling, *Windows on Day Care* (New York: National Council of Jewish Women, 1972).

Row 5: M. Bendick, Jr., "Essays on Education as a Three-Sector Industry," Ph.D. diss., Department of Economics, University of Wisconsin—Madison, 1975.

Row 6: U.S. Bureau of the Census, *Statistical Abstract of the United States: 1986* (Washington, D.C.: Government Printing Office, 1985), table 996, p. 578 (based on 1983 data).

Row 7: Source Book of Health Insurance Data, 1976–77 (New York: Insurance Institute, n.d.).

Rows 8–11: (1) U.S. Bureau of the Census, *1977 Census of Service Industries: Part 1. Selected Service Industries, U.S. Summary* (Washington, D.C.: Government Printing Office, 1979), table 1: "Summary Statistics for the U.S.: 1977," pp. 8–9, and (2) U.S. Bureau of the Census, *1977 Census of Service Industries: Part 4. Other Service Industries,* "Summary Statistics for the U.S.: 1977" (no table number), pp. x–xi. For rows 8, 9, and 11, data for tax-exempt establishments came from the second source and data for taxable establishments came from the first. Row 10 data are entirely from the second source, which had data for both taxable and tax-exempt establishments. "Tax-exempt" and "taxable" organizations are assumed to correspond to the nonprofit and for-profit categories; "taxable organizations" are defined as "establishments subject to Federal income tax" (*Part 4,* p. vii). In the case of tax-exempt service industries, the output measure is "expenses." For taxable industries, the measure is "receipts." (The two measures are assumed to be approximately the same.) Data apply to those establishments "with payroll."

a. Data apply to various years, as indicated in the sources.

b. Data for government not available.

The Nonprofit Sector around the World

Types of Nonprofits in Other Countries

Nonprofits are not uniquely American. They engage in a wide variety of activities in many countries. There are about 120,000 officially registered nonprofit charities in the United Kingdom, for example, many of them in health-related fields.[1] The hospital industry, although dominated by the government-sector National Health Service, also has a private nonprofit component, which includes the facilities operated by the Nuffield Nursing Home Trust.[2] Other nonprofit organizations in Britain include Action on Smoking and Health (ASH), which was set up in 1971 by a group of physicians with the goal of limiting smoking; its main activity is providing information to the public, doctors, media, and politicians.[3]

Half of the nursing homes and facilities for the "frail ambulant" in Israel are reported to be "nonprofit."[4] All four of the hospitals in Jerusalem are nonprofit; until March 1, 1984, all received a large share of their total revenues from private donations, but then one of the hospitals formed a partnership with the nongovernmental health insurance system operated by the (nonprofit) Histadrut labor federation.[5]

Welfare state services in the Netherlands are customarily provided by nonprofits; these include day care, facilities for the physically and mentally handicapped, and social work services. By contrast with the United States, though, the Dutch nonprofits are financed almost exclusively—90–95 percent—by government; only 5 percent of their income is from private donations or commodity sales.[6]

Nonprofits also perform a variety of social services in Spain, where a major component of the financial industry is nonprofit. "La Caixa" is a community welfare and financial institution that today is the largest savings bank in the country. "Its principal purposes are to encourage savings and to finance economic activities, and to channel its operating surplus back to the community by means of welfare projects."[7] In 1983 alone it opened 15 new cultural and welfare centers—ten of them clubs for senior citizens—and organized 41 scientific and art exhibitions; it also produced learning games for children.[8]

One specific form of nonprofit organization, the "public-interest law" (PIL) firm, has been studied in some detail. These firms, heavily supported by private foundations in the United States, rose to prominence in the 1970s. They utilize litigation and other instruments of the law for the purpose of representing people whose individual interests in some outcome—such as cleaner air or higher-quality television programming for children—are small but whose collective interests are large. In a study conducted by Joel Handler, Neil Komesar, and me, we were repeatedly told that there were no counterparts to them outside the United States.[9] Our survey, however, turned up quite similar organizations in a number of other countries. In Italy a PIL organization, the Italia Nostra, dealt with environmental preservation. In France PIL organizations, the "consumer associations," focused on consumer problems. And in Japan the "residents' movements" *(jumin undo)* and the Young Lawyers' Association *(seihokyo)* dealt with pollution-related issues.[10]

To fight Poland's serious air and water pollution problems, a group of academics and businessmen formed the Polish Ecology Club in 1980. It quickly grew to 14 branches having 20,000 members.[11]

Nonprofit organizations engage in "consumer protection" activities in many countries. They are active not only in the economically developed countries, but also in Malaysia and "in nearly every developing country, from Barbados to Bangladesh."[12]

Educational nonprofits are also widespread. They are found in the Netherlands, India, Japan, Malaysia, Sri Lanka, and Sweden.[13] Their importance in a country seems to be related systematically to the diversity of demands for education.[14]

Resource Support of Nonprofits in Other Countries

Charitable contributions are treated in a variety of ways among countries. They are not tax deductible in Sweden,[15] for example, but they are in Canada and in Japan (provided they exceed a given threshold, currently 10,000 yen, or around $60).[16] In Israel, individuals who donate to nonprofit organizations may take a *credit* for 35 percent of the donation up to an annual limit of $30,000.[17] More generally, a study by the international accounting firm Arthur Andersen and Company of the tax treatment of charitable giving across countries concluded that "direct and indirect governmental support of the private philanthropic sector varies inversely with the involvement of government itself in providing social services."[18]

Just as donations of money receive different tax treatment in different countries, so, too, is volunteer labor encouraged in different ways. In Sweden, a major report by the Swedish Secretariat for Futures Studies, "Care and Welfare at the Crossroads," recommended that care for the society's aged and handicapped be increasingly supplied by volunteers; all adults aged 19 to 65 would be required to supply 4–6 hours of care per week.[19] Of course, if legislation to this effect were enacted the labor supplied would be more like a "draft"—a tax—than like volunteered labor, but there would indeed arise a supply of labor that would be unpaid and, hence, might well not be counted in traditional labor force statistics. The motivations for the unpriced labor would be quite different in the draft case than in the volunteer case, and for this reason some of the productivity effects would differ.

The Israel Voluntary Services Agency was created—with governmental support—in 1972 to organize and coordinate volunteer workers in such areas as education, health care, and social services.[20] Little is known, however, about its effectiveness or about the overall quantitative importance of volunteer labor in Israeli society or, for that matter, throughout the world.

What estimates of donated labor do exist show a wide range of relative levels. For example, a recent survey in Austria found that the full-time equivalent amount of volunteer labor was about 7.8 percent of the regular labor force, although two-thirds of this was of an "informal" sort—that is, work "done outside traditional voluntary organizations."[21] In Sri Lanka, on the other hand, volunteer labor is a far more important source of resources for the nonprofit sector—more important, at least, relative to monetary donations—than it is even in the United States. It has been estimated as 400 percent of domestic contributions of money,[22] compared with 140 percent in the U.S.[23]

The utilization of volunteers in the Netherlands is in sharp contrast: "a commitment to the use of volunteers does not find support either in the professional or the organizational ideologies of the [voluntary] sector."[24] When the executives of 23 Dutch organizations were questioned about their use of volunteers, few "seemed to regard the work of volunteers as particularly important. While the . . . organizations were generally satisfied with their limited use of volunteers, there were no formal programs of recruiting, training, assigning, supervising, or the evaluation of volunteers."[25] This low level of involvement of volunteer workers in Holland is particularly intriguing in the light of the major overall role of the nonprofit sector in that country, as noted above.

Financing Nonprofits

Table C.1   Charitable donations, by source, 1970–1985

Year	Individuals		Foundations	Corporations	
	Amount (billion dollars)	Percent of Personal Income	Amount (billion dollars)	Amount (billion dollars)	Percent of Pretax Profit
1970	16.2	1.95	1.9	0.8	1.05
1971	17.6	1.97	2.0	0.9	0.99
1972	19.4	1.97	2.0	1.0	1.00
1973	20.5	1.86	2.0	1.2	0.93
1974	21.6	1.79	2.1	1.2	0.87
1975	23.5	1.79	1.7	1.2	0.90
1976	26.3	1.81	1.9	1.5	0.89
1977	29.6	1.84	2.0	1.8	0.92
1978	32.1	1.77	2.2	2.1	0.91
1979	36.6	1.80	2.4	2.3	0.91
1980	40.7	1.80	2.8	2.4	1.01
1981	46.4	1.84	3.1	2.5	1.14
1982	48.5	1.82	3.2	2.9	1.76
1983	53.5	1.89	3.6	3.3	1.62
1984	60.7	1.95	4.0	3.8	1.61
1985	66.1	2.01	4.3	4.3	1.89

Source: American Association of Fund-Raising Counsel, *Giving USA* (New York: American Association of Fund-Raising Counsel, 1986), 15, 20, 33.

Table C.2   Private contributions to nonprofit organizations, 1955–1984

Year	Total^a (billion dollars)	Percent of National Income	Percent of Organizational Expenditures
1984	73.3	2.41	32.7
1983	65.0	2.39	31.2
1982	60.1	2.46	33.1
1981	55.9	2.36	34.5
1980	49.1	2.32	34.3
1979	43.7	2.22	34.8
1978	39.0	2.21	34.8
1977	36.3	2.34	36.6
1976	32.1	2.32	35.0
1975	28.6	2.31	34.2
1974	27.0	2.32	35.9
1973	25.7	2.37	37.9
1972	24.5	2.54	39.6
1971	23.4	2.69	41.9
1970	21.0	2.59	41.6
1969	20.8	2.67	45.7
1968	19.0	2.62	48.0
1967	17.0	2.57	48.8
1966	15.8	2.52	50.8
1965	14.8	2.58	53.4
1964	13.7	2.61	54.2
1963	13.2	2.70	57.2
1962	11.9	2.57	55.8
1961	11.4	2.65	58.3
1960	10.9	2.63	60.0
1959	10.4	2.59	64.8
1958	9.5	2.59	66.0
1957	9.3	2.54	70.7
1956	8.3	2.38	70.6
1955	7.7	2.33	70.6

Source: Virginia Ann Hodgkinson and Murray S. Weitzman, *Dimensions of the Independent Sector: A Statistical Profile,* 2d ed. (Washington, D.C.: Independent Sector, 1986), table 3.1, at 52.

a. Contributions include bequests as well as gifts from living individuals, foundations, and corporations.

Table C.3 Responsiveness of donations, by industry, 1973–1976[a]

Industry (Activity Code)	Elasticity				Sample Size	R^2
	Price of Donating	Total Fund-raising Expenditures	Age of Organization	Constant		
Library (061)	−1.06* (.47)	−.53 (5.52)	+.03* (.02)	4.18* (.86)	554	.07
Art exhibit, museum, zoo, etc. (060, 091)	−2.65* (1.05)	−1.80 (17.92)	+.09* (.02)	3.48* (.64)	283	.24
Goods and services to the poor and aged (560, 575)	−.73 (.54)	−1.40 (11.90)	+.03 (.04)	6.17* (.77)	219	.08
Hospital (150)[b]	−1.28* (.26)	−.44 (2.46)	+.07* (.01)	3.12* (.35)	2615	.15
Aid to handicapped (160)	−.79* (.33)	−.76 (10.98)	+.01 (.01)	6.31 (.33)	1411	.16
Scientific research (diseases) (161)	−.81* (.30)	−.42 (9.91)	+.04* (.01)	4.07 (.30)	2060	.18
School, college, trade school (30)[c]	−1.07* (.41)	−.50 (5.07)	−.02 (.01)	4.06 (.73)	572	.15

Source: Burton A. Weisbrod and Nestor D. Dominguez, "Demand for Collective Goods in Private Nonprofit Markets: Can Fundraising Expenditures Help Overcome Free-Rider Behavior?" *Journal of Public Economics* 30 (June 1986), 83–95.

a. Elasticity is the percent change in donations (the dependent variable) associated with a 1 percent change in each of the independent variables—the price of donating (defined as 1 minus the marginal income tax rate; see the discussion at the beginning of Chapter 5), the level of fund-raising expenditures, and the age of the organization. Elasticities shown are ordinary least squares (OLS) estimates, and the constant is the intercept of the OLS estimates. Numbers in parentheses are standard errors of the estimates.

b. 75 percent sample.

c. 20 percent sample.

* Significant at 0.10 level or better.

Table C.4 Sources of receipts by nonprofit organization, by industry, as a percent of total receipts, 1980

Industry	Private Giving	Government	Service Fees and Other Income
Religion	93	0	7
Civic and social action	44	44	12
Culture	39	10	51
Health services	9	43	48
Human services	25	43	32
Education and research	12	9	79
Total	25	25	50

Source: Bruce Smith and Nelson Rosenbaum, "The Fiscal Capacity of the Voluntary Sector," paper prepared for the Brookings Institution Seminar, "The Response of the Private Sector to Government Retrenchment," Washington, D.C., December 9, 1981, 20.

Table C.5 Changes in federal support of nonprofit organizations, 1980–1986

Type of Organization	Federal Support in FY 1980 (billion dollars)	Percent Change, FY 1986 vs. 1980 (constant 1980 dollars)
Social service	6.5	−52
Community development	2.3	−48
Education/research	5.5	−27
Health care	24.9	− 9
International	0.8	−24
Arts	0.4	−66
Total	40.3	−22

Source: Nonprofit Sector Project, The Urban Institute, "Serving Community Needs: The Nonprofit Sector in an Era of Governmental Retrenchment," Progress Report No. 3 (Washington, D.C.: The Urban Institute, 1983), 5.

Table C.6 Contributions, gifts, and grants (CGG) as a percent of total revenues, for tax-deductible —501(c)(3)—nonprofit organizations, 1973–1975

CGG as Percent of Total Revenue	Percent of Organizations
10 and under	38
11–20	9
21–30	5
31–40	5
41–50	4
51–60	3
61–70	4
71–80	5
81–90	6
91–100	21

Source: Random sample of 274 IRS form 990 tax returns.

Table C.7 Revenues from sales and receipts as a percent of total revenues, nonprofit organizations, by industry, 1973–1976

Industry	Sales and Receipts as Percent of Revenues
Legal aid	3
Civil rights	35
Inner city and community development	49
Conservation and environment	54
Welfare	57
Advocacy groups	60
Housing	61
Youth activities	65
Culture	73
Education	82
Legislative and political action	82
Scientific research	86
Health	92
Business and professions	95
Sports	96

Source: IRS form 990 data tapes.

Table C.8 Market shares of proprietary and private nonprofit organizations in health care, education, and social services, mid-1970s

Industry	Percent of Industry Owned[a] by		Unit of Measure
	Proprietaries	Nonprofits	
Health			
Nursing homes	68	21	Beds
General hospitals	8	70	Beds
Renal dialysis centers	21	57	Facilities
Blood banks	63	6	Facilities
Education			
Secondary schools	4	14	Revenues
Child day care	51	41	Children
Other services			
Research and development	68	16	Revenues
Think tanks	50	33	Facilities
Family planning clinics	1	33	Facilities

Source: Various governmental documents, as presented in Mark Schlesinger, "Public, For-Profit and Private Nonprofit Enterprises: A Study of Mixed Industries," Ph.D. diss., Department of Economics, University of Wisconsin—Madison, 1984.

a. Excluded from this table are data on the portion of each industry that is owned by government.

Restrictions on Lobbying by Nonprofits

Currently, an organization that would otherwise qualify for tax-deductible status will not receive or retain it if a "substantial part of [its] activities . . . [involve] carrying on propaganda, or otherwise attempting to influence legislation, and [the organization may] not attempt to participate or intervene in any political campaign."[1] The restriction on lobbying is understandable. Why should public policy subsidize special interests to carry their cases to legislators? Is there not already too much political pressure from these sources, too much money for campaign contributions from "political action" groups, trade associations, labor unions, and so on? On the other hand, is there not too little representation of "interest groups" that are diffuse and poorly organized—such as consumers, the poor, and the victims of employment discrimination—whose concerns are individually small but collectively large?[2]

Congress appears to have reached a middle ground on these questions. Some legislative lobbying—determined on the sliding scale described in Chapter 6, ranging up to 20 percent of a nonprofit's total expenditures—is an acceptable use of donated funds; but lobbying beyond the sliding scale is presumed to serve the public interest to a lesser degree, perhaps not at all. Penalties for excessive expenditures on lobbying include a 25 percent tax on the excess and, ultimately, loss of the organization's tax-exempt status.[3] Donors do not receive tax deductibility for donations to a nonprofit that spends more than the permitted level.

The issue of lobbying illustrates in yet another way the complexity of social policy decisions toward nonprofits. Which goals of nonprofits should be encouraged is simply one question to be resolved. Which methods should be permitted in pursuit of those goals is another. A third is what policy should be toward a nonprofit that does some things that society wishes to encourage—providing collective and trust goods to the public—but also some other things that it does not.

Current policy on lobbying by nonprofits poses yet another set of issues: Why should an activity—lobbying, for example—be deemed appropriate but only in limited amounts? And why should such limits be defined relative to the level of other activities undertaken by each particular nonprofit, rather than relative to some overall activity level? The social value of lobbying can be debated, but certain things seem clear: (1) increases in lobbying are not likely to have equal social value in all activities—

education, charity, scientific research, health care, operating a museum, and so forth; (2) the value of lobbying, as an informational activity, in any particular activity area would seem to depend on the total amount undertaken by all organizations, not on either the amount per nonprofit organization nor the percentage of a nonprofit's total expenditures devoted to it. If 30 percent of one nonprofit's expenditures is a "socially excessive" level of lobbying, why is it not excessive to have the same absolute amount spent on lobbying divided between two or more nonprofit organizations, each spending less than 20 percent?

Volunteer Labor

Table E.1   Volunteer labor, by sector, 1977–1985

Sector	Full-Time Equivalent Volunteers (millions)[a]		
	1977	1980	1985
Private nonprofit	3.6	4.6	5.3
Business	0.1	0.2	0.2
Government	0.8	1.1	1.2
Total (excluding informal volunteering)	4.6	5.9	6.7

Source: Virginia Ann Hodgkinson and Murray S. Weitzman, *Dimensions of the Independent Sector: A Statistical Profile,* 2d ed. (Washington, D.C.: Independent Sector, 1986), table 2.3, at 34; and Independent Sector, *Americans Volunteer 1985* (Washington, D.C.: Independent Sector, 1986) table 8, at 18.

a. Full-time equivalence is calculated on the basis of 1,700 hours per year. Volunteering in other than formal settings is excluded. Data are for persons 14 years old or older.

Table E.2 Value of volunteer labor, by type of organization, 1980 and 1985

	1980		1985	
Type of Organization	Value of Volunteer Labor (billion dollars)	Percent of Total	Value of Volunteer Labor (billion dollars)	Percent of Total
Religious	13.7	21	34.3	34
Health	8.7	14	12.0	12
Educational	8.4	13	10.3	10
Recreational	5.3	8	6.9	7
General fund raising	4.7	7	8.6	8
Citizenship	4.7	7	6.9	7
Political	4.6	7	5.2	5
Community action	4.3	7	3.4	3
Work-related	4.0	6	1.7	2
Social welfare	3.2	5	8.6	8
Cultural	2.2	4	3.4	3
Justice-related	0.7	1	*	*
Total	64.5	100	101.2	100

Source: Independent Sector, *Americans Volunteer 1981* (Washington, D.C.: Independent Sector, 1982), not paginated; and Independent Sector, *Americans Volunteer 1985* (Washington, D.C.: Independent Sector, 1986), 19.

* Not reported; less than 0.5 percent.

Table E.3 Value of volunteer labor relative to paid labor, for selected types of organizations, 1980–1981

Type of Organization	Wages and Salaries Paid (billion dollars)	Value of Volunteer Labor as Percent of Wages and Salaries
Religious	6.0	228
Cultural	1.0	220
Educational	15.0	56
Social welfare	7.5	43
Health	39.0	22

Source: Calculated from 1980 data in Table E.2 and from Virginia Ann Hodgkinson and Murray S. Weitzman, *Dimensions of the Independent Sector: A Statistical Profile* (Washington, D.C.: Independent Sector, 1984), table 3.10, at 55, using 1981 data for wages and salaries paid.

Table E.4 Number of volunteers (1983) and of fund-raising volunteers (1982), selected national agencies

Organization	Total Volunteers	Fund-raising Volunteers
American Heart Association	3,000,000[a]	2,418,000[a]
American Cancer Society	2,500,000	2,150,425
United Cerebral Palsy Association	2,050,000[a]	1,875,000
Muscular Dystrophy Association	2,010,000[a]	1,615,000[a]
National Council, Boy Scouts of America	1,117,961	382,612[a]
Boys' Club of America	111,605	106,050
Camp Fire	105,000[a]	15,000
USO World Headquarters	40,000	375

Source: Abridged from *Giving USA, 1984 Annual Report* (New York: American Association of Fund-Raising Counsel, 1984), 98.
  a. Estimated.

Table E.5 Percent of volunteers performing a given task, 1973

Activity	Percent
Clerical/manual	47
Leadership	41
Fund raising	35
Teaching	25
Counseling/visitation	16
Professional	9
Miscellaneous (organizing, usher/choir, other)	12

Source: University of Michigan Survey Research Center, *Survey of Giving* (Ann Arbor, Mich.: Survey Research Center, 1974).
Note: Total adds to more than 100 percent because some volunteers are active in more than one way.

For-profit and Nonprofit Behavior in Three Long-Term-Care Industries

Definition of Variables

PRICE	Average charge per patient, per month (in analyses of satisfaction) or per year (in other analyses), for institutional care.
LOS	Patient's length of stay, in months.
GOVT	A dummy variable that equals one if the institution is operated by a federal, state, county, or local government, zero otherwise.
CHURCH	A dummy variable that equals one if the institution is operated by a religious organization, zero otherwise.
OTHER	A dummy variable that equals one if the institution is operated by a nonreligious nonprofit organization or corporation, zero otherwise.
LOSGOV	Patient's length of stay in government institutions, in months.
LOSCHURCH	Patient's length of stay in religious institutions, in months.
LOSNON	Patient's length of stay in nonreligious nonprofit institutions, in months.
SIZE	Size of institution, in number of beds.
AGE	Average age of patients in the institution, in years.
OFTEN	A dummy variable that equals one if a family member or guardian visits patient at least once per week, zero otherwise.
RARELY	A dummy variable that equals one if a family member or guardian visits patient less than once every six months.
FTMD	Number of full-time MDs employed by the institution.
FTRN	Number of full-time RNs employed by the institution.
FTMAIN	Number of full-time maintenance workers employed by the institution.
FTADM	Number of full-time administrators employed by the institution.
VOLS	Number of volunteers working at least once per month in the institution.
MEDR	Proportion of patients in the institution covered by Medicare.
MEDC	Proportion of patients in the institution covered by Medicaid.
CONSTANT	The intercept term in the regression equation.

Table F.1 Determinants of whether an institution maintains a waiting list

Variables[b]	Coefficients[a]		
	Nursing Homes	Facilities for Care of Mentally Handicapped	Facilities for Psychiatric Care
GOVT	−.20	−.23	−1.038
	(−.32)	(−.33)	(−1.32)
CHURCH	2.01*	34.15*	.58
	(1.85)	(2.62)	(.47)
OTHER	.33	1.30*	−.39
	(.67)	(2.51)	(−.58)
SIZE	−.002	.0027*	−.0035
	(−.86)	(1.98)	(−1.64)
AGE	.01	.0053	.013
	(1.16)	(.42)	(1.54)
FTMD	−12.00	−108.69*	33.04
	(−1.52)	(−2.17)	(.62)
FTRN	7.33	−.65	−5.40
	(1.04)	(−.29)	(−.89)
MEDR	.13	−.34	−.36
	(.24)	(−.34)	(−.27)
MEDC	.41	1.55	−.87
	(.87)	(1.33)	(−.98)
PRICE	.000042*	.000059	.000042
	(2.63)	(1.25)	(1.23)
CONSTANT·	.23	−.73	.95
	(.72)	(−1.49)	(1.34)
Number of observations	190	123	112

a. Asymptotic *t*-statistics are in parentheses.

b. Logit specification. For all variables containing a dummy for institutional form, the omitted comparison group consists of for-profit firms. Thus, a positive sign implies that the particular form of institution has a larger association with the dependent variable than does the for-profit form of institution, and a negative implies a smaller association.

* Significant at the 0.10 level or better.

Table F.2 Determinants of length of waiting lists[a]

| | Coefficients[b] | | |
| | Nursing Homes | Facilities for Care of Mentally Handicapped | Facilities for Psychiatric Care |
Variables[c]			
GOVT	24.24* (1.79)	122.19* (1.98)	1.78 (.25)
CHURCH	38.49* (3.36)	33.19 (.64)	1.36 (.18)
OTHER	13.37 (1.38)	−7.57 (−.16)	3.50 (.61)
SIZE	.14* (3.79)	.061 (.89)	.080* (3.58)
AGE	−.25 (−1.45)	−1.34 (−1.31)	−.11* (−1.63)
FTMD	−222.85 (−.56)	548.10 (.12)	129.30 (.32)
FTRN	92.39 (.79)	−36.25 (−.053)	−161.72* (−1.93)
MEDR	−17.82* (−1.69)	−1.49 (−.014)	−96.65 (−.000027)
MEDC	−.60 (−.064)	−97.18 (−.85)	2.23 (.24)
PRICE	.00030 (.24)	−.0043 (−1.14)	.00064* (2.03)
CONSTANT	−9.02 (−.96)	55.21 (1.16)	−4.90 (−.81)
Number of observations	138	74	73

a. For organizations maintaining a waiting list.

b. Asymptotic *t*-statistics are in parentheses.

c. Tobit specification. For all variables containing a dummy for institutional form, the omitted comparison group consists of for-profit firms. Thus, a positive sign implies that the particular form of institution has a larger association with the dependent variable than does the for-profit form of institution, and a negative implies a smaller association.

* Significant at the 0.10 level or better.

Table F.3 Determinants of awareness by family member that facility makes periodic reviews of each patient's needs

Variables[a]	Coefficients[b]		
	Nursing Homes	Facilities for Care of Mentally Handicapped	Facilities for Psychiatric Care
GOVT	.33	1.28*	.17
	(.95)	(3.47)	(.33)
CHURCH	.39	1.34*	.78
	(.96)	(3.24)	(.78)
OTHER	.069	.62*	.024
	(.24)	(1.66)	(.050)
SIZE	.00042	−.00085*	.00065
	(.52)	(−2.03)	(.61)
LOS	.0050	.0038	.0058
	(1.41)	(1.25)	(.76)
LOSGOVT	−.0081*	−.002	−.0078
	(−1.64)	(−.89)	(−.96)
LOSCHURCH	−.0032	−.0054	.082
	(−.59)	(−1.11)	(.80)
LOSOTHER	−.0075	−.0018	.0085
	(−1.33)	(−.49)	(.71)
OFTEN	.39*	.21	.084
	(2.11)	(.78)	(.25)
RARELY	−.68*	−.87*	−1.06*
	(−2.09)	(−4.15)	(−4.02)
CONSTANT	−1.44*	−1.09*	−.79
	(−4.97)	(−2.74)	(−1.23)
Number of observations	841	549	320

a. Logit specification. For all variables containing a dummy for institutional form, the omitted comparison group consists of for-profit firms. Thus, a positive sign implies that the particular form of institution has a larger association with the dependent variable than does the for-profit form of institution, and a negative implies a smaller association. That is, a positive coefficient on CHURCH, for example, indicates that residence in a church-owned nonprofit facility is more likely to be associated with family members' knowledge that the facility makes periodic case reviews than is residence in a proprietary facility.

b. Asymptotic *t*-statistics are in parentheses.

* Significant at the 0.10 level or better.

Table F.4 Determinants of number of various types of workers in nursing homes

Independent Variables[a]	Mean (standard deviation)[c]	Coefficients of Dependent Variables[b]			
		FTRN	FTMAIN	VOLS[d]	FTADM
GOVT	.085 (.28)	.0092 (.94)	.047* (1.61)	24.45* (2.38)	-.0075 (-.86)
CHURCH	.067 (.25)	.0093 (.90)	.064* (2.07)	12.53 (1.06)	-.0004 (-.045)
OTHER	.18 (.39)	.0014 (.22)	.011 (.56)	21.22* (2.64)	-.0011 (-.19)
SIZE	100.39 (72.64)	-.000035 (-1.02)	-.00014 (-1.35)	.094* (3.08)	-.000* (-5.47)
AGE	16.13 (19.93)	-.00010 (-.74)	.000079 (.19)	-.23 (-1.52)	-.000 (-.13)
PRICE	6729.8 (3094.5)	.0000052* (6.27)	.0000071* (2.89)	.00069 (.77)	-.000* (-2.02)
CONSTANT		-.00051 (-.075)	.085* (4.18)	-27.64* (-1.66)	.052* (8.68)
Standard error of estimate		.031	.092	75.6	.027
R^2		.47	.30	.55	.47
Number of observations	164				

a. Ordinary least-squares estimates. For all variables containing a dummy for institutional form, the omitted comparison group consists of for-profit firms. Thus, a positive sign implies that the particular form of institution has a larger association with the dependent variable than does the for-profit form of institution, and a negative implies a smaller association.

b. Asymptotic t-statistics are in parentheses.

c. The means for the various institutional types indicate the proportion of all facilities that are of each type. The reported numbers total 0.33, indicating that 0.67 of all nursing homes surveyed were proprietary.

d. In the volunteers equation one other independent variable was included—the number of social activities (such as sports, dancing, cards, movies, art classes) that the institution makes available to patients. Volunteers often play a major role in these activities. The resulting coefficient was 2.44* (2.00).

* Significant at the 0.10 level or better.

Table F.5 Determinants of reported claims of overall satisfaction

Independent Variables	Coefficients[a]		
	Nursing Homes	Facilities for Care of Mentally Handicapped	Facilities for Psychiatric Care
PRICE	0.0000	−0.0004*	0.0001
	(0.03)	(−1.87)	(0.35)
LOS	0.0062*	−0.0001	0.0133
	(1.86)	(−0.07)	(0.84)
LOSGOV	0.0001	0.0023	−0.0100
	(0.03)	(1.01)	(−0.62)
LOSCHURCH	0.0083	0.0169	2.003
	(0.98)	(1.41)	(0.00)
LOSNON	0.0144	0.0068	−.0080
	(1.44)	(1.53)	(−.47)
CONSTANT	1.192*	1.564*	1.259*
	(6.60)	(8.66)	(6.35)
Number of observations	791	487	228

a. Probit model. For a discussion of the interpretation of probit coefficients, see G. S. Maddala, *Limited Dependent and Qualitative Variables in Econometrics* (New York: Cambridge University Press, 1983), 22–27. For all variables containing a dummy for institutional form, the omitted comparison group consists of for-profit firms. Thus, a positive sign implies that the particular form of institution has a larger association with the dependent variable than does the for-profit form of institution, and a negative implies a smaller association. Asymptotic *t*-statistics are in parentheses.

* Significant at the 0.10 level or better.

Table F.6 Determinants of reported claims of satisfaction with building and grounds

Independent Variables	Coefficients[a]		
	Nursing Homes	Facilities for Care of Mentally Handicapped	Facilities for Psychiatric Care
PRICE	0.0004	−0.0003	0.0006*
	(1.70)	(−1.19)	(4.12)
LOS	−0.0039*	−0.0003	0.0024
	(−1.74)	(−1.58)	(0.48)
LOSGOV	0.0013	0.0030*	−.0024
	(0.54)	(1.80)	(−1.48)
LOSCHURCH	0.0059*	0.0355*	0.0243
	(1.65)	(1.80)	(0.83)
LOSNON	0.0125*	0.0059*	0.0028
	(2.20)	(2.14)	(0.42)
CONSTANT	1.6978*	1.892*	1.311*
	(10.18)	(10.80)	(7.65)
Number of observations	791	487	228

a. Probit model. For a discussion of the interpretation of probit coefficients, see G. S. Maddala, *Limited Dependent and Qualitative Variables in Econometrics* (New York: Cambridge University Press, 1983), 22–27. For all variables containing a dummy for institutional form, the omitted comparison group consists of for-profit firms. Thus, a positive sign implies that the particular form of institution has a larger association with the dependent variable than does the for-profit form of institution, and a negative implies a smaller association. Asymptotic *t*-statistics are in parentheses.

* Significant at the 0.10 level or better.

Table F.7 Determinants of reported claims of satisfaction with rooms and furnishings

Independent Variables	Coefficients[a]		
	Nursing Homes[b]	Facilities for Care of Mentally Handicapped	Facilities for Psychiatric Care
PRICE		−0.0002	−0.0004*
		(−1.47)	(3.68)
LOS		−0.0020	0.0407*
		(−1.41)	(1.98)
LOSGOV		0.0018	−0.0406*
		(1.14)	(−1.99)
LOSCHURCH		0.0080*	−0.0159
		(2.05)	(−0.49)
LOSNON		0.0054*	−.0332*
		(2.14)	(−1.62)
CONSTANT		1.706*	1.351*
		(11.304)	(7.74)
Number of observations		487	228

a. Probit model. For a discussion of the interpretation of probit coefficients, see G. S. Maddala, *Limited Dependent and Qualitative Variables in Econometrics* (New York: Cambridge University Press, 1983), 22–27. For all variables containing a dummy for institutional form, the omitted comparison group consists of for-profit firms. Thus, a positive sign implies that the particular form of institution has a larger association with the dependent variable than does the for-profit form of institution, and a negative implies a smaller association. Asymptotic t-statistics are in parentheses.

b. The matrix of second derivatives of the likelihood function was almost singular. Hence, the maximum likelihood estimates are not reliable, and test statistics are not available. (In other words, there was essentially no variance in responses among residents of nursing homes—virtually all respondents indicated satisfaction.)

* Significant at the 0.10 level or better.

Table F.8   Determinants of reported claims of satisfaction with treatment services

	Coefficients[a]		
Independent Variables	Nursing Homes	Facilities for Care of Mentally Handicapped	Facilities for Psychiatric Care
PRICE	0.0002 (1.11)	−0.0009 (−0.53)	0.0008* (5.10)
LOS	−0.015 (−0.72)	−0.0012 (−0.83)	0.0355* (1.89)
LOSGOV	0.0013 (0.50)	0.0020 (1.27)	−0.0345* (−1.95)
LOSCHURCH	0.0107* (2.15)	0.0046 (1.53)	0.134 (1.54)
LOSNON	0.0116* (2.69)	0.0047* (2.00)	−0.0320* (−1.80)
CONSTANT	1.254* (9.23)	1.750* (11.31)	1.523* (7.50)
Number of observations	791	487	228

a. Probit model. For a discussion of the interpretation of probit coefficients, see G. S. Maddala, *Limited Dependent and Qualitative Variables in Econometrics* (New York: Cambridge University Press, 1983), 22–27. For all variables containing a dummy for institutional form, the omitted comparison group consists of for-profit firms. Thus, a positive sign implies that the particular form of institution has a larger association with the dependent variable than does the for-profit form of institution, and a negative implies a smaller association. Asymptotic *t*-statistics are in parentheses.

* Significant at the 0.10 level or better.

Table F.9 Determinants of reported claims of satisfaction with relations with staff

Independent Variables	Coefficients[a]		
	Nursing Homes	Facilities for Care of Mentally Handicapped	Facilities for Psychiatric Care
PRICE	0.0002	−0.0001	0.0007*
	(0.75)	(−0.52)	(4.36)
LOS	−0.0025	−0.0018	0.0449*
	(−1.07)	(−1.19)	(1.78)
LOSGOV	−0.0002	0.0022	−0.0445*
	(−0.080)	(1.27)	(−1.81)
LOSCHURCH	0.0240*	0.018*	1.73
	(1.88)	(1.93)	(0.00)
LOSNON	0.0111*	0.0028	−0.0597
	(2.00)	(1.34)	(−1.58)
CONSTANT	1.85*	1.96*	1.54*
	(10.92)	(11.92)	(7.40)
Number of observations	791	487	228

a. Probit model. For a discussion of the interpretation of probit coefficients, see G. S. Maddala, *Limited Dependent and Qualitative Variables in Econometrics* (New York: Cambridge University Press, 1983), 22–27. For all variables containing a dummy for institutional form, the omitted comparison group consists of for-profit firms. Thus, a positive sign implies that the particular form of institution has a larger association with the dependent variable than does the for-profit form of institution, and a negative implies a smaller association. Asymptotic *t*-statistics are in parentheses.

* Significant at the 0.10 level or better.

Table F.10 Determinants of reported claims of satisfaction with social activities

Independent Variables	Coefficients[a]		
	Nursing Homes	Facilities for Care of Mentally Handicapped	Facilities for Psychiatric Care
PRICE	0.0002	−0.0001	0.0006*
	(0.96)	(−0.60)	(4.21)
LOS	0.0009	−0.0004	0.0025
	(0.44)	(−0.29)	(0.56)
LOSGOV	−0.0015	0.0001	−0.0040
	(−0.74)	(0.04)	(−0.91)
LOSCHURCH	0.0114*	0.0020	2.11
	(2.27)	(0.78)	(0.00)
LOSNON	0.0054*	0.0010	−0.0001
	(1.65)	(0.49)	(−0.01)
CONSTANT	1.408*	2.014*	1.588*
	(10.71)	(12.33)	(8.00)
Number of observations	791	487	228

a. Probit model. For a discussion of the interpretation of probit coefficients, see G. S. Maddala, *Limited Dependent and Qualitative Variables in Econometrics* (New York: Cambridge University Press, 1983), 22–27. For all variables containing a dummy for institutional form, the omitted comparison group consists of for-profit firms. Thus, a positive sign implies that the particular form of institution has a larger association with the dependent variable than does the for-profit form of institution, and a negative implies a smaller association. Asymptotic *t*-statistics are in parentheses.

* Significant at the 0.10 level or better.

Table F.11 Number of facilities surveyed, and means and standard deviations (in parentheses) of variables for analysis of satisfaction

Number of Facilities Operated by	Nursing Homes	Facilities for Care of Mentally Handicapped	Facilities for Psychiatric Care
Government	147	198	75
Religious organizations	69	79	18
Nonreligious nonprofits	137	117	109
For-profit firms	438	93	26
Number of facilities sampled	791	487	228

Independent Variables	Nursing Homes	Facilities for Care of Mentally Handicapped	Facilities for Psychiatric Care
PRICE	602.24 (329.01)	475.78 (422.00)	769.73 (778.45)
LOSGOV	57.18 (68.57)	93.15 (81.13)	58.68 (117.76)
LOSCHURCH	51.72 (50.92)	58.95 (60.66)	10.78 (7.71)
LOSNON	31.80 (33.67)	72.14 (180.39)	19.69 (42.20)
LOS, for-profit	29.97 (28.53)	71.41 (76.64)	45.73 (44.77)

Notes

1. Nonprofits in a Mixed Economy

1. The following works are suggested for the reader who has little formal background in economics: Walter W. Powell, ed., *The Nonprofit Sector* (New Haven, Conn.: Yale University Press, 1987); Susan Rose-Ackerman, ed., *The Non-profit Sector: Economic Theory and Public Policy* (New York: Oxford University Press, 1986); Burton A. Weisbrod, *The Voluntary Nonprofit Sector: Economic Theory and Public Policy* (Lexington, Mass.: Lexington Press, 1977); Michelle J. White, ed., *Nonprofit Firms in a Three Sector Economy* (Washington, D.C.: Urban Institute, 1981); Dennis Young, *If Not for Profit, for What?* (Lexington, Mass.: D. C. Heath, 1983). Economists are referred to the more extensive bibliography that accompanies my entry "Nonprofit organizations" in *The New Palgrave: A Dictionary of Economics,* ed. John Eatwell, Murray Milgate, and Peter Newman (New York: Stockton Press, 1987).

2. Murray Weidenbaum, *The Modern Public Sector* (New York: Basic Books, 1969), 93.

3. For example, it recently announced that it would give an award and a $15,000 grant to the nonprofit organization in Nashville (where its corporate headquarters are located) that best exemplifies excellence in management. Council on Foundations *Newsletter* 4 (May 28, 1985).

4. Downtown Research and Development Center, New York, *Downtown Idea Exchange* 32 (February 1, 1985), 1.

5. Staff reporter, "National Medical Enterprises to Build Facilities at University," *Wall Street Journal,* February 7, 1985, 10; Udayan Gupta, "Hospitals Enlist Profit-Minded Partners for Ventures to Generate New Business," *Wall Street Journal,* January 23, 1987, 19.

6. "1985 Survey of Nonprofit Case Law," *University of San Francisco Law Review* 20 (Summer 1986), 949–953.

7. Regina E. Herzlinger and William S. Krasker, "Who Profits from Nonprofits?" *Harvard Business Review,* January–February 1987, 93–106 at 98.

8. Congressional Research Service, Library of Congress, "1985 Tax Reform Options and Charitable Contributions," *Philanthropy Monthly* 18 (May 1985), 23–31 at 24.

9. W. K. Jordan, *Philanthropy in England, 1480–1660* (London: George Allen and Unwin, 1959), passim.

10. Robert Nelson, "An Address to Persons of Quality and Estate, Ways and Methods of Doing Good" (1715), cited by B. Kirkman Gray in *A History of English Philanthropy* (London: Frank Cass and Company, 1905), 95.

11. Thomas W. Still, "Wisconsin Non-profit Groups Ordered to Speak Up or Fold Up," *Wisconsin State Journal,* July 6, 1985, 1.

12. For a broad historical perspective on institutional choice, see Lance E. Davis and Douglass C. North, *Institutional Change and American Economic Growth* (London: Cambridge University Press, 1971).

13. Ministry of Finance, Hungary, *Introduction of New Management-Forms in State Enterprises* (Budapest: Secretariate of the Ministry of Finance, 1985), 21. The report refers to the "spectacular results" achieved by the cooperatives, especially in agriculture, "with the help of self-government by their members, and the quick reaction of their elected managers" (pp. 5–6).

14. Dennis Young, *If Not for Profit, for What?* (Lexington, Mass.: D. C. Heath, 1983), especially 97–99.

15. Whether nonprofits should also be permitted to engage in other, "unrelated," activities, is a separate—but quite controversial—matter. See Chapter 6.

16. Economists have tended to emphasize—unduly, I believe—the "fiduciary" functions of nonprofit organizations, which I have termed "trust" functions. They have generally not seen fiduciary activities as a means, albeit an important one, of promoting the collective good. Henry B. Hansmann, for example, appears to have seen the fiduciary and collective-good roles as quite distinct. See his important work, "The Role of Non-profit Enterprise," *Yale Law Journal* 89 (April 1980), 835–901 at 849, n. 46. See also David Easley and Maureen O'Hara, "The Economic Role of the Nonprofit Firm," *Bell Journal of Economics* 14 (Autumn 1983), 531–538.

17. For a theoretic analysis of clubs, although not in the context of nonprofits, see James Buchanan, "An Economic Theory of Clubs," *Economica* 32 (February 1965), 1–14.

18. The distinction between nonprofits that are clubs and those that are collectives is clearer conceptually than it is in reality. The difference lies in the degree to which activities of the organization benefit only those who contribute to its support. Trade associations and labor unions are seemingly of the club type; yet firms and workers who do not join may benefit from their activities. (It is also possible, though, that nonmembers may be harmed by the group activities.)

19. Some other organizations have tax-deductible status: veterans' organizations, domestic fraternal societies, and cemetery organizations, for example.

20. Estelle James analyzes "cross subsidies" from one activity to another within a given organization. Her principal illustration, however—undergraduate education subsidizing graduate education—involves activities that are both ordinarily tax exempt for the school; that is, both are "related" to the organization's tax-exempt purpose.

See "How Non-profits Grow: A Model," *Journal of Policy Analysis and Management* 2 (Spring 1983), 350–365.

21. See discussion in Chapter 6; see also U.S. Small Business Administration, *Unfair Competition by Nonprofit Organizations with Small Business: An Issue for the 1980s* (Washington, D.C.: U.S. Small Business Administration, November 1983).

22. At the theoretic level this position has been taken by a number of writers in recent years. Examples include Burton A. Weisbrod, "Economics of Institutional Choice," working paper, University of Wisconsin–Madison, 1979; Hansmann, "The Role of Nonprofit Enterprise"; and, at a more formal level, Easley and O'Hara, "The Economic Role of the Nonprofit Firm."

23. Receiving a growing number of complaints about competition from nonprofits, the U.S. Small Business Administration held a symposium on the subject on July 27, 1983. The ensuing report referred to "the growing problem of nonprofit organizations engaged in commercial activities in competition with for-profit small businesses." Prominent examples included activities of nonprofit universities in the production and distribution of audiovisual materials and computer software and in making travel arrangements, and sales of hearing aids by nonprofit hospitals and clinics. U.S. Small Business Administration, *Unfair Competition by Nonprofit Organizations,* 28. See also Chapter 6, below.

24. "Wish Lists, 1986 and 1980," *Wall Street Journal,* August 18, 1986, 23.

25. Steven P. Galante and Sanford L. Jacobs, "Liability-Insurance Woes Promise to Be Delegates' Primary Concern," *Wall Street Journal,* August 18, 1986, 23.

26. Enforcement problems aside, the constraint against distribution of profits implies that market prices will be paid for all resources purchased from persons associated with the nonprofit, managers included, and so any payment in excess would be an illegal distribution of profit. Operational determination of such market prices is, obviously, hard.

27. Amitai Etzioni and Pamela Doty argue that such payments are common. See their "Profit in Not-for-Profit Corporations: The Example of Health Care," *Political Science Quarterly* 91 (Fall 1976), 433–453.

28. The director of the Office of Supervision for the program overseeing the education of the handicapped, Dr. Robert L. Guarino, complained that there had been insufficient funds for monitoring. See "Levitt Audit Finds Overpayments to Private Schools for Handicapped," *New York Times,* December 18, 1977, 76.

29. President's Task Force on Food Assistance, *Report of the President's Task Force on Food Assistance* (Washington, D.C.: The Task Force, January 1984), 187.

30. Jeffrey H. Birnbaum, "Bitter Harvest: Charity That Delivers Surplus Food to Needy Is Split by Accusations," *Wall Street Journal,* October 25, 1982, 1, 20.

31. They may deduct as an expense not only the cost of producing the donated products—presumably an average cost, which could exceed the actual marginal cost of production—but also half of the difference between the cost and the fair market value of the product.

32. Birnbaum, "Bitter Harvest," 20.

33. Sari Horwitz, "Boat America Closely Tied to Nonprofit Association," *Washington Post,* September 17, 1984, Business Section, 1, 30, 31. In 1983 Boat

America earned profit of $611,000 on sales of $20.5 million. "Under the stock offering issued in May [1984], Schwartz and Ellison together stood to earn more than $2 million by selling part of their stake in the company they founded" (p. 1).

34. For further analysis of long-run competition between nonprofit and for-profit organizations when there are various types of nonprofits, see Jerald Schiff, "Expansion, Entry and Exits in the Nonprofit Sector: The Long and Short Run of It," Department of Economics, Tulane University, October 1985.

35. The original model of this process was presented by George Akerlof, "The Market for 'Lemons': Qualitative Uncertainty and the Market Mechanism," *Quarterly Journal of Economics* 74 (August 1970), 484–494.

2. Options among Institutional Forms

1. Legislation may require that services be purchased from nonprofits. In 1985, for example, the U.S. Department of Health and Human Services was directed by the House of Representatives to arrange for a "Study of the Delivery of Health Care Services to Homeless Individuals" (July 15, 1985)—the work to be done by a "public or nonprofit entity"—and for a "Study of the Role of Allied Health Personnel in Health Care Delivery" (Public Law No. 99-129, Section 223, October 22, 1985; see *U.S. Statutes at Large* 99 Stat. 523)—to be carried out by a "nonprofit private entity."

2. See, for example, Wladimir Andreff, "Redéploiement ou renouveau de l'économie hongroise? Point de vue d'un 'Outsider' " *Revue d'Etudes Comparatives Est-Ouest* 12 (December 1981), 15–16. (I thank David Granick for this citation.)

3. *Yearbook of Home Trade, 1980*, Central Statistical Office, Budapest, Hungary, 1981.

4. Government decree 38/September 30, 1980. I thank Professor János Timar, of Karl Marx University, in Budapest, for this information about the Hungarian reform.

5. *New Types of Economic Organizations, 1982*, Central Statistical Office, Budapest, 1983.

6. Personal communication from J. Timar, February 10, 1984.

7. Personal communication from J. Timar. On the Hungarian economic reforms more generally, see Xavier Richet, "Reforme dans la reforme? La nouvelle politique economique hongroise au seuil des années 1980," *Revue d'Etudes Comparatives Est-Ouest* 12 (December 1981), 31–60 at 53–54. I thank David Granick for this and the subsequent references to the role of the private sector in socialist economies.

8. V. Z. Rogovin, Senior Research Associate at the USSR Academy of Science Sociological Research Institute, in *Sotsiologicheskiye issledovania*, no. 1 (January–March 1982), 7–18, as referred to in the *Current Digest of the Soviet Press* 34 (April 7, 1982), 6.

9. Questioner in round-table discussion conducted by V. Petrov and V. Iakovlev. In *Sovietskaia Rossiia*, October 17, 1981, 2, as referred to in the *Current Digest of the Soviet Press* 33 (January 27, 1982), 14–15; it was noted that there was no objection to these "facts" by participants in the discussion, who included the Director of the Russian Republic Automotive Service Association, the Volga Automotive Plant Deputy General Director for Automotive Services, the General Director of the Moscow Automotive Service Association, and the Deputy Director of the Moscow

Administration for Combatting the Embezzlement of Socialist Property and Speculation.

10. Thomas Borcherding, Werner Pommerehne, and Friedrich Schneider, "Comparing the Efficiency of Private and Public Production: The Evidence from Five Countries," *Zeitschrift für Nationalökonomie* (Journal of Economics), Supplement 2 (1982), 127–156 at 135.

11. Peter H. Aranson and Peter C. Ordeshook, "Public Interest, Private Interest and the Democratic Polity," in Roger Benjamin and Stephen L. Elkin, eds., *The Democratic State* (Lawrence: University Press of Kansas, 1985), 87–263.

12. Diploma mills illustrate an unusual form of inequality, for the buyers and sellers are presumably well informed about what they are doing. The inequality is not between them, but with third parties who assume that the degree reflects academic accomplishments. The FBI recently ended a three-year investigation of diploma mills. Operation "Dipscam" probed 36 colleges that "provided degrees with little or no work required . . . FBI agents bought a total of 23 degrees for an average cost of about $1100. Writing skill was demonstrated by one agent who had to submit a five-paragraph paper on 'The Psychology of Embezzlement.' " "The FBI Springs 'Dipscam,' " *Newsweek*, May 23, 1983, 72.

13. Whether a tax or a subsidy is more appropriate is another matter; the decision hinges, in significant degree, on two matters: the equity of each, and the comparative costs of the alternative regulatory routes. Costs depend largely on the ease or difficulty of actually determining whether regulatory rules have been followed, in order to determine whether a firm qualifies for the subsidy or the tax penalty.

14. To a profit maximizer, the importance of regulatory restrictions depends only on the expected benefits and costs of violating them—including the probability of being detected in violation and the size of the penalty if detection occurs. The probability of being detected depends, in turn, on the difficulty of detection, and on the amount and quality of resources devoted to it.

15. Regulation of particular occupations provides an interesting illustration of a number of these monitoring-cost issues. The bulk of occupations that are subject to licensure or regulation involve consumer-protection claims. They include a preponderance of occupations in the healing arts or in activities involving "hands-on" relations with the buyer, patient, or client. (The effectiveness of licensure in providing such protection is another matter.) The following occupations are commonly licensed, and in fact are regulated in two states, Massachusetts and Wisconsin: accountants, funeral directors, podiatrists, architects, medical professionals, physical therapists, barbers, nurses, psychologists, chiropractors, nursing home administrators, realtors, dentists, optometrists, veterinarians, engineers, pharmacists.

16. The implications of "transactions costs"—including monitoring performance—are examined by Oliver E. Williamson in several books: *Markets and Hierarchies: Analysis and Antitrust Organization* (New York: Free Press, 1975); *The Economic Institutions of Capitalism: Firms, Markets, Relational Contracting* (New York: Free Press, 1985); *Economic Organizations: Firms, Markets and Policy Control* (New York: New York University Press, 1986).

17. "Private Philanthropy: Vital and Innovative or Passive and Irrelevant? The

Donee Group Report and Recommendations," in U.S. Department of the Treasury, *Research Papers Sponsored by the Commission on Private Philanthropy and Public Needs* (Washington, D.C.: Department of the Treasury, 1977), 59.

18. Waldemar Nielsen, *The Third Sector: Keystone of a Caring Society* (Washington, D.C.: Independent Sector, 1980), 5.

19. Richard Nelson and Michael Krashinsky claim that "profit [in these industries] is being mentally associated with exploitation rather than with responsible services." "Two Major Issues of Public Policy: Public Subsidy and Organization of Supply," in Dennis Young and Richard Nelson, eds., *Public Policy for Day Care for Young Children* (Lexington, Mass.: Lexington Books, 1973), at 55–56. In medical care, Kenneth Arrow has observed that "the very word, 'profit,' is a signal that denies the trust relations." "Uncertainty and the Welfare Economics of Medical Care," *American Economic Review* 53 (December 1963), 941–973 at 965.

20. See Yoram Ben-Porath, "The F-Connection—Families, Friends, and Firms and the Organization of Exchange," *Population and Demographic Review* 6 (1980), 1–30; and Kenneth Boulding, *The Economy of Love and Fear* (Belmont, Mass.: Wadsworth Publishing Co., 1973).

21. These sellers may have the incentive to be honest because of frequent transactions with the buyer or, in the case of nonprofits, because the nondistribution constraint eliminates the incentive to take advantage of consumers.

22. For further discussion of loyalty (and complaint) as an alternative to consumer mobility, see Albert Hirschman, *Exit, Voice, and Loyalty* (Cambridge, Mass.: Harvard University Press, 1970). Even if most buyers are underinformed and immobile, the switching by those who are better informed and more mobile sends signals to sellers, and so do complaints—with their implied threats to switch unless some corrective actions are taken.

23. The notion that one form of institution might be more trustworthy than another is not part of mainstream thinking in economics, but it may well affect consumer actions. Few people are inclined to donate to for-profit organizations; it is difficult for a donor to verify what is being done with a contribution, and fears that a for-profit firm will find ways to "pocket" the contribution discourage donations from private as well as governmental sources. The tax advantage of giving to a nonprofit rather than a proprietary organization is, of course, another reason for private, although not for governmental, donors to prefer a nonprofit. Even when tax considerations are irrelevant, however, there appears to be a preference for giving to nonprofits; as I will show later, for example, volunteer labor is given overwhelmingly more to nonprofit than to proprietary organizations.

24. Joseph P. Newhouse, "Toward a Theory of Nonprofit Institutions: An Economic Model of a Hospital," *American Economic Review* 60 (March 1970), 64–74.

25. Dennis R. Young and Stephen J. Finch, *Foster Care and Nonprofit Agencies* (Lexington, Mass.: Lexington Books, 1977), 229.

26. In an often-cited article, Armen Alchian and Harold Demsetz make the point explicitly: "in nonprofit corporations, colleges, churches, country clubs, mutual savings banks, mutual insurance companies, and 'coops,' the future consequences of improved management are not capitalized . . . One should, therefore, find greater shirking in

nonprofit, mutually owned enterprises." "Production, Information Costs, and Economic Organization," *American Economic Review* 62 (December 1972), 777–795.

27. Mary Adelaide Mendelson, *Tender Loving Greed* (New York: Vintage Books, 1974), 195. A somewhat different view, however, is Bruce Vladeck's: "On the whole, public agencies and their clients have been better served by nonprofit nursing homes than by profit-seeking ones, although in the great middle range of nursing home quality there is often not a dime's worth of difference between the two." *Unloving Care* (New York: Basic Books, 1980), 249.

28. Donald McNaughten, chairman of the nation's largest hospital chain, Health Corporation of America, on *The MacNeil/Lehrer News Hour,* Television Station WNET, New York City, November 3, 1983, Transcript #2114.

29. Henry Hansmann coined the term for this constraint; see "The Role of Nonprofit Enterprise," *Yale Law Review* 89 (April 1980), 835–899.

30. Hansmann (ibid.) has argued, in effect, that they are alternatives. He seemingly overlooked the fact that the nondistribution constraint is binding on governmental as well as on private nonprofit organizations. As a result, informational asymmetries are a potential justification for society choosing a form of institution other than a for-profit, but they are not a sufficient basis for choosing between government and nonprofits.

31. The problems of balancing these effects—unintentionally including some persons not targeted for inclusion and unintentionally excluding some target-group members—have been discussed in the context of access to health care programs, in Ralph Andreano and Burton A. Weisbrod, *American Health Policy* (Chicago: Rand McNally, 1974), 44–46.

32. This would not be true if it were possible, and acceptable, for government to discriminate among consumers, charging each a tax price that left each one satisfied with the level of governmental services. These "Lindahl prices" are a possibility discussed in theoretic economics, but at this point, not more.

33. This process was first discussed in conceptual terms by Charles Tiebout, "A Pure Theory of Local Expenditures," *Journal of Political Economy* 64 (1956), 416–424.

34. Diversity in demand is examined in Burton A. Weisbrod, "Toward a Theory of the Voluntary Non-profit Sector in a Three-Sector Economy," in Edmund Phelps, ed., *Altruism, Morality, and Economic Theory* (New York: Russell Sage Foundation, 1975), 171–195.

35. Ibid., 177–181.

36. "Does the Non-profit Form Fit the Hospital Industry?" *Harvard Law Review* 93 (May 1980), 1416–1489 at 1438.

37. These ideas are developed further in the chapters by Weisbrod, Marc Bendick, Jr., A. James Lee, and Stephen H. Long, in *The Voluntary Nonprofit Sector,* ed. Burton A. Weisbrod (Lexington, Mass.: Lexington Books, 1977).

38. Y. Nishimura, "Figuring Out Japan: Are Japanese Tightfisted?" *Japan Times,* October 19, 1983.

39. Differences in tax laws, reliance on the extended family, and other factors are also at work.

40. Kenneth Arrow, *The Limits of Organization* (New York: W. W. Norton, 1974), 26.

41. The notion that the act of giving can itself bestow personal utility was discussed by Thomas R. Ireland, in Ireland and David B. Johnson, *The Economics of Charity* (Blacksburg, Va.: Center for the Study of Public Choice, 1970), 20; for a more recent and more theoretic treatment see James Andreoni, "Impure Altruism and Donations to Public Goods: A Theory of 'Warm Glow' Giving," working paper, Department of Economics, University of Michigan, October 1985.

42. It has been contended that a subsidy is not enough—only compulsion would cause a rational person to contribute to any provider of collective goods, nonprofit or other—after all, subsidies are far less than 100 percent. Mancur Olson, *The Logic of Collective Action* (Cambridge, Mass.: Harvard University Press, 1965), 11.

43. For tax policy on charitable gifts in the United Kingdom and elsewhere, see Charles T. Clotfelter, *Federal Tax Policy and Charitable Giving* (Chicago: University of Chicago Press, 1985), 96–98.

44. Arrow, *Limits of Organization*, 28.

45. Gerald Marwell and Ruth E. Ames, "Economists Free Ride, Does Anyone Else?" *Journal of Public Economics* 15 (June 1981), 295–310; and Earl Brubaker, "Sixty-Eight Percent Free Revelation and Thirty-Two Percent Free Ride?" in Vernon L. Smith, ed., *Research in Experimental Economics*, vol. 2 (Greenwich, Conn.: JAI Press, 1982), 151–166.

46. Burton A. Weisbrod and Nestor Dominguez, "Demand for Collective Goods in Private Nonprofit Markets: Can Fundraising Expenditures Help Overcome Free-Rider Behavior?" *Journal of Public Economics* 30 (June 1986), 83–95.

47. To some extent this is what was involved in the 1985 tax-reform proposal of the Reagan Administration; it would have eliminated federal tax deductibility for state and local taxes. These taxes paid to lower-level governments have some of the same character as voluntary contributions to nonprofits to supplement a particular government's provision of some collective good.

48. Joann S. Lublin, "Labor Letter," *Wall Street Journal*, March 13, 1984, 1.

49. James R. Rawls, Robert A. Ullrich, and Oscar T. Nelson, Jr., "A Comparison of Managers Entering or Reentering the Profit and Nonprofit Sectors," *Academy of Management Journal* 18 (September 1975), 616–623.

50. For examinations of these and other PIL activities see Burton A. Weisbrod, in collaboration with Joel F. Handler and Neil K. Komesar, *Public Interest Law* (Berkeley: University of California Press, 1978). The concept of underrepresented-group interests is discussed at 80–88. The data used in this study, for 1973–1974, are described in Joel F. Handler, Ellen Jane Hollingsworth, and Howard S. Erlanger, *Lawyers and the Pursuit of Legal Rights* (New York: Academic Press, 1978).

51. These wage differentials were analyzed in Burton A. Weisbrod, "Nonprofit and Proprietary Sector Behavior: Wage Differentials among Lawyers," *Journal of Labor Economics* 1 (June 1983), 246–263.

52. A recent analysis of rather similar data for lawyers estimated markedly smaller income differentials, although it too found evidence of systematic sorting according to preferences. John H. Goddeeris, "Compensating Differentials and Self-Selection;

an Application to Lawyers," Department of Economics, Michigan State University, East Lansing, February 1987.

53. U.S. Department of Health and Human Services, National Center for Health Statistics, *Health, United States, 1983*, DHHS Publication No. (PHS) 84–1232 (Washington, D.C.: Government Printing Office, 1983), 166.

54. Quality may have many dimensions; I assume here, for simplicity, that they can be translated into a one-dimensional index.

55. E. S. Savas, "Policy Analysis for Local Government: Public vs. Private Refuse Collection," *Policy Analysis*, Winter 1977, 49–74.

56. Douglas W. Caves and Laurits R. Christensen, "The Relative Efficiency of Public and Private Firms in a Competitive Environment: The Case of Canadian Railroads," *Journal of Political Economy* 88 (1980), 958–976.

57. Ibid., 958.

58. Ibid., 961, 962.

59. Perhaps the two goals can be pursued separately at lower cost than through a single activity, but that is a factual matter to be determined.

60. *The Economist*, June 16, 1984, 48.

61. "Loyalties Clog," *The Economist*, June 30, 1984, 15–16.

62. Maintenance of "unprofitable" mines is, in part, a means for in-kind compensation of workers who would otherwise bear costs. In "When Government Programs Create Inequities: A Guide to Compensation Policies," *Journal of Policy Analysis and Management* 4 (Winter 1985), 178–195, Joseph Cordes and Burton Weisbrod examined a variety of compensation mechanisms, including "implicit" compensation through program design and delayed implementation; such governmental mechanisms increase the cost of the "basic" program but achieve other social goals.

63. Kim Foltz, with Ann McDaniel, Joanne Harrison, and Marilyn Achiron, "The Corporate Warden," *Newsweek*, May 7, 1984, 80.

64. Ibid.

65. Ibid.

66. It could represent neither. For example, it could reflect a temporary policy of pricing at a loss in order to gain access to the market.

67. James Hirsch, "What's New in Private Prisons," *New York Times*, April 26, 1987, 17. The quotation is attributed to Mark A. Cunniff.

3. Incentives and Performance

1. Richard Titmuss, *The Gift Relationship* (New York: Vintage Books, Random House, 1971). A more recent, rather different perspective on the blood market— but one that still gives major weight to informational problems—is Alvin W. Drake, Stan N. Finkelstein, and Harvey M. Sapolsky, *The American Blood Supply* (Cambridge, Mass.: MIT Press, 1982).

2. This is not the place to evaluate the quality of Titmuss's statistics or the way he analyzed and interpreted them—both of which deserve criticism. See, for example,

Kenneth Arrow, "Gifts and Exchanges," in Edmund S. Phelps, ed., *Altruism, Morality and Economic Theory* (New York: Russell Sage Foundation, 1975), 13–28.

3. Adam Smith, *The Wealth of Nations* (New York: Random House, 1937), 14.

4. A recent newspaper advertisement shows that private firms are aware of and address the consumer-information problem and the resulting demand for trustworthy sellers: "If you don't know roofing, know your roofer. You can trust your house to Sears." *Capital Times,* Madison, Wisconsin, June 7, 1983, 2.

5. In the market for over-the-counter drugs, for example, the Federal Trade Commission recently ordered two drug companies to cease claiming that their nonprescription products—Bufferin, Excedrin, Bayer Aspirin, Cope, Vanquish, and Midol—are "better or safer than similar products" unless they have "well-controlled clinical tests to prove it." Associated Press report, published in the *Wisconsin State Journal,* July 14, 1983, 13.

6. Lee Benham and Alexandra Benham, "Regulating through the Professions: A Perspective on Information Control," *Journal of Law and Economics* 18 (October 1975), 421–427.

7. How far it can be closed is clearly a matter of degree. It has been noted that when "the customer cannot test the product before consuming it, . . . there is an element of trust in the relation." Kenneth Arrow, "Uncertainty and the Welfare Economics of Medical Care," *American Economic Review* 53 (December 1963), 941–973 at 949. Arrow also notes that in the case of medical services profit "arouses suspicion and antagonism on the part of patients and referring physicians, so they do prefer nonprofit institutions." Also, "the very word, 'profit,' is a signal that denies the trust relations." Ibid., 950, 965.

8. The consumer-information problem can be thought of as one of writing a contract—to what extent are consumers well enough informed to know the relevant dimensions of a contract, and if they are well informed, can all relevant contingencies be covered in a contract? The better informed they are, the greater their ability to determine and reward satisfactory performance, and the stronger the case for utilizing the proprietary form of institution.

9. Nearly four decades ago, Tibor Scitovsky recognized that consumer ignorance is an obstacle to the efficient functioning of proprietary markets. "Ignorance as a Source of Oligopoly Power," *American Economic Review* 40 (May 1950), 48–53.

10. Under some circumstances, outputs may be more easily monitored in the proprietary sector, where consumers can affect seller behavior. Cotton Lindsay, comparing proprietary with governmental (but not nonprofit) organizations, has argued that some attributes of output are "invisible" to Congress but are clear to individual consumers. He cites evidence in the hospital industry, where governmental (Veterans Administration) hospitals have a lower ratio of total staff to patients—a measure of limited value that is nevertheless easily available to Congress. "A Theory of Government Enterprise," *Journal of Political Economy* 5 (October 1976), 1061–1077 at 1068.

11. For a review see Hal G. Rainey, Robert W. Backoff, and Charles H. Levine, "Comparing Public and Private Organizations," *Public Administration Review* 37 (March–April 1976), 233–244; quotation is at 239.

12. This has also been argued by Bruno S. Frey and Werner W. Pommerehne,

"Public vs. Private Production: A Dissenting View," mimeograph, University of Zurich, Department of Economics, n.d. (probably 1983). Also see Thomas E. Borcherding, Werner W. Pommerehne, and Friedrich Schneider, "Comparing the Efficiency of Private and Public Production: The Evidence from Five Countries," *Zeitschrift für Nationalökonomie* (Journal of Economics), Supplement 2 (1982), 127–156.

13. Steve H. Hanke, in a review of R. Joseph Monsen and Kenneth D. Walters, *Nationalized Companies* (New York: McGraw-Hill, 1983), summarizing the authors' (and his own) views, in "The Failure of National Industrial Policies," *Wall Street Journal,* January 4, 1984, 22.

14. In the context of measuring the quality of health care, Avedis Donabedian proposed these three approaches. See his "Evaluating the Quality of Medical Care," *Milbank Memorial Fund Quarterly* 44, part 2 (1966), 166–206. In the economics literature on "industrial organization" related distinctions have been made among structure, conduct, and performance. For discussion see F. M. Scherer, *Industrial Market Structure and Economic Performance,* 2d ed. (Chicago: Rand McNally, 1980).

15. For brief but illuminating discussions of these matters see, for the health area, Robert H. Brook, "The Use of Outcome Data in EMS Research," *Emergency Medical Services Research Methodology Workshop 2,* DHEW Publication No. (PHS) 79-3225-2 (Washington, D.C.: Government Printing Office, 1979). More generally, see Frey and Pommerehne, "Public vs. Private Production." It has even been argued that if the available measures of outcomes are sufficiently limited, it may be preferable to use only procedural measures. In the 1976 case of Ethyl Corporation v. EPA (541 F.2d 1), Circuit Court Judges Bazelon and McGowan wrote that "in cases of great technological complexity, the best way for courts to guard against unreasonable or erroneous administrative decisions is not for the judges themselves to scrutinize the technical merits of each decision. Rather, it is to establish a decision-making *process*" (emphasis added).

16. The Commission on the Humanities, *The Humanities in American Life* (Berkeley: University of California Press, 1980); the phrase quoted is from " 'An Opportunity, Not a Disaster': Report of the Rockefeller Commission on the Humanities," Wisconsin Humanities Council, *Perspectives* 8 (Winter 1981), 7–8.

17. Furthermore, it is claimed that the "president of the Federation of Teachers in a large city predicts that teacher-assisted cheating, already a widespread problem, will increase as [for example,] elementary-school teachers leave the multiplication charts on the walls [and] teachers walk around the classroom during tests and nod or shake their heads." Dorothy Wickenden, "Merit Pay Won't Work," *New Republic* 189 (November 7, 1983), 12–15.

18. Sweatt v. Painter (339 U.S. 629), argued in October term, 1949, emphasis added.

19. There is, more generally, a continuum of costs; I consider only two levels of cost merely for simplicity.

20. This language appeared in an advertisement by an organization that claimed to be "the finest nursing home ever built" and that also stated that "dignity, privacy and self-respect [other type-2 attributes] are never lost." "There's more to us than meets the eye"—added the advertisement, in seeming recognition of the distinction

between type-1 and type-2 characteristics of their service. Ad for Whitehall Boca Raton in the *Miami Herald,* January 9, 1984, section BM, 15.

21. This ratio may differ among consumers, but that is not critical to the issue at hand.

22. George Akerlof, "The Market for 'Lemons': Qualitative Uncertainty and the Market Mechanism," *Quarterly Journal of Economics* 74 (August 1970), 484–494.

23. "Merit Pay for Good Teachers?" *U.S. News and World Report,* June 20, 1983, 61–62, interview with Willard McGuire.

24. William Raspberry, "Flaw in Teacher Merit Pay," *Miami Herald,* January 12, 1984, 25A.

25. See, for example, "Officers Cite Penalty for Too Few Tickets," *Milwaukee Journal,* November 1, 1981, 1.

26. Leslie Maitland Werner, in the *New York Times,* September 18, 1983, 4E.

27. Whenever true performance is rewarded poorly, behavior will be distorted increasingly as time passes. With experience, the people or organizations affected learn how to succeed in terms of the measures used to gauge performance—that is, they learn how to obtain rewards—even without actually succeeding in achieving the goals for which the proxy measures were devised.

28. Martin Feldstein, "Consequences of Hospital Controls," *Wall Street Journal,* April 12, 1979, 24.

29. Robert Pear, "U.S. Panel Urges 4-Point Program to Reduce Hunger," *New York Times,* January 11, 1984, 1, 10.

30. "Excerpts from Final Report of the Presidential Panel on Food Assistance," *New York Times,* January 11, 1984, 10.

31. The role of nonprofits when there is "difficulty . . . in defining the quality of the performance" is also examined in Richard M. Cyert, *The Management of Nonprofit Organizations* (Lexington, Mass.: Lexington Books, 1975), 9.

32. Russell E. Palmer, "Making Government Accountable," *Business Week,* February 11, 1980, 21.

33. Cyert, *Management of Nonprofit Organizations,* 15.

34. In practice, academic tenure often involves a "guarantee" of employment but not of any particular salary. This is obviously a weaker form of tenure—and is less neutral in its effect on scholarship—than would be a full guarantee of all job-related rewards. Salary schedules in some systems, however, provide little or no flexibility of rewards; in such cases, an individual who has tenure may confront a salary schedule that depends only on, say, years of service or on factors that are essentially independent of measured performance.

35. Stuart Taylor, Jr., "Justice Stevens Is Sharply Critical of Supreme Court Conservatives," *New York Times,* August 5, 1984, 1, 17.

36. A television reporter, in a "Satirical Commentary," recognized the seeming futility of attempting to measure the subtle elements of productivity in the political realm: "President Reagan has proposed rewarding teachers for meritorious performance; he should now propose to reward U.S. Senators and Congressmen for merit." Dick Flavin, Cable News Network, June 23, 1983, at 1:40 MDT.

37. Similarly, in a study of the comparative efficiency of public and proprietary airlines in Australia, David Davies, "The Efficiency of Public versus Private Firms,

the Case of Australia's Two Airlines," *Journal of Law and Economics* 14 (April 1971), 149–165, noted that the airlines were required by law to use the same type of aircraft and to serve the same markets. Because the airlines were so limited, it was not possible for their behavior to differ in the regulated dimensions. Had it not been for these restrictions, the public and private, proprietary airlines might (or might not) have acted differently in those respects.

4. Anatomy of the Voluntary Nonprofit Sector

1. *New York Times* News Service, "Kickbacks to Salvation Army Officers Probed," as published in *Wisconsin State Journal,* Madison, May 25, 1985, 4.

2. *United States Master Tax Guide,* 67th ed. (Chicago: Commerce Clearing House, 1983), section 501, pp. 180–186 at 181.

3. Ibid., 181.

4. The distinction between these two classes of nonprofit philanthropic organizations was made by Gabriel Rudney and Murray Weitzman, "Significance of Employment and Earnings in the Philanthropic Sector, 1972–1982," Program on Non-Profit Organizations, Yale University, November 1983, table 1.

5. U.S. Small Business Administration, Office of Advocacy, "Statistical Profile of the Nonprofit Sector," Publication No. CT85-3, April 1985, 2.

6. The 36,000–38,000 annual entry of nonprofits in the late 1970s and early 1980s was more than 40 percent as great as the approximately 90,000 annual private-business starts during the same period: 1979—87,729; 1980—90,840; 1981—92,161; 1982—90,757; 1983—100,868; 1984—102,329. Dun & Bradstreet Corp. (D&B), as reported in the *Wall Street Journal,* May 20, 1985, 92C. (The D&B data imply less growth in the total number of private enterprises than is reported by the U.S. Department of Commerce; see Table A.1 in Appendix A.)

7. The definition of the nonprofit sector on which these Commerce Department data are based is somewhat broader than nonprofit organizations alone; until 1978 it also encompassed "compensation of employees in private households." Although such compensation amounted to only about 5 percent of the total in recent years, its inclusion shows again the lack of consistency in data on the nonprofit sector. Of the other data reported in this chapter only the national income data include the household sector.

8. It would be a mistake to judge the importance, from the perspective of social welfare, of the nonprofit sector simply in terms of its relevance to the national income, as that is measured. From the perspective of national-income accounting, the contribution of a nonprofit organization that is helping the poor and needy is measured essentially by the wages it pays to its workers; no explicit valuation is made of the benefits to the recipients. Similarly, the contribution of the medical research funded by nonprofits is measured by the wages of the administrators and researchers, not by an explicit social valuation of the outcomes of the research. This limitation of the way the "nonmarket"—private nonprofit and governmental—sectors are handled in the national-income accounts underscores the incompleteness of any single indicator of the nonprofit sector's social importance.

9. U.S. Bureau of the Census, *1977 Census of Service Industries: Other Service Industries* (Washington, D.C.: Government Printing Office, 1979), x.

10. A church need not file if it has no income except from its church-related activities.

11. These figures are based on my tabulation of total nonprofit-sector revenue— from the IRS form 990 tax return tapes for 1976—of $143 billion. For more detail on the estimation procedure see Burton A. Weisbrod, "Assets and Employment in the Nonprofit Sector," *Public Finance Quarterly* 10 (October 1982), 403–426. Also see Table A.6.

12. Given the great contribution of volunteers in the nonprofit sector, and its presumed reflection in my estimates of total (paid plus unpaid) employment, it is not surprising that both the Commerce Department estimate of 4.95 million FTE workers and other estimates of only paid employment are markedly lower than my estimates. Gabriel Rudney recently estimated paid employment in the nonprofit sector in 1980, and he, too, found considerably less—6.3 million *paid* employees in the nonprofit sector (5.4 million excluding religious organizations)—than I estimated for *total* employment in the sector in 1976. See Rudney, "A Quantitative Profile of the Nonprofit Sector," PONPO Working Paper 40, Program on Non-Profit Organizations, Yale University, November 1981.

13. See Chapter 7 and, especially, Table E.1 in Appendix E. The survey was carried out by the Gallup Organization, for Independent Sector.

14. U.S. Bureau of the Census, *Statistical Abstract of the United States: 1986*, 106th ed. (Washington, D.C.: Government Printing Office, 1985), 391.

15. National Commission on Employment and Unemployment Statistics, *Counting the Labor Force* (Washington, D.C.: The Commission, 1979), 5, 85.

16. The comparisons of revenues with GNP, however, does not imply that the nonprofit sector is the source of the cited percentage of the nation's output. Organizational revenues and expenditures normally exceed their contribution to GNP, largely because a sizable portion of revenues is channeled to other organizations; as such those expenditures are financial transfers and, like purchases from other firms, are not outputs or "value added."

17. Data for hospitals, nursing homes, and other organizations in the service industries shown in Table 4.1 are in Appendix A, in Table A.11, for 1977.

18. These figures imply that their workers are paid markedly less than the average for the entire nonprofit service sector.

19. A careful analysis of public support for the arts in the United States is the Twentieth Century Fund Study by Dick Netzer, *The Subsidized Muse* (New York: Cambridge University Press, 1978). Also see Henry Hansmann, "Nonprofit Enterprise in the Performing Arts," *Bell Journal of Economics* 12 (Autumn 1981), 341–361, and Paul J. DiMaggio, ed., *Nonprofit Enterprise in the Arts* (New York: Oxford University Press, 1986).

20. *Non-profit Service Organizations: 1982*, as Assembled by the National Center for Charitable Statistics, from the 1982 Census of Service Industries Conducted by the U.S. Bureau of the Census (Washington, D.C.: National Center for Charitable Statistics, May 1985), v and vi.

21. For further discussion of the collectiveness index see Burton A. Weisbrod,

"Private Goods, Collective Goods: The Role of the Nonprofit Sector," in Kenneth Clarkson and Donald Martin, eds., *Research in Law and Economics,* Supplement 1 (Greenwich, Conn.: JAI Press, 1980), 139–177. The distinctions among "sales," "dues," and "contributions, gifts, and grants" should not be drawn too sharply. Actual data do not always correspond precisely to these categories. "Sales" or "dues" may include an element of CGG—as when a buyer knowingly pays more than he or she would pay for the private good alone, regarding the additional sum as a gift to the organization. Conversely, reported CGG may represent, to some extent, sales of private goods—as when a consumer in a high marginal income tax bracket takes a tax deduction for a charitable "donation" to an exempt organization in return for a valuable "gift"; the fact that this is not legal does not gainsay that it occurs and, in the process, contaminates the data on CGG.

22. These data are from the 1981 form 990 tax return filed by each organization with the IRS. For Common Cause the true proportion is even greater; affiliates provide most of its national revenue, but these transfers are reported as "dues and assessments, from members and affiliates," even though they were initially received as CGG.

23. More than twenty years ago, sociologist Arthur L. Stinchcombe wrote about "spurts" in the rate of formation of a particular type of organization. He cited, for example, the founding of most universities in the United States between 1870 and 1900 and the founding of most men's national social fraternities in three periods, 1840–1850, 1865–1870, and 1900–1920. While not referring explicitly to nonprofit organizations, Stinchcombe did refer to "new organizational forms," raised the question of how competition works among forms of organizations, and called for, but did not provide, "a complete theory of the correlation between age and structure of organizations." "Social Structure and Organizations," in *Handbook of Organizations,* ed. James G. March (Chicago: Rand McNally, 1965), 142–193 at 154 and 160.

24. In all these industries the tax-deductible organizations were substantially younger than were the nondeductible organizations that reported engaging in the same activity. The fact that both deductible and nondeductible nonprofits report the same activity does not imply that they are providing essentially identical services; data are not available to distinguish their respective activities in detail, but the differences in their IRS subsection status, as well as differences in their collectivity indexes, are evidence that significant differences exist.

25. By referring to concentration among nonprofits I am implying that whereas competition among nonprofits is important, competition between nonprofits and proprietary firms is significantly less so. It is true, as I have already shown, that nonprofits and proprietaries coexist in many industries. If data were available on their combined activities in particular cities I would also have examined the aggregated concentration ratios. Still, there is merit in focusing on the nonprofit sector alone, for there are likely to be systematic differences between the kinds of outputs of the nonprofit and proprietary providers, even when they are ostensibly in the same "industry."

26. Concentration would be even greater if the industries were defined more narrowly. There is presumably little competition between, say, a nonprofit library and a nonprofit zoo—but both are grouped by the IRS as "cultural" organizations.

27. These data reflect only the limited range of services covered by the 1977 Census Bureau Survey discussed earlier.

28. A. Sirrocco: "Nursing and Related Care Homes as Reported from the 1980 NMFI Survey," *Vital and Health Statistics,* Series 14, No. 29, DHHS Publication No. (PHS) 84–1824 (Washington, D.C.: Government Printing Office, December 1983), table 5, p. 10.

29. The relative importance of governmental nursing home beds also varies regionally—they constitute about 3 percent in the West, 6 percent in the South, and 11 percent in the North Central and Northeast regions. Sirrocco, "Nursing and Related Care Homes," table 6, p. 11.

30. See Alan Deutschman, "Profit Isn't against the Rules at This High School," *Wall Street Journal,* September 24, 1985, 34.

31. These figures were calculated from the IRS form 990 tax return data tapes for the years 1971–1977.

32. *Non-profit Service Organizations: 1982,* 20. The data are from the 1982 Census of Service Industries, conducted by the U.S. Bureau of the Census. As previously noted, these data are incomplete.

5. Charitable Donations

1. "PM Newsletter," *Philanthropy Monthly* 18 (June 1985), 3.

2. Robert Gurenther, "Loan Fund for Poor Lures Small Savers," *Wall Street Journal,* January 7, 1987, 21.

3. Lester M. Salamon and Alan J. Abramson, "The Nonprofit Sector," in *The Reagan Experiment,* ed. John L. Palmer and Isabel V. Sawhill (Washington, D.C.: Urban Institute Press, 1982), 219–243 at 239–240.

4. U.S. Postal Rate Commission, as reported in *Philanthropy Monthly* 19 (June 1986), cover, 5.

5. The strong version has been stated by Mancur Olson, Jr., *The Logic of Collective Action* (Cambridge, Mass.: Harvard University Press, 1965), 11: "any . . . organization, working in the interest of a large group . . . would get *no* assistance from the rational, self-interested individuals" (emphasis added). Olson was referring to groups of firms or workers, but his assertion would seem to cover a broad range of activities, including the nonprofit-sector activities we have been discussing, in which free-rider behavior is likely.

6. See, for example, Earl Brubaker, "68% Free Revelation and 32% Free Ride?" in *Research in Experimental Economics,* ed. Vernon Smith (Greenwich, Conn.: JAI Press, 1982), 151–166; and Gerald Marwell and Ruth Ames, "Economists Free Ride, Does Anyone Else: Experiments on the Provision of Public Goods, IV," *Journal of Public Economics* 15 (June 1981), 295–310.

7. Martin Feldstein and Charles T. Clotfelter, "Tax Incentives and Charitable Contributions in the U.S.: A Microeconometric Analysis," *Journal of Public Economics* 5 (January 1976), 1–26.

8. Under the Economic Recovery Act of 1981, charitable deductions were allowed even for taxpayers who did not itemize deductions. In 1982 and 1983 nonitemizers could deduct a maximum of 25 percent of the first $100 of contributions; in 1984,

up to 25 percent of the first $300 was deductible; in 1985, 50 percent of all donations, and in 1986, 100 percent of all donations were deductible. Beginning with 1987, however, the tax law eliminated this option for nonitemizers.

9. For estimates of the quantitative effect of income tax rates on charitable giving see Michael K. Taussig, "Economic Aspects of the Personal Income Tax Treatment of Charitable Contributions," *National Tax Journal* 20 (March 1967), 1–19; Martin Feldstein, "The Income Tax and Charitable Contributions: Part 1—Aggregate and Distributional Effects," *National Tax Journal* 28 (March 1975), 81–100; and Charles T. Clotfelter, "Tax Incentives and Charitable Giving," *National Tax Journal* 35 (June 1982), 81–100. For a survey of these and other studies see Charles T. Clotfelter, *Federal Tax Policy and Charitable Giving* (Chicago: University of Chicago Press, 1985), table 2.12, 57–59.

10. Congressional Research Service, Library of Congress, "1985 Tax Reform Options and Charitable Contributions," *Philanthropy Monthly* 18 (May 1985), 23–31 at 24.

11. "Charitable Deduction for 80 Percent of Taxpayers Missing in Reagan Tax Plan," Independent Sector News Release, May 28, 1985.

12. The number of itemizers has been declining for a number of years, from a peak of 48 percent in 1970, to 35 percent in 1982. *Statistics of Income, 1982, Individual Income Tax Returns* (Washington, D.C.: Department of the Treasury, 1984), table 1.2, at 39.

13. For a recent comprehensive study of taxation issues as they relate to donations, see Clotfelter, *Federal Tax Policy and Charitable Giving*.

14. Jerald Schiff and Burton A. Weisbrod, "State Income Tax Reform and Charitable Giving—The Case of Wisconsin," *Philanthropy Monthly* 18 (July/August 1985), 17–22.

15. Henry C. Suhrke, editor's introduction to "Munson" (the Supreme Court's decision in the Munson case), *Philanthropy Monthly* 17 (June 1984), 5–19 at 5.

16. J. John Stevenson, "More on Munson: State Laws Unconstitutional," *Philanthropy Monthly* 17 (July/August 1984), 17–19.

17. Ibid.

18. *Wall Street Journal,* October 29, 1982, 30.

19. *Wall Street Journal,* September 14, 1984, 25.

20. Richard Steinberg, "Should Donors Care about Fundraising?" in *The Economics of Nonprofit Institutions,* ed. Susan Rose-Ackerman (New York: Oxford University Press, 1986), 347–364. Donors would also not be affected by the fund-raising percentage if they are quite sophisticated, recognizing that even if all of their contribution went into fund raising, if it were spent wisely, it could generate a much larger amount of funds that could be spent on the organization's charitable activities. This type of model, as well as one in which donors disapprove of high fund-raising percentages, and another in which donors are insensitive to that percentage, are considered by Susan Rose-Ackerman, "Charitable Giving and 'Excessive' Fundraising," *Quarterly Journal of Economics* 97 (May 1982), 193–212.

21. Burton A. Weisbrod and Nestor D. Dominguez, "Demand for Collective Goods in Private Nonprofit Markets: Can Advertising Overcome Free-Riding Behavior?" *Journal of Public Economics* 30 (June 1986), 83–95. The paper contains substantial detail not presented here.

22. Charles Clotfelter has noted, similarly, that the "final output" resulting from an individual's contribution depends on "the proportion of an organization's budget devoted to administration and fund raising." He concluded, however, that the unavailability of data precludes such analysis; apparently he was unaware of the IRS data being analyzed at the time by Steinberg and by Weisbrod and Dominguez, as discussed in this chapter. See Clotfelter, *Federal Tax Policy and Charitable Giving*, 50.

23. Steinberg, "Should Donors Care."

24. Weisbrod and Dominguez, "Demand for Collective Goods." The donor's marginal income tax rate can be disregarded as irrelevant to the allocation of donations among the recipient organizations, since donations to every one of the organizations considered in this study were tax deductible.

25. We used data averaged across years for each organization, because the tax years of firms do not span the same calendar periods and thus may introduce seasonal factors; moreover, there is some arbitrariness in what is included in one year or in the next one, which has the effect of making year-to-year variation spurious.

26. We included only nonprofits for which contributions were tax deductible—that is, 501(c)(3) organizations—because we believe that the nature of their activities is significantly different from those of nondeductible organizations. With the exception of hospitals and schools, for which the data are random samples of organizations on the IRS records, the data encompass all of the tax-deductible nonprofit organizations that filed tax returns in all four years, 1973–1976.

27. Details on the actual level of statistical significance and on the magnitudes of the coefficients may be found in Weisbrod and Dominguez, "Demand for Collective Goods." See also Table C.3, in Appendix C.

28. William Niskanen, "Bureaucrats and Politicians," *Journal of Law and Economics* 18 (1975), 617–643.

29. This analysis assumes that fund raising and receipt of donations have no effect on the success of an organization's efforts to generate resources through other means—sales, dues, volunteer labor. Although the total fund-raising responses are uniformly not significantly different from zero across the seven industries, all the estimates are negative (Table 5.1, column 2). Nonprofit organizations tend to carry their fund raising to levels that are, if anything, somewhat beyond those that generate maximum revenues. If an organization found that raising and spending additional donations helped it to sell outputs or to attract volunteers, it would have an incentive to spend more on fund raising than what would lead to maximum donations.

30. Steinberg, "Should Donors Care."

31. This effect has two components in our statistical model; there is a direct effect of age/goodwill on donations, and there is an indirect effect on the productivity of the organization's fund-raising expenditures. Both operate in the same direction.

32. Private contributions come from a variety of sources. For a survey of econometric studies of the effect of tax laws specifically on corporate giving, charitable bequests, and foundation giving, see Clotfelter, *Federal Tax Policy*, chapters 5–7.

33. The data on religious organizations are only for those filing the form 990 tax return, and most do not, since they are required to do so only if they have "unrelated business income."

34. Virginia Ann Hodgkinson and Murray S. Weitzman, *Dimensions of the Independent Sector: A Statistical Profile* (Washington, D.C.: Independent Sector, 1984), table 3.1, 45. The 1986 edition does not update the data on payments for services.

35. The question of whether the cuts actually occurred is hard to answer, given that government grants to nonprofits are difficult to separate from government purchases from nonprofits. The total of the two forms of governmental support, however, actually has increased, from $45.5 billion in 1980 to $68.2 billion in 1984— a sizable increase even after adjusting for inflation. Virginia Ann Hodgkinson and Murray S. Weitzman, *Dimensions of the Independent Sector: A Statistical Profile*, 2d ed. (Washington, D.C.: Independent Sector, 1986), table 2.1, at 32.

36. Peter G. Warr, "Pareto Optimal Redistribution and Private Charity," *Journal of Public Economics* 18 (October 1982), 131–138; and Russell D. Roberts, "A Positive Model of Private Charity and Public Transfers," *Journal of Political Economy* 92 (February 1984), 136–148.

37. But see Jeffrey H. Weiss, "The Ambivalent Value of Voluntary Provision of Public Goods in a Political Economy," in *Nonprofit Firms in a Three Sector Economy*, ed. Michelle J. White (Washington, D.C.: Urban Institute, 1981), 11–33, and Jeffrey H. Weiss, "Donations: Can They Reduce a Donor's Welfare?" in *The Economics of Nonprofit Institutions*, ed. Susan Rose-Ackerman, 45–54.

38. See Susan Rose-Ackerman, "Do Government Grants to Charity Reduce Private Donations?" in *Nonprofit Firms in a Three Sector Economy*, ed. Michelle J. White, 95–114.

39. Burton A. Abrams and Mark D. Schmitz, "The Crowding-Out Effect of Governmental Transfers on Private Charitable Contributions," *Public Choice* 33 (February 1978), 29–37. See also their later study, "The Crowding-Out Effect of Governmental Transfers on Private Charitable Contributions: Cross-Section Evidence," *National Tax Journal* 37 (December 1984), 563–568, which reports roughly similar magnitudes of crowding out.

40. William S. Reece, "Charitable Contributions: New Evidence on Household Behavior," *American Economic Review* 69 (March 1979), 142–151.

41. Jerald Schiff, "Government Output, Government Grants and Charitable Donations," Department of Economics, Tulane University, August 1984.

42. Schiff, ibid., also examines this relationship.

6. Revenues from Sales

1. These data are from my random sample of 274 tax-deductible—501(c)(3)— organizations for the tax years 1973–1975. The distribution of organizations, by the percentage of revenue coming from donations, is shown in Table C.6 in Appendix C.

2. Frank Swain, *SBA News*, no. 83-41 (Washington, D.C.: U.S. Small Business Administration, 1983).

3. Susan T. Schmidt, "Survival of Nonprofits May Depend on Their Entrepreneurial Savvy," *Washington Post*, July 27, 1983; and Small Business Administration (SBA), *Unfair Competition by Nonprofit Organizations with Small*

Business: An Issue for the 1980s (Washington, D.C.: U.S. Small Business Administration, November 1983).

4. Jack Norman, "Lean Times for Largesse," *Milwaukee Journal,* October 17, 1982, Business Section, 1.

5. Meg Cox, "At Some Eateries, People Just Eat; At This Cafe, They Also Do Good," *Wall Street Journal,* September 18, 1985, 25.

6. The Grantsmanship Center, *Business Ventures for Nonprofits, 1984 Schedule* (Los Angeles: The Grantsmanship Center, 1984), 2.

7. William Fulton, "The Robin Hood of Real Estate," *Planning,* May 1985, 4–10.

8. Jane Mayer, "Survival Tactics: Cuts in Federal Aid Lead Public TV to Try a Bit of Free Enterprise," *Wall Street Journal,* March 10, 1982, 1.

9. James C. Crimmins and Mary Keil, *Enterprise in the Nonprofit Sector* (Washington, D.C.: Partners for Livable Places and The Rockefeller Brothers Fund, 1983), 14.

10. The conference was held at Copper Mountain, Colorado, June 5–9, 1983.

11. Announcement of conference, "Marketing for Nonprofit Organizations," Shoreham Hotel, Washington, D.C., March 13–15, 1984.

12. The Grantsmanship Center, *Business Ventures for Nonprofits, 1984 Schedule.*

13. Edward Skloot, "Enterprise and Commerce in Nonprofit Organizations," in *The Nonprofit Sector,* ed. Walter W. Powell (New Haven, Conn.: Yale University Press, 1987), 380–393.

14. For a number of examples of nonprofits that have formed for-profit subsidiaries, and the reasons for their doing so, see Robert Mier and Wim Wiewel, "Business Activities of Not-for-Profit Organizations," *American Planning Association Journal,* Summer 1983, 316–325.

15. John C. Finch, "Where Is IRS Likely to Look in 'Unrelated Business Income' Audits?" *Philanthropy Monthly* 85 (September 1985), 13–16, at 13, 15. Also see a later GAO report, *Tax Policy: Competition between Taxable Businesses and Tax-Exempt Organizations* (United States General Accounting Office, Washington, D.C., 1987), report GAO/GGD-87-40BR.

16. Some forms of income are, under current law, not subject to this test of relatedness. These include investment income, income from the sale of donated merchandise, among other forms.

17. Jerald Schiff and Burton A. Weisbrod, "Government Social Welfare Spending and the Private Nonprofit Sector: Crowding Out, and More," November 1986.

18. The four equations can be described, in general terms, as follows:

$$\begin{aligned} \text{CONTR} &= a\,(GVT, STATE, \text{EXPSO}, CHAR, \text{ORGS}) + e_1 \\ \text{SALES} &= b\,(GVT, STATE, \text{EXPSO}, CHAR, \text{ORGS}) + e_2 \\ \text{EXPSO} &= c\,(GVT, STATE, CHAR, \text{ORGS}) + e_3 \\ \text{ORGS} &= d\,(GVT, STATE) + e_4 \end{aligned}$$

where *GVT* is a vector of government-expenditure variables reflecting the form of the welfare expenditures—for example, cash grants or payments for goods and services purchased; *STATE* is a vector of characteristics of the state in which the nonprofit operates, such as per capita income and the proportion of population officially classified as poor; *CHAR* is a vector of characteristics of the nonprofit organization, such as its age and level of fund-raising expenditures; a–d are coefficients; and e_1–e_4 are error terms. CONTR is the average contribution (donation) to nonprofit welfare organizations in a state; SALES is the average sales revenues of those nonprofits; EXPSO is the average expenditure of those nonprofits on solicitation of funds; and ORGS is the total number of nonprofit welfare organizations in a state. We assume that each state is, in effect, a separate market, and that a welfare nonprofit serves only within its own state and raises revenue only within the state; any federal funds received are thus assumed to be allocated randomly across states, independently of the variables listed above.

19. That is, starting with a system of four structural equations positing the factors affecting an average nonprofit's receipts from donations (CONTR) and from sales (SALES) its level of fund-raising expenditures (EXPSO), and the total number of welfare nonprofits in a state (ORGS), Schiff and I estimated reduced-form equations that reflect the interactive effects. The methodology is described in detail in Schiff and Weisbrod, "Government Social Welfare Spending."

20. Scott R. Schmedel, "Does Charity Trespass on Business's Territory, or Vice Versa, or Both?" *Wall Street Journal*, March 18, 1987, 1.

21. Susan J. Duncan, *Unfair Competition: How Government Gives the Edge to Nonprofits in the Communications Business* (Fairfax, Va.: National Audio-Visual Association, 1983), 15, as cited in SBA, *Unfair Competition*, 15.

22. Statement of Bennett Schultz, sales executive, DCA Educational Products, before the Symposium on Nonprofits Competition with Small Business, July 27, 1983, as presented in SBA, *Unfair Competition*, 15–16.

23. Statement of Hannah Gratz, Bristol Travel Service, before the Symposium on Nonprofits Competition with Small Business, July 27, 1983, as presented in SBA, *Unfair Competition*, 19.

24. Statement of Charles Garber, president of Structure Probe, Inc., West Chester, Pennsylvania, before the Symposium on Nonprofits Competition with Small Business, July 27, 1983, as presented in SBA, *Unfair Competition*, 21. (The statement made no mention of "overhead" payments to universities for research performed by faculty.)

25. Statement of James Lovell, National Hearing Aid Society, before the Symposium on Nonprofits Competition with Small Business, July 27, 1983, as presented in SBA, *Unfair Competition*, 23.

26. SBA, *Unfair Competition*, 24.

27. I say "probably" because it is possible for proprietary firms to receive donations that would be used to do much of what nonprofits do with those revenues; some natural gas utilities solicit private donations to help poor people pay their bills. The principal problem, however, is the difficulty donors have in monitoring the outputs and to whom they are distributed.

28. Internal Revenue Code section 513.

29. Susan Rose-Ackerman, "Unfair Competition and Corporate Income Taxation," *Stanford Law Review* 34 (May 1982), 1017–1039.

30. The legislative history stated explicitly that "the problem at which the tax on unrelated business income is directed is primarily that of unfair competition." Senate Report No. 2375, 81st Cong., 2d Sess. 28–29 (1950).

31. *Hi-Plains Hospital v. United States,* 670 F.2d 528 (5th Cir., 1982).

32. L. Maloney, "Special Report: For Many There Are Big Profits in 'Nonprofits,'" *U.S. News and World Report,* November 6, 1978, 7.

33. Statement by Gerald Sack, of the Exempt Organizations Division, IRS, at the Symposium on Nonprofits Competition with Small Business, July 27, 1983.

34. Executive Office of the President, Office of Management and Budget, *Supplement, OMB Circular No. A-76 (Revised), Performance of Commercial Activities,* August 1983, IV-35-36.

35. *IRS Exempt Organizations Handbook,* (IRM 7751) section 342.1(1), as quoted in Bruce R. Hopkins, *The Law of Tax Exempt Organizations,* 2d ed. (Washington, D.C.: Lerner Law Book Company, 1977), 128.

36. Knight-Ridder News Service, "IRS Seeking Big Cutbacks in Tax-exempt Status of PTL," *St. Paul Pioneer Press Dispatch,* April 28, 1987, 3A (emphasis added).

37. "Small Labs Chip Away at UL in Market for Product Testing," *Wall Street Journal,* November 10, 1986, 21.

38. Hopkins, *Law of Tax Exempt Organizations,* 154.

39. Ibid., 143.

40. Ibid., 145.

41. Ibid., 149.

42. Scott R. Schmedel, "Charities Lobby Hard to Save Their Right to Lobby," *Wall Street Journal,* March 11, 1987, 1.

43. "A Little Learning Doesn't Go Far Enough to Pass the IRS's Exemption Test," *Wall Street Journal,* December 3, 1986, 1.

44. Hopkins, *Law of Tax Exempt Organizations,* 45.

45. Richard L. Berke, "Key Figure Admits Fraud Conspiracy on Contra Funds," *New York Times,* April 30, 1987, 1, 8.

46. *Presbyterian and Reformed Publishing Co. v. Commissioner,* 54 A.F.T.R.2d 84-5730 (3rd Cir., 1984), as described in MacKenzie Canter, III, "Federal Tax Update," *Philanthropy Monthly* 17 (September 1984), 33–34.

47. Internal Revenue Code section 512(b)(12).

48. For Social Security exemptions, see 42 U.S.C. section 410(a)(8)(B)(1976); unemployment insurance, 26 U.S.C. sections 3306(b)(5)(A), (c)(8)(1976); minimum wage, 29 U.S.C. section 203(r)(1976), 29 C.F.R. section 779.214(1982); securities regulations, 15 U.S.C. section 77c(a)(4)(1982); bankruptcy, 11 U.S.C. section 303(a)(1982); antitrust, see *Marjorie Webster Junior College v. Middle States Association of Colleges and Secondary Schools,* 432 F.2d 650 (D.C. Cir. 1970), *cert. denied,* 400 U.S. 965 (1970); unfair competition, 15 U.S.C. sections 44, 45 (1982); copyright, 17 U.S.C. sections 110, 111(a)(4), 112(b), 118(d)(3)(1976); postal rates, 39 U.S.C. section 3626(1976).

49. Letter from U.S. Senator Lowell Weicker, Jr., to the *Wall Street Journal,* September 29, 1982, 33.

50. Hopkins, *Law of Tax Exempt Organizations,* 18.

51. Henry Hansmann, "The Effect of Tax Exemption and Other Factors on Competition between Nonprofit and For-Profit Enterprise," Program on Nonprofit Organizations, Yale University, July 1985.

52. Institute of Medicine, National Academy of Sciences, *For-profit Enterprise in*

Health Care (Washington, D.C.: National Academy Press, 1986), ed. Bradford H. Gray; and Burton Weisbrod and Mark Schlesinger, "Public, Private, Nonprofit Ownership and the Response to Asymmetric Information: The Case of Nursing Homes," in *The Economics of Nonprofit Institutions,* ed. Susan Rose-Ackerman (New York: Oxford University Press, 1986), 133–151.

53. The source of the quotation is not given, but the quotation appears in J. John Stevenson, "What the Supreme Court Said about Allocating Fund Raising Costs," *Philanthropy Monthly* 17 (September 1984), 36–37 at 36.

54. See Henry C. Suhrke, "Joint Costs Accounting a Key Issue in the Supreme Court's *Munson* Decision," *Philanthropy Monthly* 18 (April 1985), 25–27 at 25.

55. Ibid.

56. Whether the nonprofit "provides" the service directly or contracts it out is not important. Even in the latter case the nonprofit would presumably benefit virtually as much from the rent it could realize as from the profit it could earn.

57. These and other measures designed to make it more difficult for nonprofits to compete with for-profit firms are discussed in SBA, *Unfair Competition,* 37–41.

58. *United States v. American College of Physicians* (106 S.Ct. 1591), 1986.

59. "PM Newsletter," *Philanthropy Monthly* 19 (May 1986), 3–4 at 3. See also *United States v. American Bar Endowment et al.* (106 S.Ct. 2426), 1986.

60. *United States v. American College of Physicians* (106 S.Ct. 1591), 1986.

61. Schmedel, "Does Charity Trespass."

62. Initiatives for Not-for-Profit Entrepreneurship, "Competition: Nonprofits vs. For-profits," *INE Reports,* May 1987, 1–2.

7. Volunteer Labor

1. Nonprofit Sector Project, Urban Institute, "Serving Community Needs: The Nonprofit Sector in an Era of Governmental Retrenchment," Progress Report No. 3 (Washington, D.C.: Urban Institute, 1983), 4.

2. Independent Sector, *Americans Volunteer 1985* (Washington, D.C.: Independent Sector, 1986), table 3, at 11. This is a summary report of a survey published by the Gallup Organization, also called *Americans Volunteer 1985* (Princeton, N.J.: Gallup Organization, 1986).

3. Gallup Organization, *Americans Volunteer 1985,* 8–9; Virginia Ann Hodgkinson and Murray S. Weitzman, *Dimensions of the Independent Sector: A Statistical Profile,* 2d ed. (Washington, D.C.: Independent Sector, 1986), table 2.3, at 34; and U.S. Bureau of the Census, *Statistical Abstract of the United States: 1986* (Washington, D.C.: Government Printing Office, 1985), 390.

4. Hodgkinson and Weitzman, *Dimensions,* table 2.3, at 34; and Independent Sector, *Americans Volunteer 1985,* 18.

5. Table E.1 in Appendix E shows the growing number of FTE volunteer workers since 1977 and their distribution among the government, private businesses, and private nonprofit organizations. Also see Gallup Organization, *Americans Volunteer 1985,* 9.

6. Hodgkinson and Weitzman, *Dimensions,* table 2.5, at 35.

7. For details see Hodgkinson and Weitzman, *Dimensions,* table 1.3, at 16.

8. Independent Sector, *Americans Volunteer 1985*, 18–19.

9. *Giving USA—1984 Annual Report* (New York: American Association of Fund-Raising Counsel, 1984), 97.

10. Independent Sector, *Americans Volunteer 1981* (Washington, D.C.: Independent Sector, 1982), not paginated, next-to-last page.

11. Independent Sector, *Americans Volunteer 1985*, 18; and Hodgkinson and Weitzman, *Dimensions*, 32.

12. Nonprofit Sector Project, "Serving Community Needs," 5.

13. The 1981 Gallup poll obtained information on reasons for volunteering, separately from teenagers and adults. See Gallup Organization, *Americans Volunteer 1981* (Princeton, N.J.: Gallup Organization, 1981), 28.

14. A study that has dealt explicitly with the supply of volunteer labor for donors whose goal is to obtain work experience (the "investment model") or, alternatively, simply to help others (the "consumption model") is Paul L. Menchik and Burton A. Weisbrod, "Volunteer Labor Supply," *Journal of Public Economics* 32 (March 1987), 159–183.

15. Ibid.

16. Gallup Organization, *Americans Volunteer 1981*, 28; and Gallup Organization, *Americans Volunteer 1985*, 38.

17. Gallup Organization, *Americans Volunteer 1985*, 39.

18. That is, the partial elasticity was -0.41, evaluated at the mean. For details, see Menchik and Weisbrod, "Volunteer Labor Supply."

19. Gallup Organization, *Americans Volunteer 1985*, 38 and 39. Note that respondents often gave more than one reason; in 1981 there was an average of 1.83 answers, and in 1985, 2.05 answers per person.

20. Paul Menchik and Burton A. Weisbrod, "Voluntary Factor Provision in the Supply of Collective Goods," in *Nonprofit Firms in a Three-Sector Economy*, ed. Michelle White (Washington, D.C.: Urban Institute, 1981), 163–181; and Jerald Schiff, "Charitable Contributions of Money and Time: The Role of Government Policies," Ph.D. diss., Department of Economics, University of Wisconsin—Madison, 1984; and Menchik and Weisbrod, "Volunteer Labor Supply."

21. The elasticity of volunteering with respect to total spending by local governments has been estimated to be 0.12. Menchik and Weisbrod, "Volunteer Labor Supply."

22. Ibid.

23. "Tax Lure for Volunteers under Study in Albany," *New York Times*, April 27, 1982, 19.

24. The defeat of the bill by the Assembly was reported in a telephone conversation with D. Bierbaum, of the New York State Tax Office.

25. Nonprofit Sector Project, "Serving Community Needs," 5.

26. A temporary provision that allowed deductibility of monetary contributions even for nonitemizers ended with the 1986 tax year.

27. Schiff, "Charitable Contributions of Money and Time."

28. Stephen H. Long, "Income Tax Effects on Donor Choice of Money and Time Contributions," *National Tax Journal* 30 (June 1977), 207–212.

29. Menchik and Weisbrod, "Volunteer Labor Supply."

30. Virginia Ann Hodgkinson and Murray S. Weitzman, *The Charitable Behavior of Americans* (Washington, D.C.: Independent Sector, 1986), 27.

31. Joan R. Heilman, in *Parade,* April 14, 1985, 10–11.

32. Rod Young, as quoted in ibid., 10.

8. Are Nonprofits Really Different?

1. For further details on the empirical studies discussed in this chapter see Burton A. Weisbrod, " 'Nonprofit' and For-profit Organizational Behavior: What Is the Difference?" Department of Economics, University of Wisconsin—Madison, November 1986.

2. Even if there were no systematic differences between proprietary and nonprofit organizations, it would not follow that institutional form is irrelevant. Competition between nonprofits and proprietaries could lead to similarities in behavior that would not exist if either form existed in isolation. It is also possible that legal restrictions prevent differences from emerging—for example, regulatory controls on output quality or on pricing and distribution practices may force organizations to behave similarly, even though they otherwise would not.

3. Indeed, the claim that for-profit firms "skim" the profitable patients and leave the unprofitable ones for the public and private nonprofit sectors has often been made, particularly in the hospital industry. See Dan Ermann and Jon Gabel, "Multihospital Systems: Issues and Empirical Findings," National Center for Health Services Research, Washington, D.C., n.d., circa 1983, 16–17; and Stanley Wohl, *The Medical Industrial Complex* (New York: Harmony Books, 1984).

4. Waiting lists could also be used by profit maximizers as the basis for price discrimination, with the highest bidder on the list being selected.

5. "Nursing homes" are facilities that identify themselves as nursing homes, nursing care units, convalescent or rest homes, or homes for the aged. "Psychiatric institutions" are treatment centers for alcoholics, drug abusers, and the emotionally disturbed. Facilities for the "mentally handicapped" are for treatment of the mentally retarded and the neurologically handicapped.

6. Throughout this chapter, "church-owned" is used to describe facilities that are either owned by or affiliated with a religious organization.

7. These findings are derived from logit regression equations with dichotomous dependent variables—either the organization did, or it did not, keep a waiting list. The results reported as "significant" were statistically significant at the 0.10 level or better. In fact, the difference between the likelihood of nonprofits and proprietary firms maintaining a waiting list was significant at better than the .05 level for both religious and other nonprofit institutions for the mentally handicapped.

8. These estimates are derived from the logit model in Table F.1 but cannot be read directly from the table.

9. This difference was significant at better than the 0.01 level.

10. The distinction between type-1 and type-2 attributes is more complex than I have implied. Consumers differ in their ability to evaluate commodities. A particular attribute, thus, can be of type 1 for some consumers and of type 2 for others.

11. For examples of such behavior in the delivery of health services, see Burton

A. Weisbrod, "America's Health-Care Dilemma," *Challenge*, September/October 1985, 30–34.

12. There are no private nonprofit airlines, but there are governmental airlines in many countries, and even proprietary airlines are heavily regulated. The increased frequency of commercial airline accidents in the United States has raised questions as to whether a contributing factor is the increased competition resulting from deregulation, which may have led to cuts in maintenance or increases in flying time of aircraft and pilots.

13. There are other possible explanations for the continued existence of mixed industries—including their being a transitional anomaly, with one form of institution driving out competitors in the long run. The long history of the nonprofit sector makes this unlikely.

14. U.S. Bureau of the Census, *1976 Survey of Institutionalized Persons*, Current Population Reports, Special Studies, Series P-23, no. 69 (Washington, D.C.: Government Printing Office, 1978). The SIP was based on a stratified random sample from a comprehensive list of all facilities in the United States providing long-term medical, nursing, or custodial care outside of hospitals. It was actually a set of three related surveys: one covered the institutions themselves, with responses being obtained from a top administrator; a second survey included a random sample of patients at the institutions; and the third involved a random sample of family members of those patients selected for the second survey.

15. There are, of course, other means by which consumers' informational handicaps might be reduced—including the direct provision of information and regulation.

16. I make the assumption that all respondents answered this Census Bureau survey truthfully, to the best of their knowledge, or, more specifically, that untruthful responses are no more likely for persons at one type of institution than another.

17. The differences are statistically significant, though, only for the providers of care for the mentally handicapped. For church-affiliated facilities for the mentally handicapped the difference is significant at better than the 0.01 level. A multiple logit model was used, with the dependent variable being dichotomous; the family member answered either yes or no.

18. These findings are based on samples of family members of 841 nursing home patients, 320 psychiatric patients, and 549 patients of facilities for the mentally handicapped.

19. This analysis is based on results provided to me by Bonnie Svarstad, School of Pharmacy, University of Wisconsin—Madison. For further details, see Bonnie L. Svarstad and Chester A. Bond, "The Use of Hypnotics in Proprietary and Church-Related Nursing Homes," School of Pharmacy, University of Wisconsin—Madison, October 1984.

20. The differences were not statistically significant, however.

21. The difference was statistically significant for church-owned nonprofits but not for others.

22. Only volunteers who contributed at least once per month were counted. The difference was significant for all nonprofits—church-related and "other" nonprofits combined, and for others, alone, but not for church-owned, alone.

23. Only one of these four differences was statistically significant. The different number of maintenance workers, however, was significant (at the 0.05 level).

24. On the notion of "experience goods," see Philip Nelson, "Information and Consumer Behavior," *Journal of Political Economy* 78 (March/April 1970), 311–329.

25. Although, technically, a patient can be thought of as purchasing service one day at a time, the physical and mental condition of patients in long-term-care facilities—particularly in nursing homes and facilities for the mentally handicapped—make an admission decision tantamount to a lifetime purchase for most patients.

26. Patients who were admitted by the court or by a welfare agency are excluded in this analysis, as these patients were given little choice about where to be admitted.

27. The results, more precisely, are the coefficients on the interaction terms, length of stay with institutional type; they indicate whether length of stay—the proxy for opportunity to gain information—is of differential importance across forms of institutions, if the average revenue per patient per month at the facility is held constant. These relationships were estimated with and without the average revenue variable, and with an average cost variable instead of the price variable. There was little qualitative difference in the results.

28. The differences were not statistically significant, though.

29. An ordered probit model was estimated. The three possible responses were "satisfied" or "like," "dissatisfied" or "dislike," and "no opinion." The findings I report are the coefficients on the interaction terms combining length of stay with type of ownership. Differences are termed significant if the level of significance is 0.10 or better; nearly one-half of the coefficients are significant at the 0.05 level.

30. The statistical findings that institutional form matters are least clear for psychiatric institutions; this is not unexpected, since it appears that patient mobility among facilities is greater for these patients than for patients of nursing homes or facilities for the mentally handicapped—although evidence on mobility is extremely limited. Among nursing homes in Wisconsin, about 8 percent of all patient discharges in 1985 were to another nursing home (*Nursing Home Utilization* [Madison: State of Wisconsin, Department of Health and Social Services, 1985], tables 3.5 and 3.6A) and some, perhaps most, of these were "involuntary" in the sense that patients ran out of funds or insurance coverage and could not remain in the institution.

31. Held constant in a tobit regression equation were: the officially certified skill level of the home's services; the proportion of the home's revenues that come from private, Medicaid, and other public sources; the average price; the number of beds; the community size; and whether the home was affiliated with a hospital. For details, see Burton A. Weisbrod and Mark Schlesinger, "Public, Private, Nonprofit Ownership and the Response to Asymmetric Information: The Case of Nursing Homes," in *The Economics of Nonprofit Institutions,* ed. Susan Rose-Ackerman (New York: Oxford University Press, 1986), 133–151.

9. Recommendations for Public Policy

1. Laura M. Heuchan, "Nonprofit Charitable Organizations, 1982," Internal Revenue Service, *Statistics of Income Bulletin* 5 (Winter 1985–86), 21–40 at 24 (figure E).

2. William Vickrey, *Agenda for Progressive Taxation* (New York: Ronald Press, 1947), recommended replacement of income tax deductibility by a flat-rate tax credit forty years ago.

3. In 1985 the Bradley-Gephardt tax reform proposal included a requirement that all charitable deductions be taken at the lowest marginal tax rate, 14 percent. Although not enacted, the proposal amounted to the substitution of a flat 14 percent tax credit for the existing sliding-scale arrangement by which the after-tax cost of a donation varies with the donor's marginal income tax bracket. It did not quite constitute a credit, however, because it would have applied only to itemizers, since it was not accompanied by a proposal to extend the credit to the nonitemizers ("above the line" donors) whose deductions for charitable giving were scheduled to be, and in fact were, ended with the 1986 tax year.

4. A proposal for a "supervisory center in the United States sympathetic to the needs of charity"—a "National Commission on Philanthropy,"—patterned on the Securities and Exchange Commission model—was made in the early 1970s, much of it attributed to Alan Pifer. See Donald R. Spuehler, "The System for Regulation and Assistance of Charity in England and Wales, with Recommendations on the Establishment of a National Commission on Philanthropy in the United States," in Commission on Private Philanthropy and Public Needs, *Research Papers* (Washington, D.C.: Department of the Treasury, 1977), 5:3045–3087, especially 3080–3087.

5. *Bob Jones University v. United States,* 461 U.S. 574 (1983) (upholding authority of the Internal Revenue Service to deny section 501(c)(3) tax-exempt status to schools that discriminated on the basis of race in admission or school policy, despite religious claims of such schools).

Appendix B. The Nonprofit Sector around the World

1. P. Falush, "Trends in the Finance of British Charities," *Westminster Bank Quarterly Review,* May 1977, S32–44.

2. "The Growing Pains of British Private Medicine," *The Economist,* December 1982, 80–81.

3. "Ten Years of ASH," *British Medical Journal,* 282 (31 January 1981), 340.

4. Rebecca Bergman et al., *Nursing the Aged: Institutional and Personal Factors Influencing the Work of Nursing Personnel in Long-Term Care Institutions* (Jerusalem: Brookdale Institute for Gerontology and Adult Human Development, May 1983), 14.

5. Margery Greenfield, "A Revolutionary Medical Deal," *Jerusalem Post International Edition,* February 12, 1984, 5.

6. Ralph Kramer, "Governmental–Voluntary Agency Relationships in the Netherlands," *Netherlands Journal of Sociology* 25 (1979), 155–173.

7. *La Caixa, Abridged Annual Report, 1983* (Barcelona, Spain), 2.

8. Ibid., 29.

9. Burton A. Weisbrod in collaboration with Joel F. Handler and Neil K. Komesar, *Public Interest Law* (Berkeley: University of California Press, 1978).

10. Ellen Sward and Burton A. Weisbrod, "Public Interest Law Activities Outside the U.S.A.," chapter 17 in *Public Interest Law,* 500–531.

11. David Brand, "Polish Ecology Club Risks Government Ire by Battling Pollution," *Wall Street Journal,* July 24, 1981, 1, 6.

12. B. Newman, "Watchdogs Abroad: Consumer Protection Is Underdeveloped in the Third World," *Wall Street Journal,* April 8, 1980, 1.

13. Estelle James, "The Nonprofit Sector in Comparative Perspective," in *The Nonprofit Sector,* ed. Walter W. Powell (New Haven, Conn.: Yale University Press, 1987), 397–415.

14. This dependence of the nonprofit sector on demand-diversity was posited earlier in Burton A. Weisbrod, "Toward a Theory of the Voluntary Nonprofit Sector in a Three-Sector Economy," in *Altruism, Morality and Economic Theory,* ed. Edmund Phelps (New York: Russell Sage Foundation, 1975), 171–195; also chapter 3 in Weisbrod, *The Voluntary Nonprofit Sector* (Lexington, Mass.: Lexington Books, 1977), 51–76.

15. Krister Andersson, "The Swedish Tax System," Brookings Institution Discussion Papers in Economics, April 1986, 10.

16. Harry M. Kitchen, "The Canadian Tax System," Brookings Institution Discussion Papers in Economics, April 1986, 6; M. Homma, T. Maeda, and K. Hashimoto, "The Japanese Tax System," Brookings Institution Discussion Papers in Economics, June 1986, 7.

17. *Israel's Outlays for Human Services 1984,* ed. Yaacov Kop (Jerusalem: Center for Social Policy Studies in Israel, 1985), 200.

18. Arthur Andersen & Co., "Overview of Governmental Support and Financial Regulation of Philanthropic Organizations in Selected Nations," *Research Papers Sponsored by the Commission on Private Philanthropy and Public Needs* (Washington, D.C.: Department of the Treasury, 1977), vol. 5, 2975–93 at 2975.

19. Denis P. Doyle, "Socialist Sweden Tries to Reinvent Philanthropy," *Wall Street Journal,* April 17, 1984, 34.

20. Eliezer D. Jaffe, *Pleaders and Protesters: The Future of Citizens' Organizations in Israel* (Jerusalem: The American Jewish Committee, 1980), 7–8.

21. Christoph Badelt, "The Voluntary Provision of Social Services—A Comparative Institutional Approach," Paper presented at the International Forum Meeting, Structural Change in the Service Sector, International Institute for Applied Systems Analysis, Laxenburg, Austria, July 20–22, 1983, 2.

22. Estelle James, "The Nonprofit Sector in International Perspective: The Case of Sri Lanka," *Journal of Comparative Economics* 6 (1982), 99–129 at 117.

23. Virginia Ann Hodgkinson and Murray S. Weitzman, *Dimensions of the Independent Sector: A Statistical Profile* (Washington, D.C.: Independent Sector, 1984), 11, 44.

24. Ralph Kramer, "Governmental–Voluntary Agency Relationships in the Netherlands," 166.

25. Ibid., 165.

Appendix D. Restrictions on Lobbying by Nonprofits

1. Internal Revenue Code section 501(c)(3).

2. The case for, and the use of, legal mechanisms such as class actions for

promoting "underrepresented interests" were examined in Burton A. Weisbrod in collaboration with Joel F. Handler and Neil K. Komesar, *Public Interest Law* (Berkeley: University of California Press, 1978).

3. See Commerce Clearing House, *1984 U.S. Master Tax Guide,* 67th ed. (Chicago: Commerce Clearing House, 1983), section 502C, pp. 183–184.

Index

Abrams, Burton A., 235*n*39
Akerlof, George, 220*n*35, 228*n*22
Alchian, Armen, 222*n*26
Andreoni, James, 224*n*41
Arrow, Kenneth, 222*n*19, 224*nn*40,44, 225*n*2, 226*n*7

Bakker, James, 119, 120
Ben-Porath, Yoram, 222*n*20
Blood banks, 44–45, 60, 71, 113
Bono, Jack, 119
Borcherding, Thomas, 221*n*10
Brook, Robert H., 227*n*15
Brubaker, Earl, 224*n*45, 232*n*6
Buchanan, James, 218*n*17
Burger, Warren, 56
Business associations, 72

Canadian National Railways, 36–37, 38, 41
Caves, Douglas W., 225*n*56
Channell, Carl R., 121
Charitable organizations, 10, 67, 119–120, 133. *See also* Collective-type nonprofits
Christensen, Laurits R., 225*n*56
Church-owned nonprofits, 144, 149–150, 241*n*8. *See also* Religious organizations
Civil service guarantees, 53–57. *See also* Tenure
Clark, Robert, 26
Clotfelter, Charles T., 224*n*43, 232*n*7, 233*nn*9,13, 234*nn*22,32
Clubs, 9–10, 73, 162, 218*n*18
Coal mines, 38–39
Collective-type nonprofits, 9–10, 59–60, 70–71, 93, 218*n*18; tax exemption of, 10; subsidization of, 70–71; tax deductibility of, 85

Collectiveness index, 59, 75–79, 230*n*21
Common Cause, 69, 77
Competition: of nonprofits with private firms, 3, 11–13, 84–86, 107, 111–129, 164, 166; and tax exemption, 116–118, 121–128; and type of output, 123–128, 164
Conservation organizations, 9, 69, 80, 82
Consumer(s): mobility, 145, 146, 147, 152; satisfaction, 151–155
Contracts, 40, 147, 152
Cooperatives, 62
Cordes, Joseph, 225*n*62
Corrections Corporation of America, 39–40
Cost interdependencies, 125–127
Country clubs, 59, 67, 81
Cross-subsidization, 110, 113–114. *See also* Revenue generation
Crowding-out effect, 103–106, 110–111. *See also* Government spending
Cultural organizations, 74
Cyert, Richard M., 228*nn*31,33

Davies, David, 228*n*37
Day care, 6, 71, 84–85, 113, 123
Demand, diversity of, 6–7, 25–31, 34, 41–42, 223*n*30; and nonprofits, 25–31, 67; and efficiency, 34
Demand interdependencies, 127, 163–164
Demsetz, Harold, 222*n*26
Dominguez, Nestor, 98, 99, 100
Donations, 3–4, 8, 12, 30–31, 77, 79, 88–106, 107, 162; deductibility of, 14, 28–30, 93–95, 192; effects of tax policy on, 28–30, 90, 93–94, 98; factors in size of, 29, 30; and free-rider behavior, 29–30, 92, 93; and informational inequalities, 30;

James, Estelle, 218*n*20, 245*n*13
Japan, 27
Johnson, Lyndon Baines, 119
Judges, 55–56

Komesar, Neil, 192
Krashinsky, Michael, 222*n*19

Labor. *See* Paid labor; Volunteer labor
Labor unions, 9, 72
Law enforcement, 51–52
Legal aid organizations, 81, 82
Lindsay, Cotton M., 226*n*10
Lobbying, 119–120
Long, Stephen H., 223*n*37, 240*n*28

Managerial sorting, 31–33, 158–159
Market failure, 6, 8, 19–20, 21, 26–27, 29–30, 145–146, 163. *See also* Information inequalities
Marwell, Gerald, 224*n*45, 232*n*6
Membership organizations, 72–74
Menchik, Paul, 134, 135, 240*nn*14,20–22,29
Merit pay, 48, 50–51
Minnesota Education Media Center, 112
Mixed industries, 40, 84–86
Mobility, consumer, 145, 146, 147, 152
Monks, Robert, 31
Mutual organizations, 61, 62

Nader, Ralph, 77
National Endowment for the Preservation of Liberty, 120–121
National Institutes of Health, 60
National Science Foundation, 17
Nelson, Richard, 222*n*19
Netzer, Dick, 230*n*19
Newhouse, Joseph, 222*n*24
Niskanen, William, 234*n*28
Nondistribution constraint, 11–12, 14, 16, 24, 31, 41, 118, 120, 159, 219*n*26; and tax exemption, 11–12, 14, 61; and output distribution, 142–144; and health care, 155–158
Nonprofit organizations: and governmental agencies, 1–2, 8, 84–86; for-profit ventures of, 2, 8, 11–13, 107–118, 123–128, 163–164; Internal Revenue Service and, 2–3, 8, 10, 90, 115, 116, 127, 165–167; competition between proprietary organizations and, 3, 11–12, 84–86, 107, 111–115, 118–129, 166; in a mixed economy, 3–4, 5–9; and diverse demand, 6–7, 25–

31, 67; advantages of, 8, 30–31, 118–122; regulation of, 8–9, 60, 82–83, 95–97, 113–114, 165–166; trustworthiness of, 11, 13, 23, 39, 41, 42, 45, 124, 146–155, 222*n*23; interlocking directorates of proprietary organizations and, 13, 164; efficiency of, 14, 18, 23–24, 33–41; limitations of, 16–17, 23, 118–120; employee incentives in, 23, 31, 33, 53–57, 101–102; rationale for, 23–31; lack of political constraints in, 24–25; entry conditions for, 67, 81, 87, 161; revenue generation in, 69–70, 76–79, 89–90; life cycle of, 80–83, 101, 231*nn*23,24; size and number of, 81–82, 231*nn*25,26; geographic distribution of, 83–84, 86–87, 123. *See also* Donations; Efficiency; Revenue generation; Sales; Tax deductibility; Tax exemption; Volunteer Labor
Nonprofit sector: growth of, 69–70, 182; size of, 62–67, 176–177, 178, 179–181, 229*n*8; in international economy, 191–193
North, Oliver L., 121
Nursing homes, 6, 24, 60, 71, 81, 82, 83, 85, 123, 241*n*5; regulation of, 22; growth of, 72, 74, 82; waiting lists in, 143–144, 206–207; proprietary vs. nonprofit, 146–155; patient review in, 147–149; use of sedatives in, 149–151; satisfaction with, 151–155; church-owned, 154, 210–216

O'Hara, Maureen, 218*n*16, 219*n*22
Olson, Mancur, 224*n*42, 232*n*5
Opportunism, 45, 83, 145, 146, 149. *See also* Free-rider behavior; Information inequalities; Trustworthiness
Outputs: distribution of, 21–22, 142–144, 221*n*13; type of, and efficiency, 33, 36–41; and performance, 36, 48–53; monitoring of, 36–37, 46–53, 82, 142, 144–155, 226*n*10; related or unrelated to nonprofits' tax-exempt purpose, 114–117, 123–129. *See also* Goods, collective; Goods, private; Services; Type-1 outputs; Type-2 outputs

Paid labor, 64–67, 72–73, 130–131. *See also* Volunteer labor
Performance: measurement of, 36, 44–48; rewarding of, 44–46; quantifiable vs. nonquantifiable, 48–53; of teachers, 48, 50, 54–56; of police service, 51–52; of hospitals, 52; of civil servants, 53–54; of judges, 55–56
Pollution, 21–22, 28
Pommerehne, Werner, 221*n*10, 226*n*12